About this book W[illegible]g that Manet's pictures must be given the first and last word, James H. Rubin uses contradictory views – from then and now – of the artist's works as a context for approaching them. Drawing on J. L. Austin's notion of the performative, which bridges the gap between language and action, or between the painted image and its social effect, Rubin reaches beyond past theorists to describe the curious ways in which Manet's paintings act on us. With these ideas as his guide, the author takes us through Manet's *œuvre*, pointing out the elements that are distinctive and consistent, notably the artist's reliance on patterns of gazes and the 'unique state of undecidability' that this strategy establishes. Rubin also examines Manet's relations with three leading critics of his day – Baudelaire, Zola and Mallarmé – giving special attention to Mallarmé's appreciation, and eventual use in his poetry, of the artist's work. Finally, Rubin uses the image of the bouquet to exemplify Manet's creative poetics through an exploration of his still-life paintings.

About the author James H. Rubin has been a Professor of Art at Stony Brook, State University of New York, since 1979. A specialist in French art of the later eighteenth and nineteenth centuries, his books include *Realism and Social Vision in Courbet and Proudhon* (1981) and *Eugène Delacroix, 'Die Dantebarke': Idealismus and Modernität* (1987).

ESSAYS IN ART AND CULTURE

In the same series

The Landscape Vision of Paul Nash
by Roger Cardinal

Looking at the Overlooked
Four Essays on Still Life Painting
by Norman Bryson

Charles Sheeler
and the Cult of the Machine
by Karen Lucic

Portraiture
by Richard Brilliant

C. R. Mackintosh
The Poetics of Workmanship
by David Brett

Image on the Edge
The Margins of Medieval Art
by Michael Camille

Illustration
by J. Hillis Miller

Francis Bacon
and the Loss of Self
by Ernst van Alphen

Paul Delvaux
Surrealizing the Nude
by David Scott

The Symptom of Beauty
by Francette Pacteau

Manet's Silence and the Poetics of Bouquets

James H. Rubin

REAKTION BOOKS

For Nana

Published by Reaktion Books Ltd
1–5 Midford Place, Tottenham Court Road
London W1P 9HH, UK

First published 1994

Cover and text designed by Humphrey Stone

Photoset by Wilmaset Ltd, Birkenhead, Wirral
Printed and bound in Great Britain by
BAS Printers, Over Wallop, Hampshire

British Library Cataloguing in Publication Data:

Rubin, James H.
Manet's Silence and the Poetics of
Bouquets. – (Essays in Art & Culture)
I. Title II. Series
759.4

ISBN 0–948462–55–8
ISBN 0–948462–56–6 (pbk)

Contents

Preface

Although this book presupposes some familiarity with nineteenth-century art, it is addressed not only to an academic audience of students and specialists but to the general reader, for whom Manet's historical importance may be as much a matter of reputation as of systematic comprehension, and for whom speculation on the meanings of his art will be a source of pleasure. Rather than presenting new documentary research on Manet, I integrate and expand recent studies of the painter toward a broad and enlightening view by framing discussion with new ideas I hope are useful for approaching him. Not, strictly speaking, a work of scholarly art history, this book includes certain terms and interpretations that tend more toward criticism and literature than history. Consequently, rather than encumber the text, I have limited the scholarly apparatus primarily to direct references, followed by a bibliography of specifically useful items.

First of all, I am most thankful to the late Louis Marin for the time to ponder matters such as representations of seeing. I still miss his seminar, and I dedicate this book to his memory. I am deeply indebted, also, to recent work on Manet and Impressionism by scholars such as Carol Armstrong, Françoise Cachin, T. J. Clark, Robert Herbert, John House, Theodore Reff and Richard Shiff, although they cannot be held responsible for my own peculiar ways of thinking, and I have certainly not tried to make a summary of or a balancing act between their various points of view. In addition, I am happy to say that this book owes something of its origins and form to several friends and colleagues to whom I am immensely grateful for their generosity and candour. Conway Lloyd Morgan first gave the practical impulse that made me think a book was possible. Klaus Herding questioned connections I made between Delacroix, Manet and *l'art pour l'art*. Harry Rand made me think seriously about putting down my own ideas on Manet and Mallarmé. Filiz Burhan outlined affinities between nineteenth-century psychology and art and set me on the paths of Taine and Ribot. Carolyn Halpin-Healy helped with some preliminary research. Don Ihde stimulated thoughts on paradigms, while André Glucksmann helped me formulate some paradoxes. Carol Armstrong offered a chance to discuss new historicism and 'neo-formalism' (though I am not sure whose term this is), and her book on Degas set an example for methodological pluralism. In addition, she and Catherine Soussloff most generously offered thorough and probing suggestions on the manuscript. I am also grateful to the anonymous readers for Reaktion Books and Harvard University Press, and to the extraordinary staff at Reaktion Books, for innumerable constructive suggestions, as I am for those of Dick Howard, Melody Davis and Brian Taylor. Finally, Jean Kendrick's secretarial help made things go more smoothly than I had any right to expect.

To Stony Brook I owe the sabbatical during which I did most of my research and began my writing, as well as opportunities to teach Manet during which I worked out many of these speculations. Since the 1970s, when I began assigning Manet and Mallarmé as an essay topic, I had thought of writing about them. After Harry Rand's *Manet's Contemplation at the 'Gare Saint-Lazare'* appeared, a book I wholeheartedly admire, I realized there was room for my own way of looking at the relationship between Manet and Mallarmé. While I was writing in Paris in 1986–7, Penny Florence's incisive *Mallarmé, Manet and Redon* appeared and became a further stimulus. In my conception of this book, in other words, the section on Manet and Mallarmé has been central.

Finally, I would like to acknowledge the many hours of pleasure I found in Robert Gordon and Andrew Forge's beautiful *The Last Flowers of Manet*; I would encourage everyone to consult the many colour illustrations in it, as well as, of course, those in the catalogue of the great Manet exhibition held at the Grand Palais and the Metropolitan Museum of Art in 1983. Obviously, this book is based on a great deal of travel and many hours of looking, for which there is no substitute. I hope it will stimulate others to do the same.

'L'Oeil, une main. . .' que je resonge.

Mallarmé, 'Edouard Manet', *Médaillons et portraits en pied*, c. 1896

Yes, I know, *we are but vain forms of the material – but so sublime . . . that I want to present to myself this spectacle of materiality, while conscious of my being, yet soaring toward that Dream which it is not, chanting the Soul and all the divine impressions we have accumulated since the early years, and proclaiming before the Nothingness which is truth, these glorious lies!*

Mallarmé to Henri Cazalis, March 1866

To put it bluntly, no one's home. We are literally absent from our own present. We are elsewhere, not in the real but in the represented. Our bodies, the flesh and blood of it all, have given way to representations . . .

Barbara Kruger, *The New York Times*, 9 September 1990

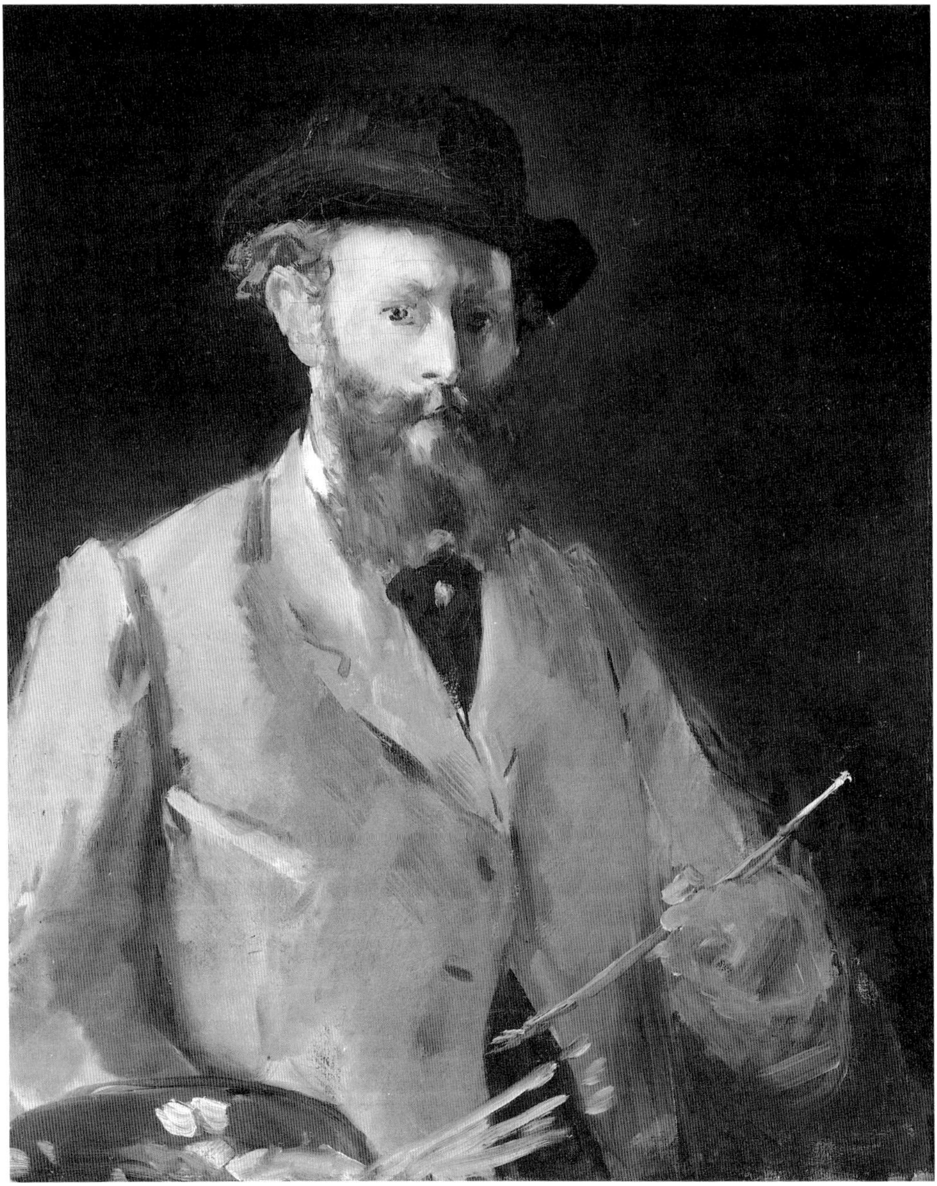

1 *Self-portrait with Palette*, 1878–9, oil on canvas. Private collection

Introduction: Performing Sight

A sense of stillness and silence pervades Manet's painting. His flattened, sometimes fragmented forms appear to exist absent-mindedly in a world seemingly removed from discourse. Our experience of Manet's art is difficult to put into words, and Manet said little about it himself. Yet few artists have generated so much critical writing, perhaps for these very reasons. Of course, we see before we say – we all know that sight precedes speech in early human development, and, later on, experience is the basis for conceptualization, data the basis for theory. Yet the history of art is often dominated by new searches for models in which aims are more articulate than in art itself, as if verbal explanations could produce certainty where looking alone cannot, or as if literary sources and documents might hold the keys to visual mysteries. True, the acquisition of language profoundly influences the way we see. But structures of consciousness are not necessarily dependent on verbal intermediaries for their influence on art. That is, in passing directly from perception to picturing, the 'inarticulate' artist may express an 'a-theoretical' consciousness – one that operates without guidelines that can be articulated. Such an artist would appear 'naive', and thus, in nineteenth-century terminology, 'sincere', the implication being that directness equals truth.

In such a sense, what follows is about the restoration of the visual in art to primacy through Manet's painting. This book is about Manet's visual poetics. By that I mean, first, the conceptual basis or system underlying Manet's visual creativity – his unspoken, perhaps unstatable theory, in effect. But I also mean that those poetics are deeply grounded in the nature of the visual – hence, the persistent ineffability of his art. Speaking of visual poetics does, of course, beg the question as to what 'poetry' is, especially when expressed through visual form. By 'poetry', then, I mean a form of language, as in a style of painting, that awakens us to its *aesthetic* presence, a presence that makes us conscious of language rather than taking it for granted. Poetry usually operates not through conventional description or narrative, but through strategies that somehow call convention into question, be it simply by using a novel word or phrase, or, in painting, an unexpected colour or pose. In Manet, the poetic is constituted by, and produces effects that enhance, our awareness that we are encountering painted signs – figurations rather than figures themselves, representations rather than their referents. Such poetry can be called semiotic (that is, referring to signs) rather than strictly mimetic. (It is also opposed to the kind of mimesis that claims to imitate the 'ideal'.) As the bearer therefore of the artist's subjective agency, this visual poetry rouses our consciousness of ourselves and of our relationship to the world.

Edouard Manet's friends remember him for an acute eye and a disdain for anything too theoretical. They say he read little and wrote even less.[1] His conscious paradigm was not philosophical, scientific or literary. On the contrary, his example reversed the relative position of art and literature: he and his friends became models for the creative act, as set forth in contemporary novels, for example the Goncourts' *Manette Salomon* (1867), or Zola's *L'Oeuvre* (1886). He rejected all that seemed too professional about the art world, namely the Académie and its high-minded concepts, but he strove to exhibit his work publicly, which meant at the official Salon (the annual, Government-sponsored, juried exhibition). Manet's outlook and practice were those of the *amateur* (literally, lover) or *homme de lettres*, but he believed such attitudes should be taken seriously. Though his manner was confident and his art filled with wit, his conduct was always discreet and well-bred. Even the pictures that most bluntly shocked and confused his public were made with an economy and deftness that demonstrate strength of mind and courage of conviction.

Manet's art was recognized as modern by the artists and writers who took him as the leader of their school. For them it exemplified a natural rather than conventional way of seeing. They responded first and foremost to its powerful visual impact (so much of which has been lost today because of colour reproductions and slides, and because the abstractions of more recent painters have gone so much farther). And they assumed that this effect was tied directly to Manet's person – his moral character, his public persona and his private personality, all at once. In other words, Manet's vision was identified as highly personal and subjective, yet at the same time – indeed, as a result – it was considered natural and accessible because it stemmed from his very nature. On this basis alone, then, I believe we are justified in being concerned primarily with the conceptions and dynamics embodied and created in Manet's art, rather than with his sources or specific aims. Comparisons from realms outside the visual will shed useful light on his achievement, but I will use them mainly to illustrate a community of vision rather than to demonstrate direct influence or intention. The painted expression of contemporary concerns will normally precede their theoretical articulation when the way of seeing is 'sincere', that is, responds directly to the seen. And for an artist, that way of seeing cannot be separated from a way of painting. So my premise will be that Manet's pictures must be given the first and final say in any interpretation. But my point of departure will be to accept conflicting views of his works – both now and as recorded in their time – as a context for approaching them. In responding to the entire artistic spectrum, from Academicism to Impressionism, from the Renaissance to Dutch and Spanish Realism, and to the spectacle of modern social life, Manet exhibited both the open-mindedness and the diffidence of an artist operating without ulterior motive. Yet far from simplicity or aimlessness, his painting has all the complexity of the individual seeking adequate and convincing forms in a changing world of competing ideologies and declining traditions.

While thus universally accepted as a watershed in the history of originality and for the development of modern art, Manet's art continues to be a focus of controversy and debate. Despite the volumes of writing about it, no one has had the last word; the territory is far from exhausted. Few agree on what constitutes its modernity, although the prevailing view is that this is connected to its self reflexivity. That is, according to this view, modernist art, in taking itself, hence its nature as an artistic medium, as the object for investigation and understanding, becomes philosophical rather than simply representational. It is an artistic enactment of the philosophical development in which consciousness takes itself as its own object. Manet's art would be the first step in this development, which, according to the traditional account, culminates in the abstract art produced after World War II. I agree with the part of this assessment that views Manet as one of the first to make selfconsciousness about the nature of art his theme, but when I say 'the nature of art' I believe we should be referring to the nature and role of subjectivity in representation rather than, too simply, to the physical properties of the artwork. The paradigm shift of modernism is to have recognized the futility of Realism and to have dedicated itself to exploring and recording the space and function of subjectivity, variously defined as imagination, creativity or perception, in visual representation. We too often think of artists as historically propelled technicians, singlemindedly solving formal problems that lead through a pre-determined development. By stressing the concept of subjectivity, the story of modern art can be recast as that of the self's self-discovery and of the mind's recognition of the role of the visual in its self-knowledge and definition.

Of course, to say that Manet's painting is 'about' the visual states the obvious; but the obvious is the result of deeply embedded philosophical and ideological beliefs. In the nineteenth century, seeing itself became a poetic act (that is, in our context, a creative one), and vision became a crucial concept for the development of modern art. Vision refers to many things. On the one hand, it is *sight*, the physiological sense common to many higher organisms but occurring within discrete individuals. On the other, it is a point of view or attitude, an ambition or conception, and it is not always limited to an individual but may be an ideology shared by a society. Vision thus always implies inseparable objective and subjective activities: it refers to sight and to insight simultaneously. A third, and no less important, referent of the word 'vision' is the image formed in the mind – the result of those physiological and ideological processes. That image, as a formation within a specific and unique consciousness, will always have a subjective dimension in addition to a public one. Representation, especially in art, whether realist or abstract, historical or fantastic, is always based on such images formed at one time through vision; but it is also overlaid by and affirms various attitudes. Imagination, which beholds images in the mind, obviously depends on vision for its material and organization, but those other attitudes generally affect its choices. Consciously or not, it accompanies artistic creation and is indeed often identified with it. But in addition, and not to be forgotten, is that among the various attitudes that affect artistic vision are those embodied by technical conventions or, as often in Manet's case, stylistic innovations. That is, the artist's vision is concomitant to and commensurate with its enactment through the materials of his art. The duality of art, its reference to both external and internal worlds, is thus inherent in vision itself, and especially in artistic vision. Without necessarily influencing Manet, theories of vision focusing increasingly on this duality, and aesthetic theories focusing increasingly on vision, help suggest a logic for his preoccupation with the gaze.

But artists have never settled for mere 'reproductions' of the visible, even if one were to assume such a possibility in art (or in any form of representation). They have always believed artistic vision to have original and personal dimensions that differentiate its product from mechanical representations and justify its spiritual value. Thereupon they founded their poetic ambitions. Traditional literary and historical themes had encouraged artists to express creativity through dramatic or didactive inventiveness. But in the late eighteenth century, artists felt constrained by the academic formulations of those approaches, with their emphasis on Antiquity and on stylistic and technical recipes. Their reaction was to claim inner vision as the sole legitimate source of art. Even if at first they expected it to reveal grand and universal truths, such vision was a guarantee of creative integrity. Gradually discarding traditional narrative subject-matter in order to look more closely at the world around them, artists began to express creativity through the act of representation as revealed through the artifices of its means. Visuality – what might most simply be called visual presence as a value in itself, or the aspect of form known to the eye without necessarily referring to anything, or apart from its references to things – would eventually become the focus of their painting. That is, in a major shift of emphasis, artists began to think about the act of seeing and their pictorial, hence material, responses to the seen, as distinguished from reality as a measurable and constant object. It was as if limiting personal vision strictly to the visual (literary and allegorical themes being judged conventional or insincere) ran the risk of rendering art subservient to the external. So the more artists relied on the act of seeing and picturing as the basis of their art, the more their art as the expression of that act bore the mark of seeing and of artistic subjectivity. Visual artistic forms came to appear more and more wedded to the subject's perception/representation of them, and the technical processes artists brought to bear on increasingly ordinary objects became the means to endow them with poetic life.

The partnership between objective and subjective in artistic representation, and indeed in all perception, has remained the foundation for aesthetics since the time of Plato and Aristotle. But more recently, analysis has focused on the social function of the arts in serving ideology and politics by affirming or establishing systems of consciousness. For example, the French linguist Emile Benveniste has distinguished between two modes of verbal representation – the 'historical' and the 'discursive'.[2] The former claims objectivity and typically uses third-person speech, whereas the latter reveals its subjectivity through the use of the first person. That is not to say one excludes the other, for we all know that historical representation is fraught with the ideology of its producer and that the subjectivity of the individual is permeated by his or her social experience. But Benveniste's paired concept is useful for understanding all forms of expression, including the visual. Post-structuralist thinkers have been concerned with how language 'constructs' the subject, that is, the way in which language, whether visual or verbal, actually shapes the sense of identity and belief system of those who share and employ it. The critical approach that is Deconstruction analyses – one might say, dismantles – those operations; Deconstruction shows how what is taken for granted – what we assume to be a natural given – is actually an element of ideology and hence part of a system to which there might therefore be alternatives, rather than being an objective fact or a transcendent truth.

In discussing the persuasiveness of Renaissance and Baroque naturalism, which corresponds to the 'classical' phase of Western thought (i.e., from the Renaissance to the Enlightenment), Louis Marin has remarked that the coexistence within the same visual work of two apparently contradictory interpretations is the foundation on which the classical system of representation is based.[3] Those two interpretations are as follows: on the one hand, a painting's flatness makes it seem a mirror reflection of our physical realm, which appears to have an objective existence, independent of our perception. It thus contains forms that appear available for our possession and control. On the other hand, as argued by Michel Foucault, a painting's three-dimensional illusionism creates the effect that what we see exists as a result of our own seeing – is our own projection. In Velázquez's *Las Meniñas*, which Foucault used as his paradigm,[4] the artist's representation is beholden to the power of Philip IV and Queen Mariana, in whose employ he operates and whose entourage his painting depicts. By showing his sovereigns reflected in the mirror on the far wall of the gallery, the painter implies that the artwork embodies their vision, hence their power over the world, and by extension, that of any viewer who stands in their place before the image. The world's signs seem the attributes of individual vision, empowering the beholder's gaze as its sovereign creator.

Jacques Derrida implicitly supports this critique of naturalist representation by pointing out the role played by the frames of pictures.[5] Although not actually part of a picture, the frame is always essential in defining it; to use Derrida's term (borrowed from Kant), it is a *parergon*; it is its absent condition. The notion of framing locates power outside the image, within a framing subject, which determines and encloses a selected parcel of reality. Whether we read across the image, project into it, or circumscribe it, these interpretations show how naturalistic art produces a viewer who takes himself to be dominant over the material realm of objects and other individuals, and how it therefore bestows sovereignty on the particular individual who through economic or political power calls it into being. They validate vision as 'panoptical', the term Foucault invoked to suggest a right of surveillance, hence authority over an objectively existing world.[6] We might say that the classical viewer is one for whom the world is 'readable', for whom it coheres, decodes, and is therefore authentic, legitimate and available. Western artistic naturalism, at least in this theoretical version, thus literally embodies – gives concrete form and power to – the ideology of man as the measure of all things. Through art, the world as it appears is given to exist of necessity, while at the same time it is susceptible to possession. The political consequence of such representations is to make the status quo appear objective. The viewer whose vision is the most panoptical will possess the most power. Hence the eye of God, or the ever-present image of the King, implies the ontological legitimacy of their reigns.

Two other concepts applied to naturalistic art are the descriptive and the theatrical. Proposed, respectively, by Svetlana Alpers and Michael Fried,[7] they are not alternatives to Marin, Foucault or Derrida, but formulations specific to art-historical experience and discourse. Both Alpers and Fried still posit the eye as omniscient and external, as the reader in fact is from the text or from any other representational production. Alpers characterizes Dutch realism as fundamentally descriptive (as opposed to allegorical), and she has shown how its descriptiveness was allied with optical sciences (the camera obscura) and cartography. In map-making in particular, the viewer is placed in a god-like position above the representation, or 'text', of reality. This position corresponds to that of the reader of written or graphic texts, who holds the book below and before his or her eyes.[8] It also matches that of the painter as framer of reality. Thus, even art without obvious narrative or underlying verbal messages, such as much still-life, may yet reduce to the paradigm of textuality or reading. The notion of theatricality (and its opposite, absorption) also places the spectator before a construct produced for the eye. Theatre is, after all, the acting out of narratives before the eye, and it served as a powerful model for history painting. According to Fried, the theatrical – an excessive playing to the spectator – eventually provoked demands for a more naturalistic counter-movement, in which scenes would be so absorbingly realistic that the spectator would forget they were 'produced' at all. For both Alpers and Fried, effects of realism or authenticity therefore depend on suppressing any signs of the external viewer's presence – on so distancing the beholder that he or she seems no longer to exist. The absence of personal imprint, of anything that marks objects as belonging to another's vision, creates what Georges Didi-Huberman has described as the absolute dominance of the referent – that which we call the subject-matter, but which is actually the object of art.[9]

Yet as Didi-Huberman also observes, the more one enters into the detail of representation, even in so-called Realist art, the less legible it becomes, the more one discovers instances of pure visuality, passages of visual presence that are undetermined as anything other than indexes of the materiality of painting. The closer we look – for in looking closer we presume to learn more and to better possess – the less transparent pictorial figuration becomes. In fact, the more it dissolves into its opposite, which might be called defiguration, the more it eludes our grasp. In such instances, the art of painting reveals itself as artifice and process.[10] Among the artists Didi-Huberman cites as his examples, Jan Vermeer has a specific relevance for us, since he exemplifies a kind of opticality that was a powerful model for nineteenth-century Realism, and, in addition, his works were rediscovered and discussed in the very milieu Manet frequented. In Manet's painting, the detail that rises to the surface to call realism into question becomes an explicit theme. Tension between figuration and defiguration is central to the character of his art.

Rather than combining the two interpretations underlying the classical system of representation (window versus mirror, or frame versus canvas), Manet's painting has torn them apart to play them against one another. In his art, there is tension between two essential, yet contradictory responses that exist for all naturalist painting. Forgetting we view pigment on a flat surface, we see a figure or an object we accept as a reality mirrored either from our own or an imagined world. This interpretation is 'realist' or 'descriptive', in that the viewer gazes on figures that seem to have an independent life in nature and to which the eye, and therefore the viewer's self, appear external. Yet, Manet's forms and figures affect us physically. Not only do we recognize and take pleasure in the materiality of the artwork and in the artist's means of handling it – in the technique and intellect underlying representation – but, in addition, and more important, Manet's figures impinge on us with their gazes, their scale and their physicality, for which the painting or aspects of it are the signs. We might call this a 'semiotic' or 'performative' *experience*, as opposed to the paradigm of *reading*, hence decoding and dominating, the work as 'text'. In it, the figures encountered by the gaze are experienced as signs that are no longer transparent to their referents in nature but are displayed as events in the materiality of painting. They make present the productive and performing activity of the artist's own practice. The artist's eye, and therefore body, seem to 'inhabit' those visual signs and have the power to affect us, even to displace us as part of the same world.

This duality corresponds on one level to Benveniste's distinction, mentioned earlier, between the 'historical' (third person) and the 'discursive' (first person), but it also adds another, powerful, dimension to it, which I have called 'performative' and which can be understood through semiotics, the study of signs, in this case visual signs. In terminology proposed by J. L. Austin, 'performative' refers to language that actually accomplishes an action in the real world, as opposed to the 'constative', which merely states or describes a thing or state of being.[11] As simple spoken performatives, one might cite Austin's classic example: 'I pronounce you man and wife', which in the proper public circumstances legally confers that status upon a couple; or 'You're fired!', if uttered by your boss. The performative thus bridges the gap between language and reality. Austin refined his concept by adducing different classifications of performative statements (primary and explicit), levels (locutive, illocutive and perlocutive), and verb types (verdictives, exercitives, behabitives, expositives, commissives). For the purposes of application to visual representation, the idea that an utterance, spoken, written or painted, can be associated with the performance of an action is key. Manet's paintings are more than simply representations with meaning (locutive); they operate with discernible force (illocutive) and sometimes powerfully affect emotions (perlocutive). Manet's frequent references to himself as the personal maker of his representations through an immediately recognizable style and through ostentatious signatures correspond respectively to the 'primary' and the 'explicit' in Austin's system. But we shall see that the performative is an even more useful concept when expanded in order to be more encompassing. For I am not interested in finding an exact parallel in visual language to the particular kind of speech acts that Austin used as his examples. Rather, I am suggesting that his term can be used to characterize painting that produces certain social effects through its pictorial forms. Just as in performative speech, where the fact of stating an effect can be the occasion by which that effect is enacted, the same is possible through art.

Since vision and meaning are always constructed within a social framework, there is always a social dimension to a dialogue of gazes and to the relationship of the eye to its object. Indeed, that dialogue may be the vehicle for positioning within both a social and an artistic context or milieu. It is inherent in both the realist and the semiotic interpretations of Manet's work, and results from their interaction. Painting as an act of seeing *qua* figuration may thus act on and so transform its social milieu. Earlier I mentioned how a work of art may be said to produce or construct its viewer – in the case of Western naturalism (in Marin's and Foucault's sweeping generalization), a viewer who is assured of power over matter. All art, like all speech, as Derrida has noted particularly in his critique of the performative,[12] ultimately has a performative level even when it masquerades as what Austin called constative. In traditional naturalism, the performative effect is concealed behind the appearance of neutrality. The work done by such images is to confirm and perpetuate a status quo by making it appear objective. Thus Western naturalism was deeply implicated in the ideology of hierarchy and authoritarianism even while it seemed to empower the viewer. Of course the authority of such representations is effective only with a kind of complicity on the part of the subject, in that the subject feels mandated to recognize their authority, as, in the examples given above, the bridal couple felt authorized and the employee censured by society. Social convention, as well as conventions of representation, therefore play an essential role in endowing certain images with performativity. The performative relies on pre-established circumstances for its power. It can be further argued, then, that even in the transformative aspect of the performative there is something of the constative, since the transformative can only perform with the acquiescence of a receiver already prepared by convention to do so, and therefore the performative, too, confirms a status quo. Having heard the Post-structuralist critique of the ideological ramifications of Western naturalism during the classical period, our question for modern art will therefore be this: How does painting enact the relationship of the viewer to the world when the viewer has discovered that there is no hierarchy, that he is himself a part of nature, over which he previously believed he had power? How can it at the same time construct the modern viewer's belief in the democratic concept of self-determination and the sovereignty of the individual? The answer lies in the fact that the ideology that Manet's performative/transformative art enacts is itself an ideology of transformation.[13]

Poetic language in the nineteenth century acted through a kind of negativity, on the margins of ordinary discourse or through its deformation.[14] Art effects social change through transgression of accepted traditions and the founding of new conventions, even while it is dependent on the old ones, which it uses as its foil. The very existence of conventions makes their violation an inherent and permanent possibility, so change is always a potential, relying on eventual public acceptance in order to establish its new order. In its dialogue with art history and its flouting of propriety, no art is more sensitive to conventions and traditions than Manet's. With Manet, the transformative aspect of the performative becomes explicit, through a display of signs or references to the action of the artist's selfconsciousness in its transformative representation. Manet's painting enacts, for all to see, conditions that had emerged but which were not necessarily recognized and whose consequences for the language of painting were not yet fully apparent. Perhaps art had been a consoling refuge for an outdated way of thinking. Manet brutally dragged it into the modern age, and in so doing visually acted out the ideology of modernity. As in performative language, the representation of that social effect through the material means of his painting was both an establishment of the effect and an act determined by it. It enacts, both in the sense of to perform and to decree, its expression and consciousness of subjectivity and personal freedom, by both exemplifying and legitimating them. As such, we need new figures of speech to account for Manet's art. It does not simply describe, it performs; it does not simply narrate, it enacts; it does not simply represent, it embodies; it does not exposit a way of thinking, it stages and teaches it. And in the very performing, enacting, embodying, staging and teaching, it exemplifies the new performative mode.

In contrast to traditional naturalism, Manet's art, since its realist effects are mediated by their coexistence with its semiotic selfconsciousness, subverts the traditional subject-as-sovereign relationship to produce, ultimately, an uncertain and ambivalent viewer. The viewing subject's presence, rather than distinct from art, is called forth by it (not simply addressed by it), and seems to recognize itself and have a life within it. As such, the power of the spectator is displaced into the world of representation; the subject becomes an aspect of matter (of the object) and matter becomes an aspect of it. In this case, then, the 'complicity' that enables a visual performative to operate can consist both (or either) in the viewer's willingness to accept his transformation or in his resistance to it. For in either case, he acknowledges not just that images have power but that visuality is at the heart of their effects.

This willingness is at least in part elicited by the reassurance Manet offers on the value of human individuality and effort through the marks his painting bears of the artist's actual engagement with the representational realm. It is as if consciousness can still shape the world from its position of congruency with it, even if it can no longer frame it from a position of exterior dominance. Signs of artistic action on matter, while on one level, as I have said, identifying matter as part of the same realm as consciousness, on another imply the possibility of their separateness, as displayed by the former's susceptibility to manipulation by the latter. The explicitness of this dialectic, as it is engaged in Manet's painting, subverts the confidence of classical man in the objective status of reality, but leaves open the possibility of human fulfilment by featuring existence as an encounter between individuals and their material realm. What was in Romanticism a heroic struggle is here an everyday, and seemingly more casual, defiance of tradition, although in the long run a far more profound one. Although the first term of the dialectic (that we are materially defined and bounded) makes of the second (absolute freedom) a false promise, the modern subject none the less appears perpetually striving to transcend his nature in order to recover a sense of worth and compensate for his sense of loss. Through its cycle of destruction and recreation, then, Manet's art visually performs for the benefit of its viewer a transformation of consciousness from the classical to the modern – from that of man as framer to man as shaper.

Manet's silence might be compared to the rapt fascination of the self contemplating its own image in a mirror. Seeing itself as an 'other' (indeed, transformed into an 'other' by its own gaze), yet with full possession of its thoughts, would appear to obviate conventional communication. But while the gaze is suspended in wonder before the apparently magic transformation of self into representation, it is troubled by the lack of reassurance it receives. For the gaze returned blankly by its mirror double can never answer the self's query, unless self-knowledge is defined as the acceptance of unknowability and the impossibility of absolute figuration. In painting, this recognition of difference assumes a poignance, for the marks of pictorial representation are constant reminders of the otherness of the image. The self accustomed to possessing the world thus discovers itself as latent object even more through painting than in the mirror. Through representation it confronts its potential to be dominated and controlled, even though its own active gaze, indexed by brushstrokes, appears at the same time to assert the autonomy that should have been guaranteed by the will to figuration. Perpetually suspended over, yet defined by, this gap between self and other, between subject and object, between figuration and defiguration, human identity in Manet's painting eludes precise articulations. That space of uncertainty between the viewer and the picture is thus the field within which Manet's painting silently operates.

In Manet's two most controversial paintings, the *Déjeuner sur l'herbe* (illus. 40) and the *Olympia* (illus. 41), we discover we are being looked at from within the painting. Moreover, the person doing the looking is a naked woman of questionable social status – Manet's model, Victorine Meurent. Rather than acquiescing to the subject's traditional role as the object of a voyeur's fantasy, she makes the viewer the object of her own sight. When our eyes meet hers, we cannot hide that she is the object of our thought; and she returns the dubious compliment. A similar play on looking and seeing is crucial to many subsequent works, though only in these two is it carried out so frontally. *La Gare Saint-Lazare*, *Boating* and *In the Conservatory* (illus. 32, 51 and 33) are all characterized by empty gazes, in which must lie a key to their conception. They raise the possibility of thought's absence and the question of whether seeing can exist without looking, of whether one can look without seeing, and of what sort of being that implies – are we object or subject, body or soul? Finally, the *Bar at the Folies-Bergère* (illus. 45) is structured by the displacement of the viewer's gaze from its traditional position at the front and centre of the work. The psychological effect is different from earlier paintings, but again, a pattern of gazes is its key. Of course the *Déjeuner* and *Olympia* use sexual roles to heighten consciousness of the visual act (and of course they presume an audience consisting primarily of heterosexual males). For if looking were not an expression of desire or an act of vicarious possession, Victorine's returned gaze would have no power and the viewer no shame. In the *Bar at the Folies-Bergère* by contrast, the displacement of the gaze problematizes the notion of Manet's barmaid as an object of sight for which sexuality is a metaphor of possession; seeing is potentially both aesthetic and dehumanizing, disinterested and knowing, as the painting displays her visuality and that of the spectacle of contemporary leisure of which she becomes a virtually undifferentiated part. To accomplish that in the charged setting of modern sociability is no less a *tour de force* than is the ostensible emotional matter-of-factness of the *Execution of Emperor Maximilian* (illus. 25) or *The Dead Toreador* (illus. 46).

Coexisting with a realist interpretation of Manet's painting is its opposite, the semiotic interpretation (for these poles are not mutually exclusive, but simply useful concepts for analysis). Returning with equal intensity the gaze encountered in *The Fifer Boy* (illus. 43) disconnects the boy's representation from its referent in reality, just as he is already detached within the frame from any context or setting. Both the image as a whole and the distinct elements that comprise it float autonomously and disjointedly against their background in an almost hallucinatory way. Moreover, the boy's eyes bear the scars of Manet's hand, of the sign of his eye's presence in them – in other words, of the sign that they are art. Their forms are identified with the manual process of their creation, which refer thus to the artist rather than to the boy. Even in works where the gaze is most transfixing, its grip is subverted by concrete elements of facture or of still life. They divert attention and invite the eye to scan the picture surface, from object to painted object, from contour to colour to brushstroke, all of which have taken on a physical presence accomplishing their divorce (or its possibility) from the referent. The frozen atemporality of the hypnotic gaze and the figure's magic spatiality are counterbalanced by a complex tracery of sequential glances responding to the plethora of technical events for which the flat canvas is the physical support. It is in this second, obviously anti-illusionistic, experience of Manet's painting that the links to artistic traditions are strongest – especially to the Spanish and the Dutch, on whose 'realism' Manet's art casts doubt by his attention to their artifice. The paradigm for this side of Manet's art is the still-life – an arrangement of autonomous forms. Paradoxically suspended between poles (which will provide parameters for our discussion, although the following sets are not exact equivalents) – figure/still-life, history/discourse, realism/aestheticism, figuration/defiguration, constative/performative – Manet's painterly gestures deconstruct traditions of representation. His art cannot be circumscribed by either 'reading' or 'experience' alone; it contains both, and unlike his predecessors Delacroix and Courbet, he himself offered no explanation that favoured either one. Manet's art produces a unique state of undecidability – in contemporary terminology, it operates through *aporia*, through figures or events whose meanings or referents cannot be fixed – which is different from saying it has no signification at all. Thus, the peculiarly non-literary poetics of Manet's art depends on the ambiguity of visuality; and Manet's silence is the appropriate sign of the inequivalence of the verbal to the visual.

I shall propose that Manet replaced what I have called 'textual' (or 'externalist') paradigms with forms corresponding to an experience of the world as 'lived within' – with what his friend, the poet Stéphane Mallarmé, referred to as 'immersion'. Although, of course, Manet built on the work of his predecessors, his painting was the most powerful expression in the nineteenth century of this change. While practising an art of ostensible emotional neutrality and naturalism, he relocated the site of representation from a position external to representation to one internal and integral to it, one informed by the experiential processes of visual figuration.[15] Manet's art results in the opposite of realist distancing, and therefore it has the potential to invert the power relationship between viewer and viewed. By injecting himself quasi-physically into his representation (and drawing us in, too), that is, by leaving on his picture surface the marks of his bodily presence, Manet invalidated, or at the very least, problematized the naturalist model we saw deconstructed by the Post-structuralists.

In Manet's art, subjective experience is what is represented as concrete and enduring (though dynamic, not static); the self, in effect, becomes the object of representation and, as such, it appears 'possessed' or informed by the world, as opposed to the classical vision in which, as I remarked earlier, the world appears as an object of dominance and control. I believe the evidence from Manet's own paintings shows conclusively that his art is primarily concerned with looking and being looked at, seeing and being seen, painting and being painted: in the broader sense, it is about vision and visuality – ultimately, about the position and experience of the eye and body in their world, about a phenomenology that is as inextricable from the psychological as it is from the social. Manet's art transcends the paradigm of external reading, moving rather toward a 'lived' visuality, that is, one that implies the eye's continuity, interaction and interdependence with the physical world, as expressed through eloquent markings made by the artist's 'visual' hand or 'handling' eye. It is 'lived' as much because it is Manet's intimate and social world as because he focuses on the visual experience of it and on the manual act of its picturing. In referring to the artistic self, then, rather than (or at least as much as) to the world, those markings, pictorial notations or signs, move toward independence from their duty to their referent in the world and acquire the potential to be manipulated and enjoyed for themselves.

I call Manet's conceptual system or visual poetics a 'poetics of bouquets' because, as embodied in his painting of still-lifes, and epitomized by his flowers, Manet's representations produce a performance of the consciousness of picture-making as much as they provide a description of the seen. Compare Manet's relatively early *Peonies in a Vase* (illus. 71) of 1864 to the later *Pinks and Clematis in a Crystal Vase* (illus. 49). The former still has a residue of literary content, for it contains both a fresh-cut flower and one that has lost its petals, as if suggesting a flower's life cycle. Although it is the latter that was painted while Manet was dying, it might seem that the earlier one, with its twist on the theme of *vanitas*, would have been more appropriate at the later time. The later one seems no more than pure visual presence devoid of discernable allegory. But there is more. As for many artists at the end of their careers, Manet's last works are products of the total freedom that approaching death often provides. Without ulterior motive, Manet's painting reverts to its practice as a physical and aesthetic activity. That practice, in the context of Manet's illness, can be seen as symptomatic of an entire *œuvre* whose focus is on the interplay between figuration and its impossibility. Confronted now with the certainty of his mortality, Manet is ineluctably drawn to the exercise, however futile, of figuration – a process that, given its compensatory nature, now has no other purpose than itself.

It is no accident that the object of that figuration is a bouquet. Painted flowers are among those categories of art whose function as painting is closest to their function as original object. In other words, a painting of flowers has for its beholder an effect parallel to a real bouquet. Both are decorative, and both display the taste of its creator for beauty and arrangement. A painting of a bouquet or still-life differs from a photograph of the same subject-matter in that photographs are often likened to mechanical reproductions, whereas paintings usually are not. Indeed, it is often assumed that painting as an art exhibits a kind of creativity similar to that displayed by *arranging* bouquets or still-lifes. To the degree, then, that painting a bouquet is like painting another work of art, it is a self-referential act. It belongs to that genre of painting that takes art as its own subject-matter. Yet we must keep in mind that flower painting is still a specific and limited branch of art – one of visual selection and arrangement, of appropriation of nature for pleasure and personal taste – that is not dependent on didacticism or allegory. In accepting its function as that of an object of delectation, indeed by taking that experience as its theme, flower painting, like still-life in general, only more so, epitomizes Manet's performative poetics. When one experiences the texture of Manet's paint, one experiences not simply the beauties of soft petals or fresh leaves but the actively ordering process of representation itself. And the discovery of that process is a source of pleasure and reassurance every bit as much as is the sight of the bouquet.

The same may be true for us today in experiencing Manet's figure paintings, even those of the 1860s. Indeed, I believe that their underlying poetics are related. In their own time, the figure paintings were so disturbing that critics writing about Manet found their received vocabulary inadequate to explain its characteristics and justify its effects. Chapter One is an account of those effects, which I describe while following the chronological development of his figure painting. In chapter Two, the idea of the 'uncertainties of the word' not only echoes the ambiguities produced by Manet's painting, but suggests the relative limitations of attempts by Manet's contemporaries, particularly Baudelaire and Zola, to define and theorize his production. On the one hand, his work was profoundly disconcerting – a characteristic many found no better term for than 'originality'. Attributed to 'temperament', however, his originality could be regarded as 'natural'. But now, in place of definitions of naturalism that stress everyday subject-matter and the non-idealized reproduction of nature, a more fundamental feature of Manet's naturalism came to be his reliance on a non-narrative language of physicality and bodily presence, which, playing off his realist subject-matter, created an apparatus of aporia. Manet's art refused the mechanism that was the recognized vehicle for official ideology. His art defied decoding; hence, while to many it was incomprehensible, to others, 'uncoded' meant 'natural'. This characteristic was complemented by Manet's apparent lack of interest in what one might call the social agenda, or the public status, of institutional artists. Yet, at the same time, his art was integral to his society of cultivated leisure, whose values it confirmed by making its characteristic activities, both public and domestic, the pre-eminent subject-matter of his painting. Manet's life became the exemplary life of the artist, not the least because the picture-making that was his principal activity seemed itself constituted by acts of leisure – by the ostensibly casual, sketch-like, unfinished and untutored brushstrokes of the non-professional. So the 'position' of Manet's eye is expressed by subjects from his world as well as by a hand that impresses their shared reality with his eye's presence in it.

In chapter Three Mallarmé emerges as the writer who most closely understood these attitudes as well as the material and performative aspects of Manet's aesthetic. Two collaborations between Manet and Mallarmé, though the resulting artworks – for Poe's 'The Raven' and Mallarmé's own 'L'Après-midi d'un faune' – are illustrations of limited significance, provide the opportunity to study a convergence of their interests. Parallels between Mallarmé's essay on Manet and his famous 'L'Après-midi d'un faune' shed light on how he interpreted and shared many of Manet's concerns. Its theme, as in so much of Manet's art, is the uncertainty of identity and the ambiguity of perception, and its approach is evocative and approximate rather than descriptive and unequivocal. In chapter Four, I rehearse Manet's chronology a second time, now illuminated by these factors, by looking primarily at still-life rather than at the figure. In the art-historical literature on Manet, which concentrates on his figure paintings, still-life has always seemed peripheral, non-essential. Yet a number of contemporary critics saw still-life as a paradigm for Manet's peculiarly original approach to forms and to pictorial composition. Indeed, if the 'content' of Manet's painting is embedded in its materiality, perhaps still-life is the way to get at its heart. It is here that I will propose that flowers and bouquets exemplify the making of nature into art practiced by Manet and (in chapter Five) his immediate followers – a poetics of bouquets. The defining element of Manet's painting – its *parergon*, to use Derrida's term – is no longer the frame but the surface, like the table-top (or the picnic blanket, the bed-sheets, or the wrapper) on which still-life compositions are set. Although hidden behind the drama of pictorial composition and technique that express the poetry of creativity, the canvas has become the stage for representation. And no longer can one so confidently refer to the painting's field as a *space* – realm or site might be more appropriate. Locating the site of representation within the painting, rather than outside it, both embodies and contributes to producing a subject who feels congruent with and integral to the realm he once felt capable of controlling. So the display of artistic agency and the gestural rhetoric of artistic freedom serve as compensatory ideological expressions for the subject's loss of external control. The artist, as I said earlier, becomes shaper rather than framer. Rather than the panoptical eye, it is the figuring hand (a motif sketched in the final chapter) that now embodies the human will.

The bouquet, like Manet's painting, is itself the bearer of a paradox. Manet's is a hedonistic and physical rather than intellectual poetics, in which art is treated not as knowledge and control over an external reality, but as the enactment, through shaping and assimilation, of the artist's presence (immersion) within it. He seems to take nature to exist for his leisure and seems to arrange it to reflect his pleasures. In social practices, bouquets often take the place of words. They may allude to a favour rendered or hoped for; they may signify a love that words are inadequate to define. Yet while celebrating the present and the material, bouquets also often allude to the opposite. Indeed, in their commemorative function, they may mourn absence and the loss of pleasure. They signify death – the negation of materiality and yet, as a result, the condition of its discovery and affirmation. The uneasy coexistence in Manet's art of the joyful and the troubling can embody this irreconcilability. So the modernity of Manet's art may reside in the paradox of its limitations and contradictions, as signs of the frailties and aspirations that in the modern world define humanity itself. Manet's silence combines both wonder and regret.

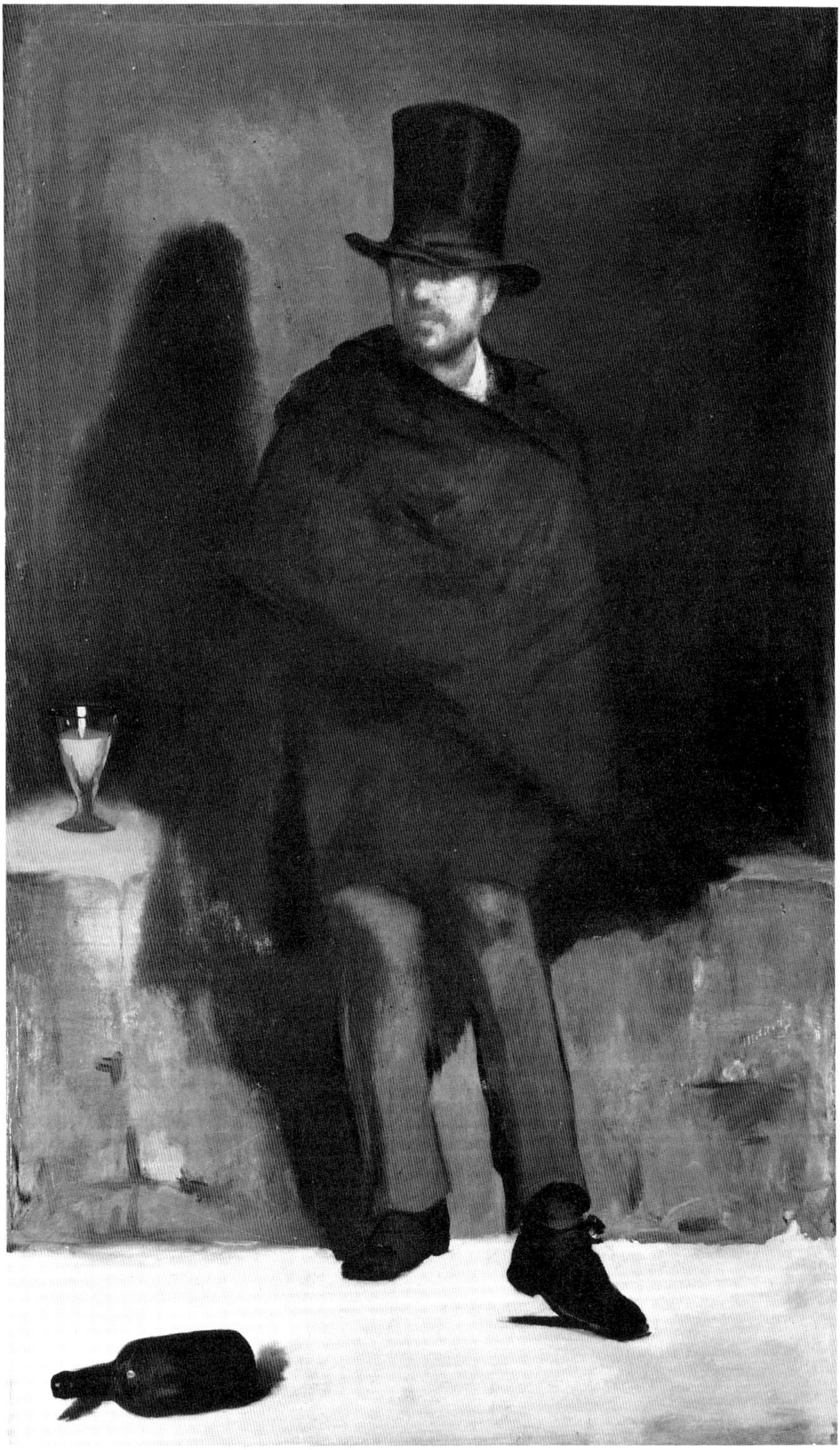

1 Paradoxes of the Visual Hand

In his essay of 1883 on Impressionism, Jules Laforgue wrote that 'the optical arts derive from the eye and solely from the eye'.[16] The phrase 'seeing is believing' is but another formula for the role of sight in the acquisition of knowledge, that is, in the activity of consciousness. But artists know better than anyone that art also derives from the hand and the body. Ever since René Descartes's essay on 'Dioptrics' (1637), in which Descartes compares the transmission of light to the eye to the way a blind man uses a cane to detect information about his physical surroundings, sight has been associated with the sense of touch.[17] Bishop George Berkeley used that relationship as the basis for his *New Theory of Vision* (1709), in which he showed that visual sensations call forth memories of tactile experience. Visual impressions were thus signs interpreted by the mind, that is, representations (re-presentations) of more primordial experiences. Michael Baxandall has demonstrated how the followers of John Locke claimed that sensations – the only means to knowledge – were themselves internal, and how their assumptions were spread in eighteenth-century France.[18] Attributes such as colour and size came to be seen as perceived internally rather than as inherent in objects themselves. Early in the nineteenth century, the British 'psychological' school of philosophers continued to explain perception as the mind's ability to associate original sensations with previous experiences. Perception was the awareness of sensation; the mind perceives only those stimuli it has had the training to recognize, a training intimately related to the sensations of the body. As Svetlana Alpers demonstrated for Dutch naturalism, the dominant model of vision in the classical age was a mechanical device, the camera obscura. In the 1820s and 1830s, however, as Jonathan Crary has pointed out,[19] the monocular model of perception collapsed in favour of one in which binocularity embodied the many visionary possibilities of the human body as 'productive observer'. The body's physiology became a central factor in producing an inherently subjective visual experience. No longer viewed

2 *The Absinthe Drinker*, 1859, oil on canvas. Ny Carlsberg Glyptotek, Copenhagen

solely as an optical device, the eye became a temperamental organ interacting with the body's network. Unlike Descartes's model, in which the observer takes for granted an accurate transmission that reproduces existing objects outside the body, the tappings of the blind man's cane can be said in the organic model to become tentative efforts through which the body, producing its own interpretations, gropes its way towards whatever image will suffice for its own uses. Perhaps with Descartes in mind, Derrida has described the origins of art as the result of blindness – of our inability to produce images equivalent to our experience.[20] But Derrida's description is, of course, based on the theoretical possibility of such reproductions, a possibility that was definitively replaced in the nineteenth century with the dynamic, as opposed to the mechanical, model of vision. It might be said, then, that the art that came to embody the human limitations discovered in the nineteenth century was the always tentative and forever experimental art of Impressionism. In it, the brush, like the blind man's cane, gropes its way toward competent approximations.

The hand translates the eye's presence and role in representation, while at the same time distancing us from the so-called 'real' or external world to which representation refers us. The mark of the hand is thus the index of a duality: it suggests physical limitations that give vision its historical ground, yet it is also the bearer of originality, of that which exceeds previous limits. As in handwriting, it is characteristic of the age, yet it distinguishes one artist's product from another's; it is the tool of vision and yet the creator of a unique visuality; it is subject to technical conventions, yet it interprets or defies, and sometimes redefines them. Like the cane of Descartes's blind man, it is both the means to possess reality and yet the sign of exclusion from it. The brush inserts the self, however uncertain, into reality but maintains reality at the distance of its tip. Such paradoxes constitute a framework for Manet's painting. Few issues are as basic to human existence as the matters of perception and expression confronted in an art of the visual. Yet they are intuited: the artist whose work most deeply involves them may have no conscious theoretical rationale. In an article in *L'Artiste* of 1868, Arsène Houssaye complained that 'Manet would be an exceptional artist if only he had a hand. . . . It is not enough to have a head that thinks and an eye that sees; you must have a hand that speaks'.[21] Perhaps he should have said 'a hand that paints', for Houssaye is suggesting that Manet's painting was too transparently naturalist – so objective that it bore no content or meaning that might follow from the evidence of painterly subjectivity. Rebutting Houssaye, Zola countered that contemporary artists were all too skilful with their hands in rendering nature according to recipes: 'their fingers are too deft, they play too easily with childish difficulties. If I were judge, I would cut them at the wrist and force open their minds and eyes with pliers'. Zola took for granted the ability of Manet's hand to express the nature of his eye (as opposed to nature itself) transparently, and he argued that other painters let mannerisms get in the way. He concluded, in spite of Houssaye's reservations, that Manet was 'a born painter'. According to Zola, then, Manet's handling of the visual and the peculiar, yet unmannered, visuality of his handling were the keys to his richness and accessibility.

MARGINALITY AND MODERN CONSCIOUSNESS

For Manet, the act of looking was never innocent or impartial, even though at first glance it may seem to have been so. The Realism of the 1840s and 1850s had popularized a taste for the picturesque. Landscapes and images of rural life extended the vistas of serious art to include a naturalism and a class of subject-matter it had traditionally excluded. The philosophical impact of art was said to lie in its truth to appearances, and the unspoiled rituals of the countryside were thought to embody an unaffected morality that was disappearing in the towns. Appearing first in publications like *Les Français peints par eux-mêmes* (The French painted by themselves), marginal figures such as ragpickers, beggars and chimney-sweeps were the urban objects of such nostalgia. They, too, were part of the world that art increasingly claimed to mirror. They were the starting point for Manet's quintessentially Parisian version of Realism.

In the second quarter of the nineteenth century Paris assumed a new position, that of the glittering capital of the cultivated world. The vast, open city we know today, with its formal parks, leafy embankments, elegant monuments and fashionable stores, was in the making during Manet's time.

Baron Haussmann's reconstruction of the central parts of the city gave it a harmonious and integrated feeling, while also serving to drive the working classes towards dingier neighbourhoods in the east and north. The tree-lined boulevards we so associate with Impressionism and with the cafés that Manet haunted were of Haussmann's making. The increasing economic power of the middle classes and their democratic institutions and ideology were sustainable as long as order was preserved and wealth increased. With France in full industrial expansion under the leadership of Napoleon III and his international bankers, many men of Manet's comfortable economic circumstances could afford the life of public gardens and cabarets. Many others, less fortunate, including immigrants from the countryside and from abroad, went to Paris in the hope of earning a share of that prosperity. For Baudelaire, the crowding of the city was a shock, relieved only by the anonymity it afforded. The subject-matter of Manet's art is almost always inseparable from this urban geography and its diverse population, as well as from the psychology peculiar to its experience.

Yet, for the subject of the first painting Manet submitted to the official art exhibition (the Salon), he chose one of the less attractive characters from city life. Although still a student in the atelier of Thomas Couture (a middle-of-the-road painter, politically liberal and possessing a sure technique), Manet seems to have wanted to outdo his teacher's conventionally Realist themes by representing something with a stronger bite. His *Absinthe Drinker* (illus. 2), which depicts a presumably derelict addict of the famous herb distillate, was certainly viewed by contemporaries as one of the more degraded possibilities in the category of urban realism. Manet may have been inspired by themes of wine and drugs in the poetry of his friend Baudelaire, whose sonnet 'Le Vin des chiffonniers' (The ragpickers' wine) appeared in the first edition of his *Fleurs du mal* (1857), and whose reputation linked him to the seamy side of Paris. Yet in the fringe neighbourhood where Manet had his studio at the time, such figures cannot have been uncommon; indeed, Manet is said to have portrayed a man named Collardet who actually did make a living collecting rags. That the painting was excluded from the Salon of 1859 is not surprising, given both the offence it would cause in a society unwilling to admit its unvarnished underside into the halls of

3 *The Guitar Player*, 1861, oil on canvas. Metropolitan Museum of Art, New York

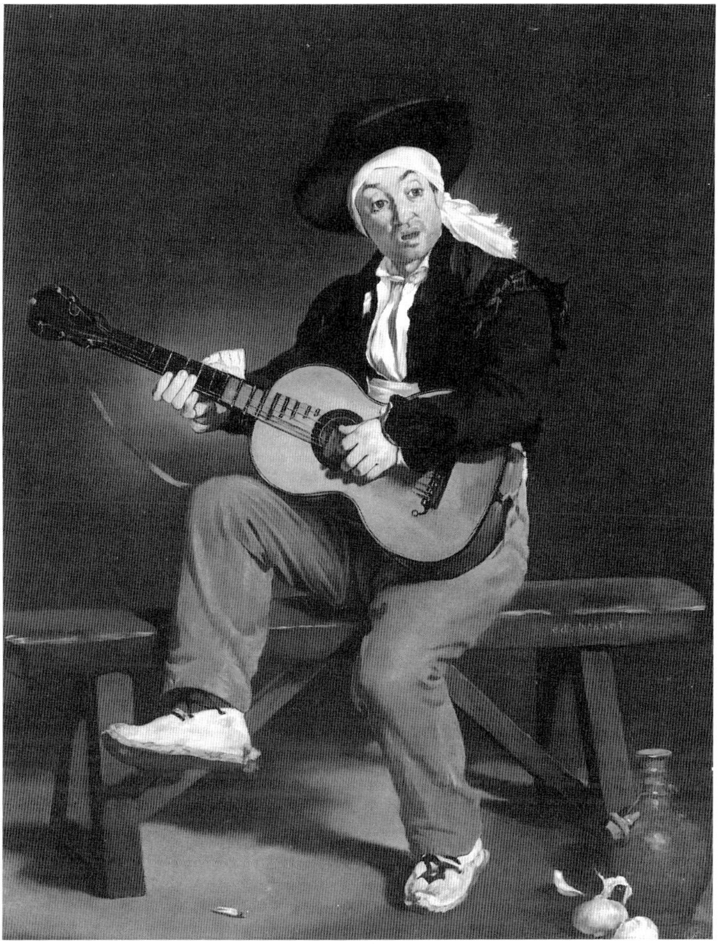

art and its technical ambiguity – the awkwardness with which the legs are joined to the figure, and its quasi-unfinished state. From the beginning, there was something odd and personal about Manet's choices and his execution.

Two years later Manet successfully entered another painting of a 'type' from the margins of society, *The Guitar Player* (illus. 3). Now the figure could be perceived as one from the world of entertainment rather than of poverty – a reflection of, rather than an affront to, Paris's self-image of prosperity. The painting combined the romantic and exotic reputation of Spain with the well-established aesthetic of Spanish Realism. With its suave colour contrasts, its signature cleverly located on the end of the bench, and its unusual still-life, it more than adequately exemplified both Manet's singularity and his painterly skills. It drew the attention of a group of young painters and writers (Henri Fantin-Latour, Alphonse Legros, Carolus-Duran, Félix Braquemond, Baudelaire, Jules Champfleury and Edmond Duranty), who together paid a visit to Manet's studio to express their admiration. Indeed, both the *Absinthe Drinker* and the *Guitar Player* exhibit the frontal and monumental directness of Manet's classic works, soon to follow, while the *Guitar Player* in particular reveals the sophisticated breadth with which Manet would typically manipulate his brush. And the *Guitar Player* already contains the elements of ambiguity that were to characterize subsequent works. The guitarist holds his instrument in reverse and strung upside down, an impossible arrangement, even for a left-handed player (with the unique exception, so far as I have been able to determine, of the American blues guitarist Albert King). Though it may be tempting to see the canvas as a mirror, even an explanation based on reflection cannot account for the reversed order of the strings. When the error was pointed out to Manet, he refused to make a change. Was he deliberately stressing artifice – that is, that the painting was a studio pose rather than a slice of life?

Over the next couple of years Manet introduced a decisive change in subject-matter. Where he continued at all to represent picturesque motifs, they began to include those more clearly familiar to his class, such as demi-mondaines rather than city street figures. More important, he began to represent members of his own class, his peers in their surroundings, dressed in their top-hats and black frock-coats, as Baudelaire would frequently observe. Manet's background was grand bourgeois (his father was a respected judge), and he was known as impeccable and urbane. His shift of emphasis from the margins to the centre of Parisian society is evident when one compares the two most important pictures he exhibited at the gallery of the engraver and dealer Louis Martinet in March 1863. *The Old Musician* (illus. 4) is a pastiche of figures from various 'realist' sources, both of the past and of the present, and which Manet seems to catalogue. They function as signs – of a realist art, in this case – yet their artificial arrangement offers a commentary on the artificiality of such art, indeed, of any art at all. The painting's seemingly unfinished background, reminiscent of a theatre backdrop, exposes Manet's utter lack of interest in producing a realistic scene. The

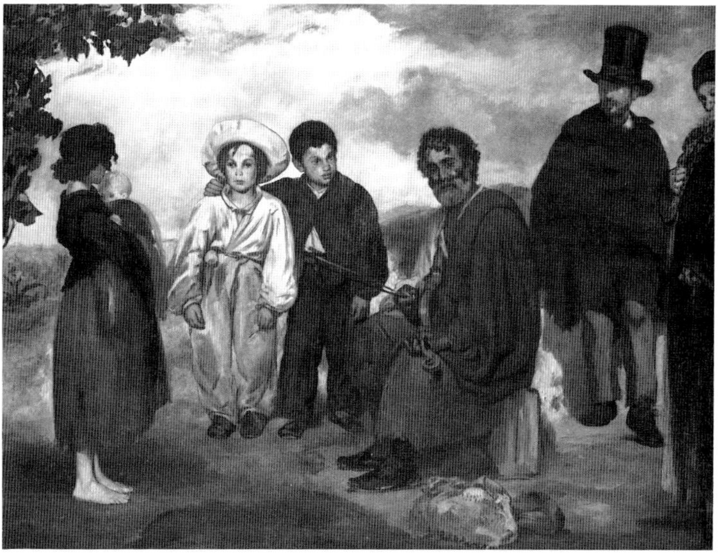

4 *The Old Musician*, 1861–2, oil on canvas. National Gallery of Art, Washington, DC

associations between the figures is what counts. Manet took the gypsy girl with her child from a popular print, the two boys from the realist traditions of eighteenth-century France (Watteau's *Gilles*) and seventeenth-century Spain (Murillo's *Ragged Boy*), and of course the absinthe drinker from his own work. The main character, a violin player, looks like the kind of figure the Le Nain brothers liked to portray, those three seventeenth-century painters of peasants whose earthy provincial directness and monumentality were instructive for Manet's great Realist predecessor, Courbet; yet *The Old Musician* is also a portrait of a junk dealer from Manet's own neighbourhood. The violinist's gaze, which prefigures that of Victorine in the *Déjeuner* and *Olympia*, acknowledges the presence of an audience on which such a purposeful assembly of the figures (one might say the objects) of picturesque realism obviously depends. Yet in so consciously displaying his mastery of the genre, Manet seems to dispose of it as well. Men like the junk dealer, the absinthe drinker and the guitar player were hardly Manet's social and cultural peers, even though they were his contemporaries. Their presence in art depended, rather, on a romantic notion of the artist's bohemianism that led many to identify with them. Indeed, a collection of etchings Manet published in 1862 on picturesque and Spanish themes strongly suggests he played on such a parallel, especially with entertainers. But the genre also safely catered to the bourgeois fascination for the exotic as a source of entertainment and consumption. (Manet would return to it only in exceptional cases, in order to introduce some new irony or subversive moral point, as in his series of 'philosophers' of 1865–7.)

Two pictures may be considered intermediaries of sorts between *The Old Musician* and the *Concert in the Tuileries* (illus. 6), the latter signalling Manet's definitive movement towards greater authenticity: both *The Spanish Ballet* (1862; Phillips Collection, Washington, DC) and *The Little Cavaliers* (illus. 5) present, like the other two, an array of figures. The cavaliers, copied from a painting in the Louvre that was, at that time, attributed to Velázquez, are contemporaries of the original painter, just as the Spanish ballet-dancers lined-up were contemporaries of Manet. Thus, the two paintings – the pseudo-Velázquez and the Manet – point away from *The Old Musician*'s aesthetic of pastiche toward actual experiences, although they do not yet go all the way. The *Little Cavaliers* obviously depends on the past, but at least that past provided a prototype for Manet's new painting of the present. And the members of the Spanish troupe that opened in Paris in August 1862 were at least a part of Manet's Parisian experience, though not his friends. Thus, it was not until the *Concert in the Tuileries* that Manet actually treated subjects with whom he shared social status and solidarity, figures whose presence did not depend on entertainment or cater to audience fantasies of possession.

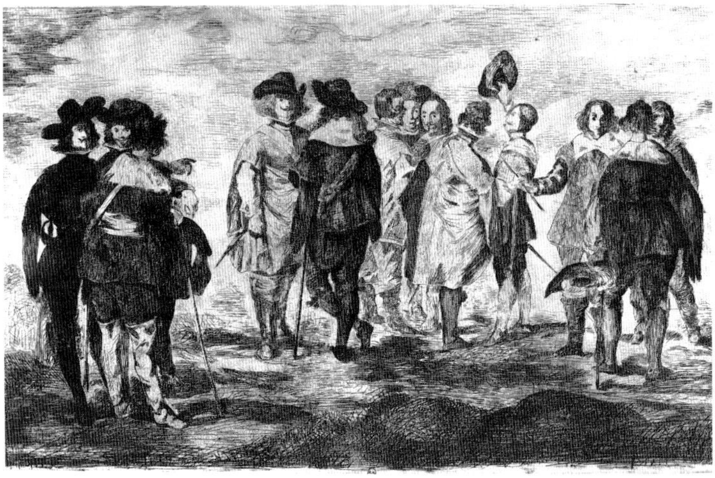

5 *The Little Cavaliers*, 1861–2, Manet's etching with drypoint after his oil copy of a painting in the Louvre formerly attributed to Velázquez. Bibliothèque Nationale, Paris

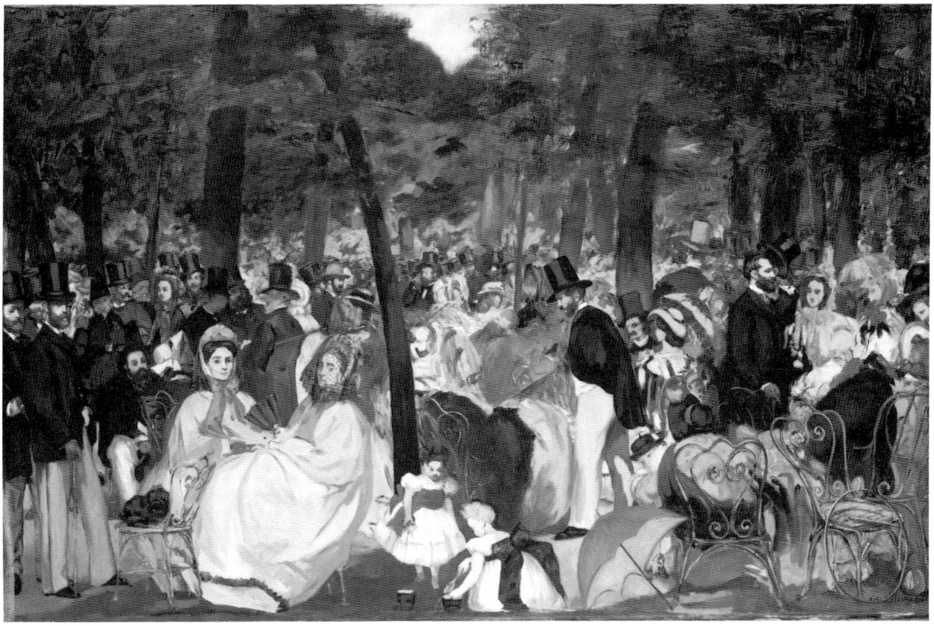

6 *The Concert in the Tuileries*, 1862, oil on canvas. National Gallery, London

Done immediately after, or perhaps concurrently with, *The Old Musician*, the *Concert in the Tuileries* is again a composite, which thus complements or serves as a foil for the other works. In it Manet has assembled the bourgeois artistic and literary intelligentsia of 1860s Paris. A series of portraits (from left to right) begins with himself, half in and half out of the picture. It is an early example of self-positioning, alluding perhaps to the ambiguous marginality of the artist as both part of a world and yet its objectively distant observer. Next to Manet, with a walking-stick, is his aristocratic friend Comte Albert de Balleroy, a painter of animals and genre scenes, with whom he had shared a studio; behind and between them is the Realist apologist and supporter of Courbet, the novelist Champfleury; seated nearby is the bearded sculptor, poet and critic Zacharie Astruc, another friend, above whom is the 'journalist of the Boulevards', Aurélien Scholl. The younger of the two prominently seated women is Mme Lejosne, wife of the Commandant in whose house Manet met Baudelaire and the fledgling painter Frédéric Bazille. With her is the wife of Jacques Offenbach, the composer of both the *Tales of Hoffmann* and popular dance-hall music, who (wearing spectacles and a moustache) is himself seated further to the right, between Manet's brother Eugène (turned to the left) and the painter

Charles Monginot (doffing his hat). The most important group is that near the large tree above Mme Lejosne. Next to the tree and facing us is Henri Fantin-Latour, a member of the Realist circle and its portraitist, who also did many flower still-lifes and was renowned for his lithographic illustrations of Wagner's *Tannhäuser*. In the group of three, engaged in conversation to Fantin-Latour's left is, at the left, Baron Taylor. A Frenchman despite his British surname, Taylor had been involved in early Realism as the editor of illustrated accounts of travels through Spain and France; later, he was commissioned by Louis-Philippe to acquire examples of Spanish art for the King's Spanish Museum. (The King considered this gallery to be his contribution to the Royal Collections until he was deposed in 1848, after which he claimed them as his own and sold off the lot!) To Taylor's right is Théophile Gautier, an important Romantic author and critic, whose open-mindedness led to some young Romantic and Realist artists receiving their first press exposure. Equally important, Gautier was a chief proponent of the theory of art for art's sake. In the preface to his novel *Mademoiselle de Maupin* (1835), Gautier opposed theories of the social utility of art, arguing that the sole purpose of art was its own creation, and hence the experience of the aesthetic. Beauty could not exist when tied to baser human interests, for it was to be their disinterested antidote. This theory, reviled by Courbet, has more to do with Manet than is generally recognized, though its role, as we shall see, is subtle and complex.

Indeed, the figure who built on and transformed Gautier's thought (and dedicated his own works to Gautier) stands in profile between him and Fantin-Latour. This was Baudelaire, who had been a friend of Manet for several years and was probably the greatest single external resource for Manet in the early to mid-1860s. Indeed, for the *Concert in the Tuileries* Manet may have drawn a great deal from Baudelaire's ideas, as embodied in his recently completed essay, *The Painter of Modern Life* (1863). (Baudelaire was looking for a publisher during the time Manet was painting this canvas.) *The Painter of Modern Life* contains so many ideas crucial to an understanding of Manet that, even though we shall return to Baudelaire later, we need here to summarize three main points especially relevant to this painting. First is Baudelaire's attempt to reconcile the ideal of classical beauty with a commitment to modernity. Beauty, he argued, contained both an eternal and a circumstantial element, the latter tied to the contemporary world's 'fashions, its morals, its emotions'. Building on ideas set out in the 1820s by Stendhal, Baudelaire saw the artist as expressing the moral disposition – the ethos – of his age. Second, and more profound, was Baudelaire's belief that through aesthetic experience man can transcend ordinary reality to reach a higher plane of existence (a way of making art for art's sake 'utilitarian' or, better, morally worthwhile). Here again was an attempt to reconcile traditional ideals with the demands of modernity. Academic theory held that art displayed its moral value by representing a world unattainable through ordinary nature. The academic artist attempted to transform and perfect nature according to 'divine', unchanging ideals that only the great classics had approached. Having disputed the exclusively eternal character of beauty, however, Baudelaire now argued it was the experience of artistic process itself – of the artifice that indexes the artist's move through imagination and beyond nature – that distanced the viewer of art from the reality that was its starting point and ostensible subject-matter. Hence art could maintain its source in the external world while emphasizing aspects of it in uplifting and pleasurable ways.

The third crucial aspect of Baudelaire's theory describes the kind of individual who would be the artist/viewer in (and of) the modern urban society he considered culturally central. For Baudelaire, the gentleman-dandy, whose means allowed him to cultivate the aesthetic and rise above the crowd, may well have been the model for Manet's new vision, as well as for his off-centre location in the *Concert in the Tuileries*. Baudelaire imagined such enviable beings as *flâneurs* – those well-dressed, leisurely observers who strolled about the town without particular direction, yet for the purpose of enjoyment, such as we might do when taking a break from work, except that their jaunts could last all day. The notion of infiltrating society in order to see up close, but maintaining distance as if observing through a spyglass, embodies both the directness and the remove we often experience in Manet's work. According to Baudelaire, such a gaze was characteristic of social circumstances peculiar to the nineteenth century, for it was the attribute of a certain class of superior people who, through their indomitable bearing, heroically resisted the rising tide of

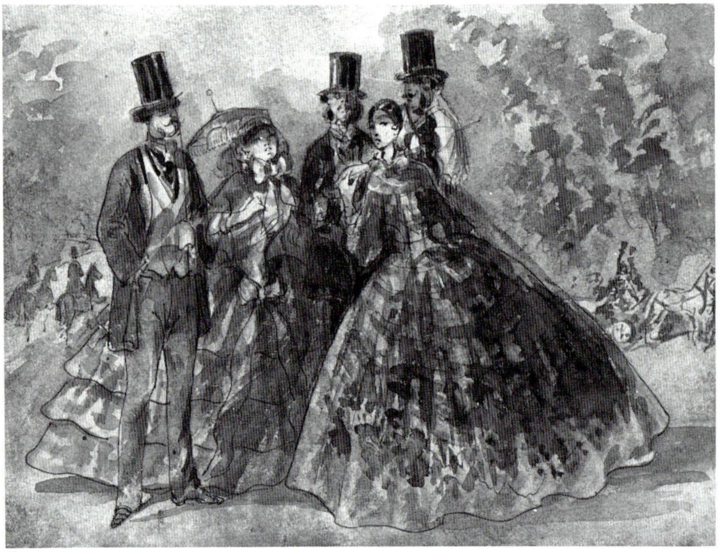

7 Constantin Guys, *Meeting in a Park*, c. 1855, watercolour. Metropolitan Museum of Art, New York

democracy at a time when the world of the aristocracy was on the verge of collapse.

The artist through whom Baudelaire exemplified his theories was the watercolourist and illustrator Constantin Guys. The rapid, sketch-like quality of Guys's style, Baudelaire claimed, embodied both the passion and fascination for seeing of the naïve observer (one unencumbered by outworn conventions) and the modern ideal of efficiency (the greatest effect with the most economy of means). We may judge Baudelaire's theory by a Guys watercolour (illus. 7). If we were to weigh the degree to which we view the work as a technically brilliant sketch against the extent to which we see it as a naturalistic denotation of its object, surely the former would be so obvious that mere representation could not be the drawing's only effect? Hence, the subject-matter is made a vehicle for art, and the artist's transformation of it offers an experience of aesthetic properties – such as the watercolour medium, or the artist's personal technical virtuosity – that outweighs the image's illusion as a form reproducing nature. In other words, one appreciates figures not as figures but for the aesthetic impact artists can impart to them. In the ghoulish children to be seen in the foreground of the *Concert in the Tuileries*, and in Manet's loose and suggestive handling generally, there may be something of Guys's spirit, as well as his technique, translated into oils. We know, by the way, that

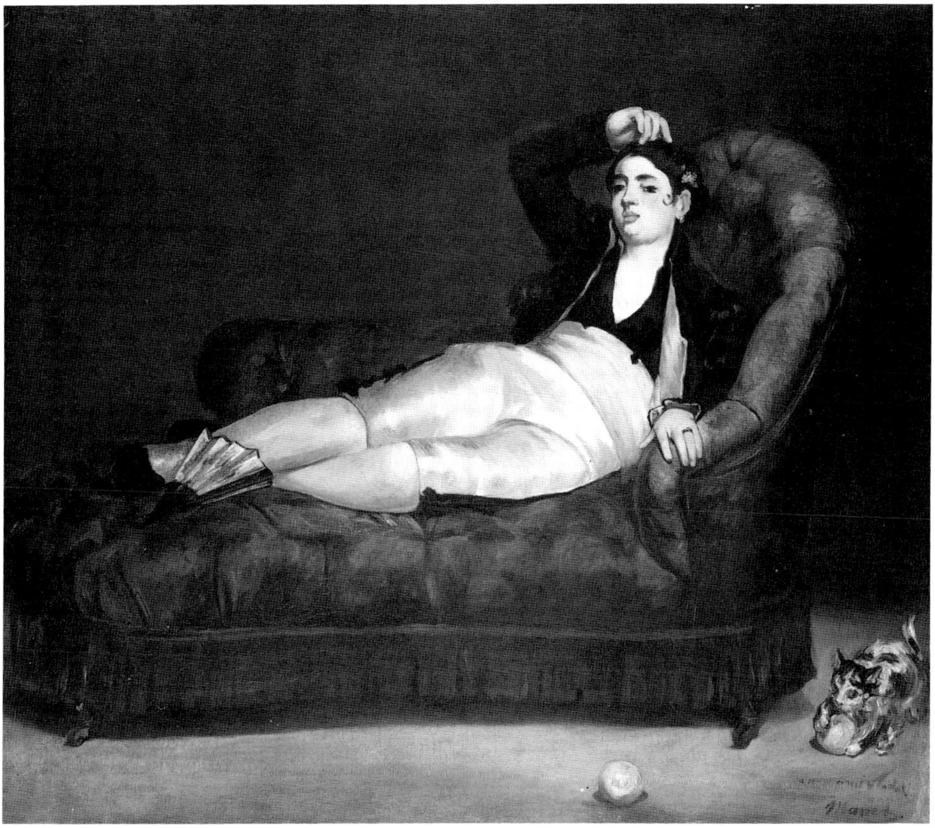

8 *Reclining Woman in Spanish Costume,* 1862, oil on canvas. Yale University Art Gallery, New Haven

Manet possessed a group of drawings by Guys. And the latter's frequent representations of women dressed as men is reflected in another painting Manet showed at Martinet's, that of the mistress of the photographer Nadar, the *Reclining Woman in Spanish Costume* (illus. 8). In any case, the marks explicitly left by Manet's hand on his painted surface bear witness to the painter's presence in the act of seeing, hence to his attitude – *à la Guys.*

Concurrent with Baudelaire's discussion of Guys, Manet thus developed a pictorial technique into which he could translate his modern vision – a vision in which distance combined with presence expresses the ambiguity of the artist's position both within and outside his world. Even more than subject-matter, style became its sign. Refusing the relatively smooth transparency of picturesque realism as practised by most other painters, including many of those who had admired the *Guitar Player*, Manet's pictorial markings

– those opaque traces of a working brush that are the tell-tale signs of the specific artist's hand – have a dual effect. They place him outside his painting by designating him as the painterly vision's creator, and yet, by the same token, they place him within it by making its peculiarity an expression of artistic personality. His marginality was not that of the bohemian's social exteriority to the represented world, but of the voyeur's perceptual exteriority and attitudinal superiority, while remaining at one with a world very much his own. It is as if on entering this world of Parisian culture and recognizing its principal practitioners close up, we discover it to be rooted in artifice and aesthetic display. Thus although the *Concert in the Tuileries* naturalistically represents Manet's intellectual and social milieu by adducing the likenesses of its members, it also records the essential subjectivity and selfconsciousness of all perceiving beings.

VICTORINE'S GAZE

While the *Old Musician*, the *Concert in the Tuileries* and other paintings were being shown at Martinet's, Manet was at work on a picture for the Salon of 1863, the now famous *Déjeuner sur l'herbe* (illus. 40). Originally known simply as *Le Bain*, the painting drew on a recent tradition of outdoor leisure enjoyed on the outskirts of Paris that had already spawned numerous images of strollers, picnickers, bathers, canoers and the like. The most notorious of these visual precedents to date was surely Courbet's *Demoiselles des bords de la Seine* of 1856–7 (Musée du Petit Palais, Paris), which showed ladies of questionable morals lying on the river-bank. Since Manet's *Déjeuner* included the naked Victorine Meurent, his professional model, it could thus easily be taken as an offensive and bizarre provocation despite – indeed, perhaps because of – its equally evident connections to prestigious traditional compositions. With its problematically disjointed foreground and background to boot, then, the *Déjeuner*, like the earlier *Absinthe Drinker*, was an obvious candidate for rejection from the official Salon. That year, however, because the jury was so severe, and the rejected artists so vociferous in their protest, Napoleon III, anxious to present his liberal side to the intelligentsia, authorized a parallel exhibition of refused works. Though for most of those who attended it the resultant

Salon des Refusés simply confirmed the jury's original good judgement, Manet's *Déjeuner* earned him tremendous notoriety, while subsequent reforms made admission to the regular Salon far easier for all.

It would not have occurred to Manet to paint for any audience other than the educated public of the Salon. It has even been argued by Pierre Bourdieu (convincingly so, at least for Manet's figure compositions) that Manet's painting constitutes a response to the institution of the museum.[22] Indeed, throughout his career Manet's painting depended for much of its intellectual consistency and focus on a dialogue with the traditions in which the museum and the Salon public's expectations were grounded. For example, though few of Manet's contemporaries could have known that his *Déjeuner* was based on a portion of an engraving by Raimondi after a lost Raphael cartoon (illus. 9), this borrowing was a wry and practically effortless means of 'combining' the classical with the contemporary. The male figures in contemporary dress are portraits of Manet's brother Eugène (to the right) and his future brother-in-law, the Dutch sculptor Ferdinand Leenhoff. The picture takes up in a much less derivative manner a theme already explored in *The Surprised Nymph* (illus. 10). In that painting, references to bathers such as Diana, Bathsheba or Susanna are all too obvious. Manet's mistress (soon-to-be-wife), named Suzanne (a near Susanna), was the model. A study for the *Surprised Nymph* shows that Manet originally intended to use accessory figures in the act of watching the nymph. The decision to exclude them from the final version accentuates the viewer's role as voyeur and, looking ahead to the *Olympia*, suggests some complicity on the part of the naked female.[23]

Far less obscure than either the lost Raphael or the theme of Susanna – and immediately recognized by Zacharie Astruc – was a more fundamentally significant art-historical source for the *Déjeuner*: Giorgione's well-known painting in the Louvre, the *Concert champêtre* (illus. 11). Since Manet is said to have wished to do a contemporary outdoor nude,[24] a comparison with this source may reveal just what he believed constituted the contemporary in his own painting. Giorgione had already combined nude and contemporarily clothed figures in a recognizable (as Venetian) landscape; hence, these features cannot in themselves define the difference between Manet's

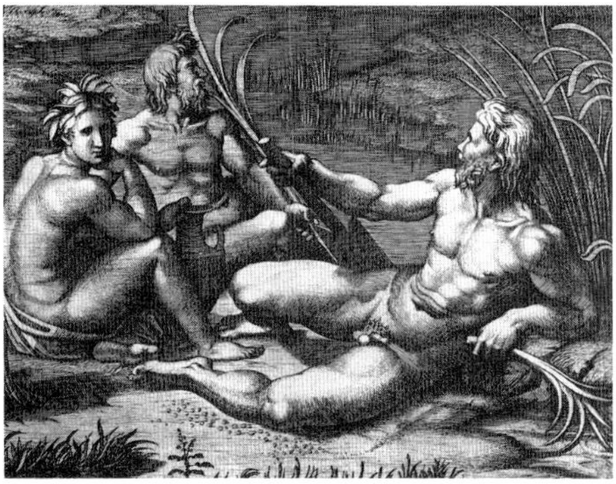

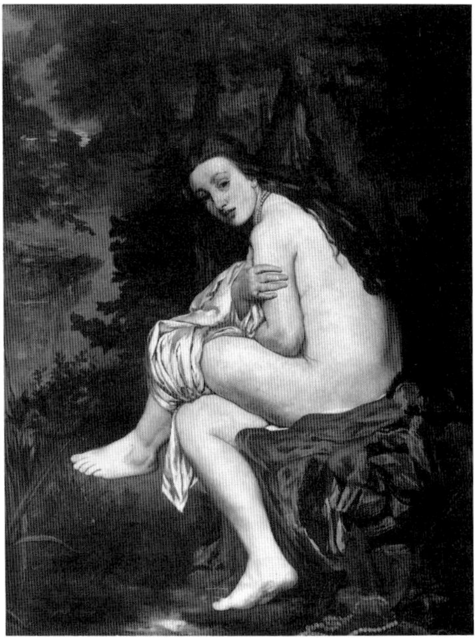

9 Marcantonio Raimondi, Detail from *The Judgement of Paris*, *c.* 1518, engraving after a lost cartoon by Raphael. Metropolitan Museum of Art, New York

10 *The Surprised Nymph*, 1859–61, oil on canvas. Museo Nacional de Bellas Artes de la Escuela, Buenos Aires

11 Giorgione, *Concert champêtre*, *c.* 1510, oil on canvas. Musée du Louvre, Paris

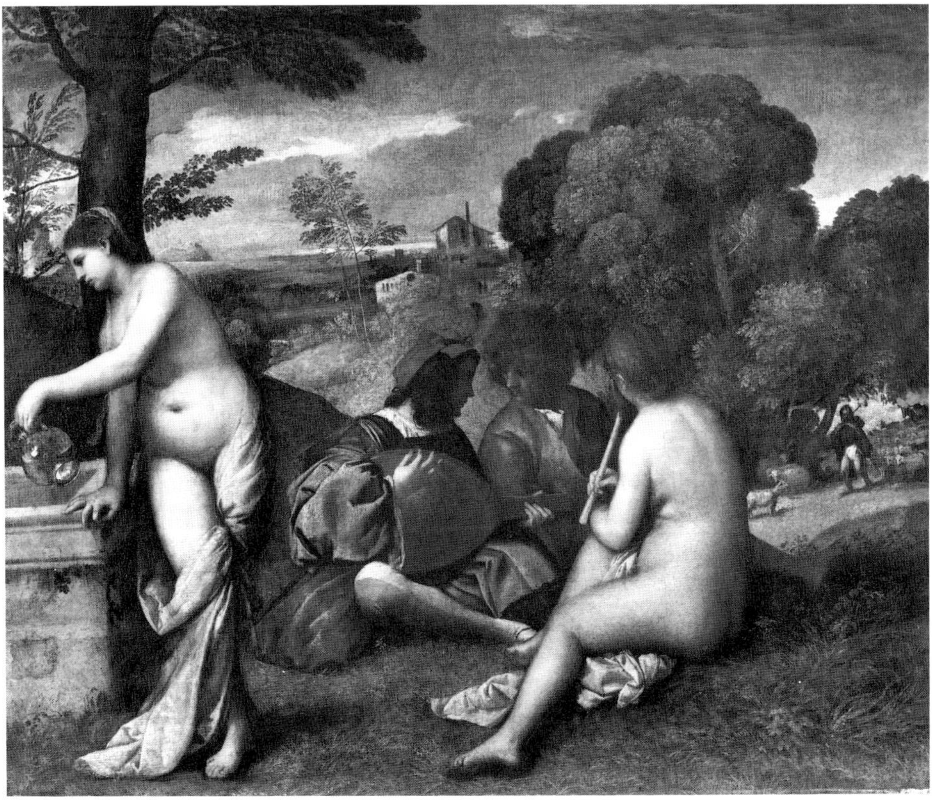

work and the earlier one. Rather, the novelty of the Manet turns on the relationship between the viewer and the painted groups. In the Venetian work, the figures are absorbed in their own world; absence of the illusion of direct contact between us and them creates a fiction of the painting as a separate and ideal realm. There, the combination of nude and clothed characters is justified by allegory, in which the women are probably muse-like figures of literary or artistic inspiration. (The Venetian reverence for nature as an artistic source is well known.) In the Manet, however, no such literary reading is possible. Our possession of its world through intellect is challenged. For one thing, Eugène makes a cryptic, possibly vulgar, but in any case incomprehensible gesture towards Victorine; for another, Victorine looks so unabashedly out at the viewer that the contact she establishes between her world and ours asserts her realm as an extension of our own, and ours as an extension of her's. Centuries of art viewing had prepared European audiences to see pictures as visual equivalents of literature, a way of viewing that Manet now ruthlessly challenged. With no possibility either of narrative to explain the figure relationships, or of escape into a pictorial fiction, the viewer is thrown back onto his own consciousness and experience of seeing as the core of the *Déjeuner*'s 'meaning'. Victorine's gaze, as the act of her consciousness seeing in its own right, embodies experience of the contemporary as much as does our own consciousness of seeing her.

Defying conventional expectations, Manet's painting was seen as morally provocative, for to deny a picture's life as fiction made its figures accountable by the standards of society. Hence, Victorine's public exposure was outrageous: Napoleon III himself declared the painting an offence to modesty. But surely the most remarkable and lasting effect of the *Déjeuner* results from the personal encounter between the eyes of the beholder and those of Victorine? For one thing, Victorine violated one of the first rules of civility: many were the books of manners that called staring an affront. Those written for ladies were explicit: the eyes must be lowered to avoid impudence. 'Modesty is the first of the graces', went the maxim.[25] Between the sexes, staring is gender-specific to men, for the aggressive role is reserved for them: women who do it are not only acting improperly, but contrary to their gender. Yet Victorine answers the voyeurism Manet had hinted at with his position in the *Concert in the Tuileries*. Now the viewer is studied from within the painting; our experience of the *Déjeuner* is that of being seen while seeing. Just as we feel discomfort when an unfamiliar person we are watching discovers us doing so, the viewer of Manet's painting feels the privacy of his perceptions violated. There is a saying that the eyes are the window of the soul, a saying that, despite our reluctance to take it too literally, admits of seeing as a social process, a two-way exchange. It suggests that he who sees reveals the inner self when his eyes are seen by another, but that, at the same time, the other person is revealed in return. We may interpret this interchange as meaning that the viewer's viewing is revealed to the viewed – a dynamic dialogue of the eyes involving social differentiation, which the person who sees performs while having it performed on him- or herself.

The act of seeing is often characterized in psychoanalytic literature as a vicarious act of possession. But, in addition, sight is connected through memory to the experience of touch. Hence, submission to the gaze may symbolically imply physical appropriation and dominance – the gaze as a projection of actual power. Confrontation between two gazes often supposes a test of wills, one of which eventually overcomes the other. This is the principle of the hypnotic gaze, which Alfred Maury discussed in 1860 in the *Revue des Deux-Mondes*, noting that the excessive impression produced by a fixed gaze could result in a vertigo-like state and loss of consciousness by the subject.[26] The hypnotist disposes freely of the victim's body. The painted Victorine is, of course, impassive. If the painting is confused with reality, as in a Realist interpretation, there can be no hope of 'victory' over her, for such an interpretation endows her with a life and will external to the viewer's consciousness, and to which the viewer is forced to submit. Seeing herself being seen, Victorine appears to seize the viewer's thought. As a viewer herself, she makes the viewer of the painting, who is external to her consciousness, nothing but her own representation; and on becoming other, the viewer experiences vulnerability, absence, even a vicarious mortality. 'Victorine-Medusa' – in the sense that her gaze deprives its object of independent life and immobilizes it as a fixed image – enacts the concept of viewing as transformation into representation and as potential for possession. The viewer experiences the dimension of the object. The viewer experiences himself as visual sign. The selfconsciousness provoked by the role reversal performed by Manet's painting is a consciousness of the duality of seeing, of how surveillance both excludes and appropriates the object of sight. Hence, in Victorine, the viewer experiences the act of seeing as a living social act rather than an act of literary fiction; he or she experiences not just vision, but visuality – an effect in the real world with a physical dimension.

Manet's audience was, and is sometimes still so today, accustomed to a Realist way of seeing. Yet precisely because of its social sensitivity, Manet's gaze had to be more complex. In real life Manet was a man of class and breeding who would never violate decorum. It could even be argued that his understanding of social conventions is proven by the way he cleverly turns the tables on them in his paintings. Manet's diffidence can translate into a treatment of the object of sight as a purely visual entity. His painting takes pains to convey the difference between art and 'external' reality. Rather than discovering in the other the consciousness he can only know in himself, Manet concentrates on his subject's visuality – which is predicated on his responses to its bodily presence. His handling of paint, like Victorine's gaze, forces us to acknowledge the painting as part of the physical world. Looking past Victorine's stare to avoid complicity, to avoid having her read one's own mind, we encounter aspects of the picture independent of psychological expression. Freed from the systematic task of producing convincing illusions of the fictive, style assumes its potential for creating experiences of the pictorial, that is, of the representational process rather than the represented referent. One need not even look closely to perceive individual brushstrokes, overlappings of which in different hues (nominal modelling) caused Manet's critics to complain that he had sullied his colours. But by ostensibly emptying the picture of experiences other than visual ones, Manet has concentrated our attention on what is left – the presence of the eye in objects *cum* the artifice of representation. As such, the exquisite still-life on the ground near Victorine, with its broad, flat, dry and carefully controlled brushwork, becomes as central to the painting's portent as any other passage. The painting is a picnic – forms spread across a surface – for the eye. (One thinks of the earlier claim by Eugène Delacroix that painting should be a feast for the eye.) Only Victorine's call to selfconsciousness is a brutal reminder that Manet's aim can hardly have been limited to the creation of aesthetic escape. Endowing the traces of vision with physicality and thus somewhat crudely insisting on associations between sight and touch, between eye and hand, Manet's hand converts the seen world to signs, to painted physical forms, like the objects of still-life, paradoxically introducing a form of distance that permits possession (as representation) even in indecorous situations. We may conclude that, like Giorgione's *Concert champêtre*, the *Déjeuner sur l'herbe* deals with the relationship between art and nature. In the earlier work, nature is the inspiration for art, whose difference from nature is expressed by the classical nudes of its muses – allegories implying that truth lies in the world as concept. In Manet there is an inversion: the difference between nature and art is expressed as that between the world as concept and the world as seen – the world bearing traces of the act of seeing, and thus inhabited or possessed by the eye.

A second picture may more successfully integrate these ramifications of Manet's interests with subject-matter and form, though a smoothing over of the *Déjeuner*'s pictorial disjunctiveness was done at the cost of greater public confusion between reality and art. Also painted in 1863, but not shown until the reformed Salon of 1865, the *Olympia* (illus. 41) places Victorine in the (for Manet's contemporaries) all-too-obvious role of a prostitute, receiving flowers from an admirer. The object of desire is overtly posed as object of consumption. Yet, in a radical role reversal, Victorine's gaze meets ours squarely, with its source in the heavily adorned head emphasized far more than in the *Déjeuner* by the flower in her hair and the velvet choker at her neck. It has been said, by the poet Paul Valéry, that the head seems psychologically severed from the body; and it is certainly true that intelligence and will seem unsentimentally in control of, rather than subject to, what is displayed as a commodity. Dominated by Victorine's gaze, we are subject to the world on her terms; we become the other (presumably the male), whose desire she exploits for profit. Rather than experiencing the artist determining the parameters of an imaginary world, the painted representation operates on ours.

Manet again plays off a classic prototype, Titian's *Venus of*

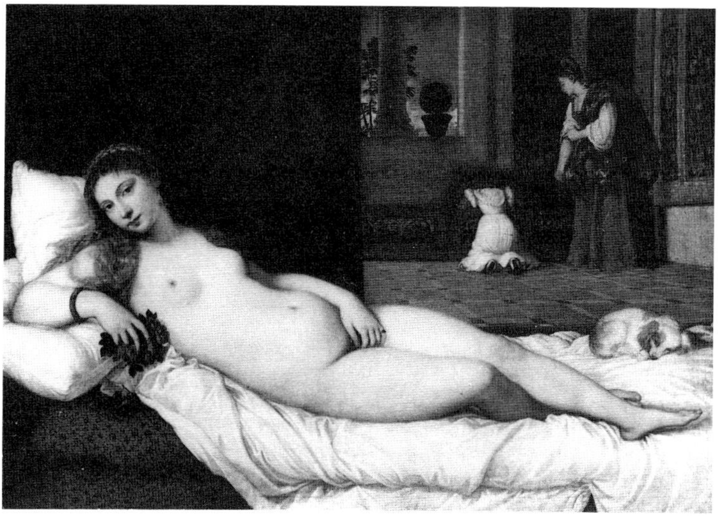

12 Titian, *The Venus of Urbino*, 1538, oil on canvas. Galleria degli Uffizi, Florence

Urbino (illus. 12), which he copied twice. Yet, in another role reversal, Titian's warm, curvaciously alluring figure, actually the Duke of Urbino's mistress under the traits of Venus (ideal love), becomes a dominatrix who casually retains her bracelet and slippers throughout her matter-of-fact display of quasi-inert and rubberized-looking flesh. The hand that hides her sex actually attracts attention to it – note its strong outlines – and acquires its properties through transference: though compared, understandably, by one reviewer to a toad, the hand actually resembles a crab (with ironic overtones of ensnarement), or perhaps a tarantula, which could suggest the orgiastic dance of the *tarantella*. Moreover, Manet has transformed the Venus's little lap-dog – symbol of fidelity – into a black cat, like the one roaming Paris rooftops in his later Japanese-style lithograph for the poster for Champfleury's book documenting the promiscuous feline life (illus. 13).

Courbet's remark, that this composition was as flat as a playing-card, may allude to Manet's Japonisme, that is, his taste, shared by many artists of the time, for the flatness, bold outlines and bright, localized colour to be found in the Japanese woodcuts that had begun to flood Europe. However, it also suggests comparison with pornographic photographs, some of which were used by prostitutes as calling-cards. Photographs, too, had their impact on the art of painting. For one thing, they certainly provided a standard by which two-dimensional visual realism could be measured; in addition,

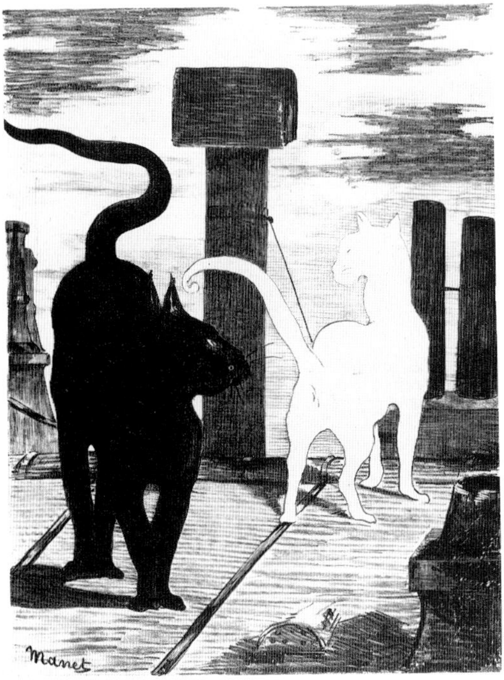

13 *Cats' Rendezvous*, lithograph for a poster for Champfleury's *Les Chats*. The New York Public Library

they introduced previously excluded subjects to the realm of visual culture. As a result, they increasingly blurred the boundaries between mass and élite forms, boundaries already under seige as graphic media, and what we now know as advertising developed and spread. Indeed, Manet's composition does partake of an aesthetic of public display, like that of abalone in a fish-shop window, posed on cloth or some similar support. It parallels the display of flowers in their wrapping held up by the maid – Olympia herself treated as a sort of still-life, as Zola eventually would imply. The painting is often contrasted to a *Birth of Venus* exhibited in 1863 by Alexandre Cabanel (illus. 14). Surely the Cabanel is a far more erotic image (for the standard male viewer, of course)? One in which the goddess's seductive undulations overtly aim at encouraging sexual thoughts. Thus the Manet is the more shocking precisely because Olympia is not a cliché male fantasy, and because there is no mythological disguise. She is from the harsh contemporary world of commerce and careerism (she could afford a maid) – a world from which conventional art was to serve as an escape, but of which Olympia, contrariwise, seemed a heartless affirmation. Critics treated Manet's

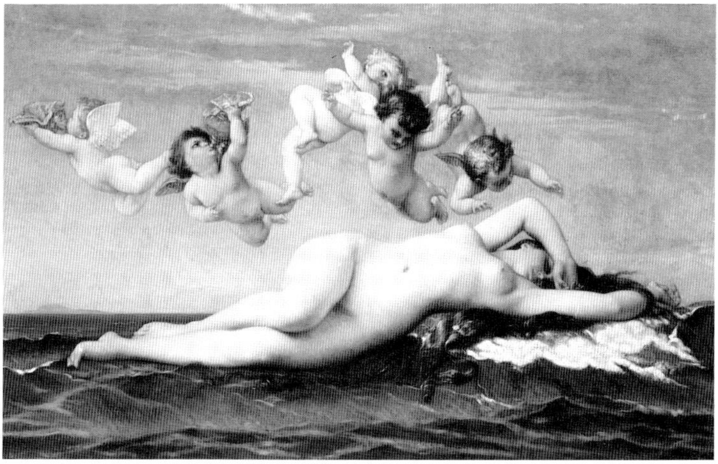

14 Alexandre Cabanel, *The Birth of Venus*, 1863, oil on canvas. Metropolitan Museum of Art, New York

painting with unmitigated disgust: 'What is this odalisque with the yellow belly, ignoble model dredged up from who knows where?'; or 'The flesh tones are filthy. . . . Shadows are indicated with strokes of shoe polish;' or 'There is an almost infantile ignorance of the basic elements of drawing [and] the painter's attitude is one of inconceivable vulgarity.' The Government was forced to post guards!

The nude courtesan with a black companion is found in innumerable odalisques, of which the ones by Ingres are merely the best known. Moreover, the name 'Olympia' had various sources, including *La Dame aux camélias* by Dumas *fils*, and the poem by Zacharie Astruc that was used in the Salon catalogue. But above all, the *Olympia* is Manet's most Baudelairian picture – and in ways that go beyond obvious reminiscences of poems from *Les Fleurs du mal*. As Walter Benjamin has written regarding the motif of the gaze in Baudelaire: 'In eyes that look at us with a mirrorlike blankness the remoteness remains complete. It is precisely for this reason that such eyes know nothing of distance. . . . When such eyes come alive, it is with the self-protective wariness of a wild animal hunting for prey. (Thus the eye of the prostitute scrutinizing the passers-by is at the same time on its guard against the police. . .).'[27] The *Olympia* also reflects Baudelaire's fascination, expressed in *The Painter of Modern Life*, for woman as 'idol, stupid perhaps, but dazzling and bewitching', who 'holds wills and destinies suspended on her glance'. Olympia echoes his description of the modern courtesan (the mistress of the rich, as opposed to the low-class prostitute), who 'has discovered for herself a provocative and barbaric sort of elegance'. Baudelaire suggested that women of the *demi-monde* had created the most current forms of beauty, both out of the necessity of their nature as sexual beings craving male attention and from an innate desire to rise above nature. Artifice is woman's way of expressing her essence as material being aspiring to divinity; more broadly, Baudelaire regarded external adornment as 'one of the signs of the primitive nobility of the human soul'. This duality of the aesthetic drive between the material and the spiritual helps explain the poet's comparisons between courtesans and artists: the artist's vision is subjugated by the external reality it describes, yet it acts on that reality to express its special character; the artist is an exhibitionist in displaying this vision to the world, yet the strategy of attracting the other's gaze through artifice enables him to rise above that on which he is dependent. Is it a coincidence that Olympia's hand both draws our attention to her sex and yet covers it up, as the artist's hand both produces reality and yet distances us from it? Manet's fusion between introspection and his intense seeing of exteriority is related. Demonstrating possession of the world through personalized vision, he creates the vehicle for a transcendent position within it. So it may not be too far-fetched to see Olympia as an indirect self-image for Manet, one confirmed by the recent discovery that the bracelet she wears belonged to Manet's mother and contained a lock of the painter's hair.[28] Perhaps in this hidden attribute of both mother and son there is embodied Manet's ambitious yet ambiguous straddle between obedience to authority and rebellious compulsion to shock.[29]

Although not as strongly as in Baudelaire's 'provocative and barbaric sort of elegance', the young Emile Zola characterized Manet's style in terms of related contradictions: 'dry but winning charm', and 'surprisingly elegant awkwardness'. To the extent that Manet's head-on compositional simplicity, his matt, slightly abrasive surfaces, his summarization of details and sternly contrasted outlines transfer their effects to characterization, his style is totally congruent with its subject-matter in creating an experience of the contradictions of modern life. But these are not simply expressive devices, nor are they to be understood as allegorizations of the characteristics of modernity. Constantly reminding us we are viewers of an artist's creation – of artifice rather than reality – such effects appropriate reality to art, transforming it into a visible sign for itself. In Victorine's gaze, distanced yet knowing, the viewer discovers the self's status as voyeur and that of the artwork, as a response to that condition, representing the position of the eye. In this deeper additional sense, Manet's image of Olympia may be considered an effective *alter ego*.

SIGNATURES AND PORTRAITS

A painting of the early 1860s, *Landscape with Fishermen* (Metropolitan Museum of Art, New York), presents Manet with his mistress in a setting reminiscent of works by the seventeenth-century Flemish painter Rubens, using historical costumes and a relatively loose painterly style as dual marks for his persona. Almost unique in its directness (Manet would do no more self-portraits until the late 1870s), the picture establishes the centrality in Manet's work of the relationship between past art and the painter's sense of his personal artistic identity. Manet's many literary and art-journalist friends formed the heart of his social and cultural world, a world Manet identified through his numerous portraits of them. During the 1860s, these portraits highlighted his own artistic interests through a dialogue with those of his models – the ego of the artist in conversation with that of the friend. They thus exemplify the way aesthetics became a medium for social exchange in the cafés in the Batignolles quarter of Paris, where a fashionable new artistic radicalism was brewing. In addition, in these works of ostensibly Realist intent, Manet more than ever displayed an equally strong will to stylistic self-expression, through deliberate contrasts between figurative and what I earlier called defigurative passages of painting.

Manet painted the first of such portraits in 1866, for his long-time friend and supporter, Zacharie Astruc (illus. 15). The composition is based on a traditional portrait type, with a curtain in the upper-right corner and the figure on one side juxtaposed with a scene on the other. Adjacent to the elegantly dressed Astruc (note his bright-red belt) is a table covered with a tapestry on which a still-life with a glass and half-peeled lemon recalls Dutch models. These and other objects – quill pens, and old and recent publications distinguished by leather or paper bindings – allude to Astruc's

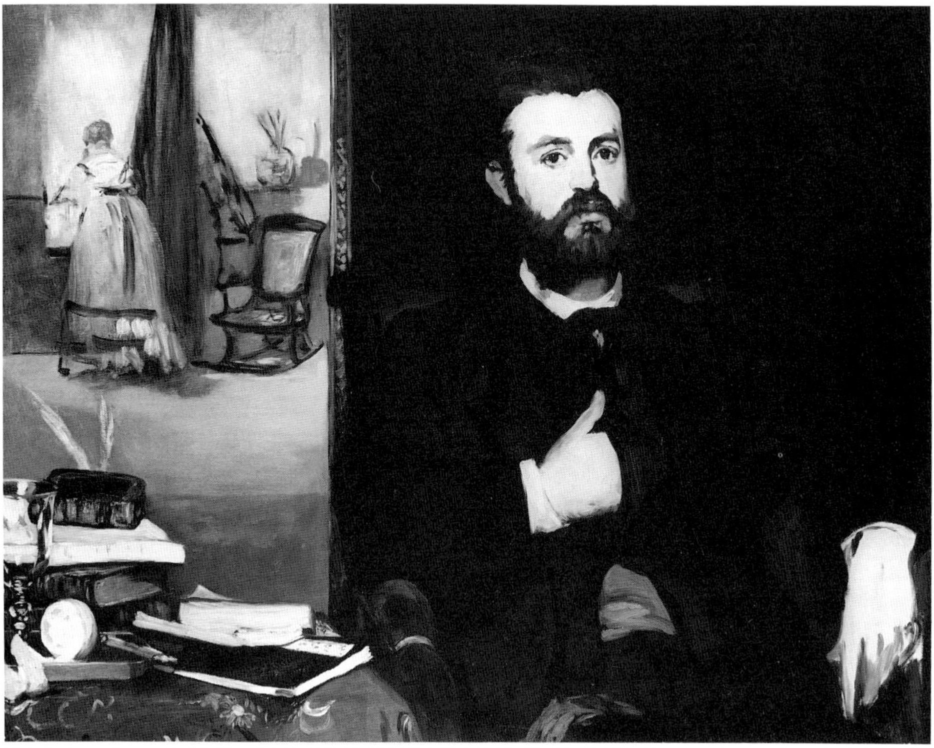

literary and artistic interests. An album of Japanese prints bears witness to Astruc's Japonisme, and a fan refers to his Hispanicism by resembling the one held by the singer Lola de Valence in Manet's painting of her (illus. 20). Astruc had composed a song about Lola, which Manet illustrated. In addition to the still-life, the painting hanging behind Astruc's table suggests Dutch art, too. It may partly be based on the background in Titian's *Venus of Urbino*, and hence bear an indirect allusion to the *Olympia*. But its blond tonalities and the perspectival relationship it creates with the rest of Manet's composition, as well as its iconography (the woman looking into the distance, the curtain and the musical instrument) are reminiscent of works by de Hooch and Vermeer, who were vaunted in articles by Théophile Thoré in the *Gazette des Beaux-Arts* that very year. Astruc made watercolours of just such subjects, though few have survived, and he had visited Holland in the 1860s.[30]

15 *Zacharie Astruc*, 1866, oil on canvas. Kunsthalle Bremen

Manet's interest at this time in Dutch art can be found in numerous still-lifes, or in pictures such as the *Boy Blowing*

Bubbles (1867; Museu Calouste Gulbenkian, Lisbon). It is obvious in Manet's very early portrait of his parents (illus. 16), and, in fact, it went back as far as the early 1850s, when he travelled to Holland and to various other parts of Europe (and, later, to Italy). His friendship with Astruc dated from the same period; the painting may, then, honour its duration. However, the combination of Titian and the Delft School also suggests Manet's theme of the classics renewed through contact with reality. Regarding this point, we should note that Manet has certainly positioned the painting within his portrait to provoke a dialogue between reality and art: at first we wonder whether we view a painting, a mirror or a scene in an adjacent room. At the opposite side of the portrait is another play on that distinction: Manet's flat, broadly brushed, unfinished-looking rendering of the writer's hand. Though partly an allusion to the art of Frans Hals, Hals is one of those artists, like Velázquez, for whom the deliberate mark of artistic process is a reminder that his picture represents an artist's vision of the world, not simply that world itself. It is a sign of self more telling than a signature, as Manet systematically draws on reminders of the materiality of painting he

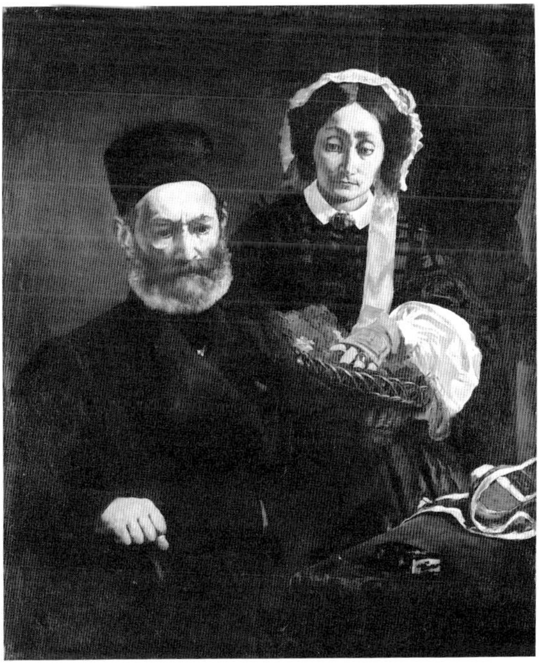

16 *M. and Mme Auguste Manet*, 1860, oil on canvas. Musée d'Orsay, Paris

found in work reputed to be Realist. If it can be said that the 'hand writing' or the 'writing hand' of the author is comparable to the painting hand of Manet, then the attention drawn to Astruc's hand ostentatiously expresses the presence of the artist's own hand as well.

The most famous of Manet's pictures of a literary friend is the portrait of Emile Zola (illus. 42), executed two years later. It translates the suggestive aspects of the Astruc portrait into an even more tightly constructed programme, while making ties to the *Olympia* more explicit. An image of the scandalous work at the upper right shows Olympia gazing benevolently toward the writer seated at his desk with an open art book. In this way, Manet conveyed his gratitude to Zola for the latter's valiant defence. Featured among the author's clutter are his inkstand, his letter-opener, his books, including one with a curiously multi-coloured binding lying on a pile on his desk, and his pamphlets on Manet – the tools and products, in fact, of his craft. The title of one pamphlet serves as Manet's signature, a visual pun obliquely echoed by the parallel between the broadly brushed quill-pen – the 'hand tool' of Zola's art – and the painter's own punning and illusion-making brush. At the time Manet made this portrait, he was not so much Zola's friend as a beneficiary of critical support that served the younger man's desire for journalistic visibility. The parallel between their careers is thus entirely credible.

Through his art criticism, which we shall study in closer detail later, Zola worked out many ideas that would be important for his far more renowned career as a novelist. His defence of Manet disregarded conventional attitudes towards subject-matter. In a felicitous definition that could apply to Manet and, eventually, to Impressionist painting, Zola had claimed that art was 'a corner of nature seen through a temperament'. He accepted as given that art begins in nature, by which he meant not some idealized abstraction but the contemporary world; and he made the artist's way of seeing the basis for his own critical judgements. The temperament, or artistic personality, of the painter, expressed through style (but also given by nature), was where the experience of art resided. Discounting conventions that sought stories, feelings or ideas in art, he located 'content' in colour combinations, fine lines and modelled surfaces. At one point he noted that Manet's attitudes toward figure painting were like those of

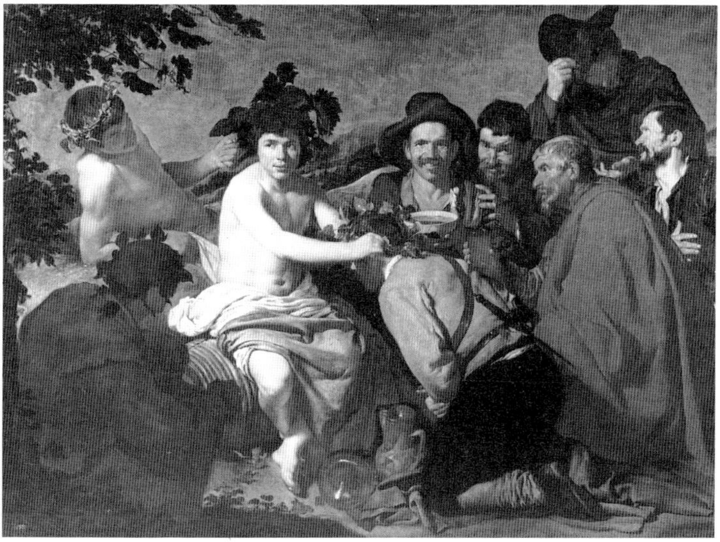

17 Diego Velázquez, *Bacchus (The Drunkards)*, *c.* 1629, oil on canvas. Museo del Prado, Madrid

academic painters towards still-life, that is that structure and form were, for Manet, the only meaningful elements of art.

But while the single-minded formalism of Zola's approach no doubt had its polemical uses, it needs to be qualified against Manet's preoccupations with past art, with significant subject-matter, and with clever signatures and other devices through which he asserted his creative presence. Adjacent, in the Zola portrait, to the *Olympia* are two images that are particularly close to such interests. The first, a Goya print after Velázquez's *Bacchus* (illus. 17) displays a connection to Spanish art. The second, a Sumo wrestler in a print by Kuniaki II (1835–88), alludes to Manet's fascination with Japanese prints.

Besides the colours and broad brushstrokes of Velázquez, Manet must certainly have admired his Spanish predecessor's frank acceptance of continuity between the realm of the viewer and that of art. In *Bacchus*, the tipsy god looks out, holding a goblet as an offer to partake of sensual pleasures – those of drink no doubt paralleling those of art. Manet's interest in Spanish art was exemplified in certain portraits of the 1860s, and focused primarily on the example of Goya. After the critical uproar over the *Olympia* in 1865, Manet consoled himself with a trip to Spain. There he met Théodore Duret, whom he painted in 1868 (illus. 18) as another tribute to a writer friend. The critic's pose is closely based on portraits by Goya, such as that of Manuel Lapeña (1799; Hispanic Society

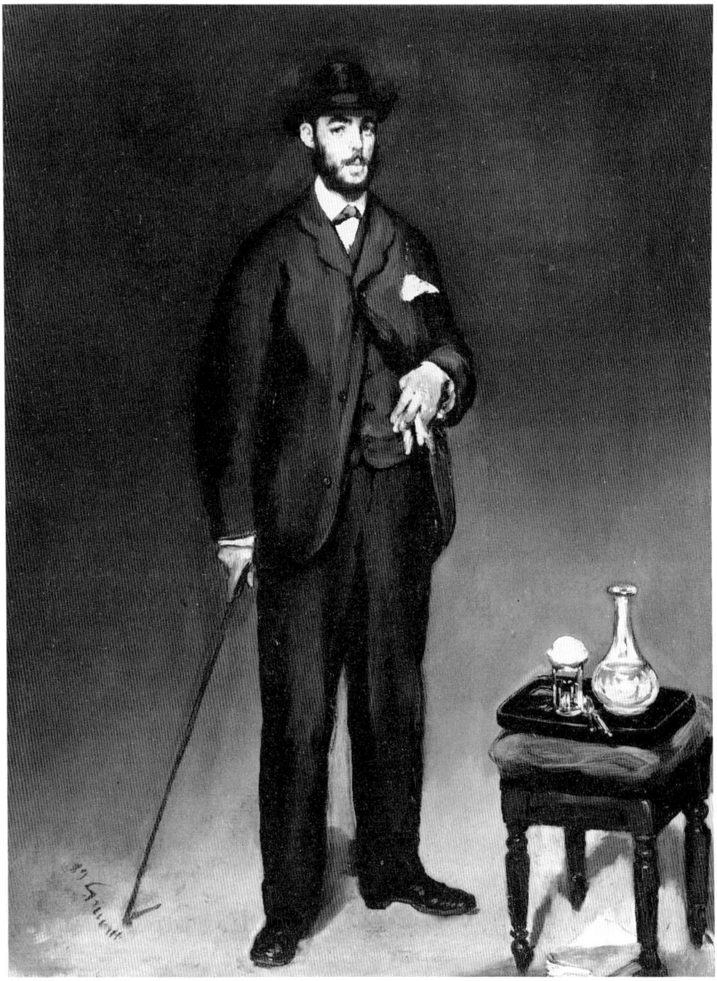

18 *Théodore Duret*, 1868, oil on canvas. Musée du Petit Palais, Paris

of America, New York). Manet's again playful signature, indicated by the tip of Duret's cane touching the ground, was also inspired by Goya, whose *Duchess of Alba* (illus. 19), on which Manet had modelled his *Lola de Valence* of 1862 (illus. 20), points to Goya's signature traced on the ground. The same device occurs in the portrait of *Philibert Rouvière as a Tragic Actor* (illus. 21). Rouvière, about whom Baudelaire had written as the epitome of theatrical make-up and selfconsciousness, points downward, perhaps because the pattern formed by his legs, their shadows and the sword more or less suggests an 'M'. The performer points to the artist's performing presence.

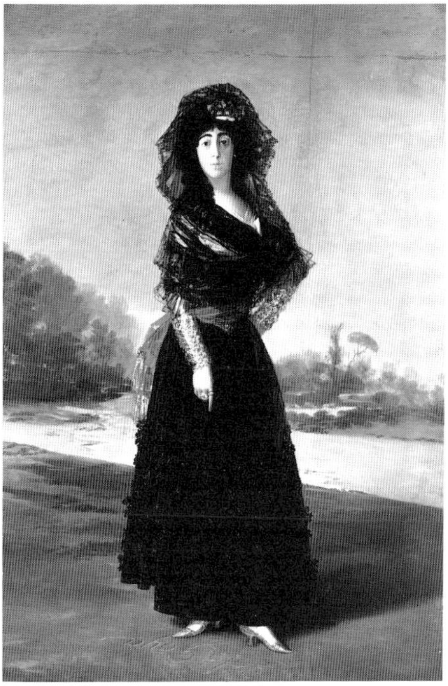

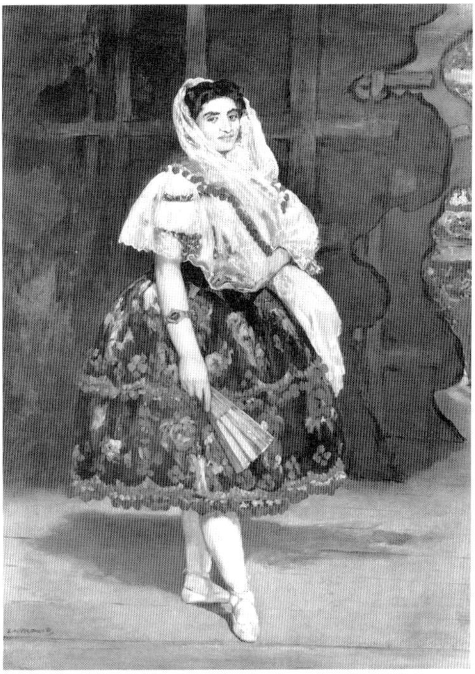

19 Francisco de Goya, *The Duchess of Alba*, 1797, oil on canvas. Collection of The Hispanic Society of America, New York

20 *Lola de Valence*, 1862, oil on canvas. Musée d'Orsay, Paris

21 *Philibert Rouvière as a Tragic Actor*, 1865–6, oil on canvas National Gallery of Art, Washington, DC

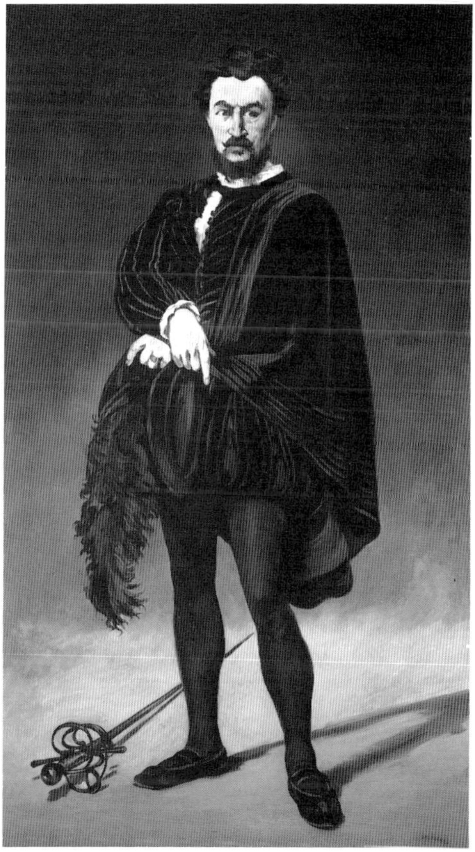

In the Zola portrait, the print of a Sumo wrestler alludes to the phenomenon of Japanese prints, which were a popular discovery among painters of Manet's generation. Both stylistically and in their themes, such works appeared to the Western eye to be free from the burden of traditions that weighed down on painting (forgetting that the Japanese certainly relied upon their own traditions). Unaffected by demands for Renaissance illusionism or classical prototypes, Japanese prints embodied the possibility of an alternative visual culture to that of Europe. They treated subjects from contemporary life with bold lines and colours that expressed a joy in the aesthetic possibilities of their medium. The Japanese artist's method seemed to exemplify Zola's criterion that an artwork be nothing more than fine lines and colour combinations done according to the artistic personality of their creator. Rather than denying the material presence of the support through efforts to create the illusion of looking through a window, as Western artists had done since the Renaissance, Japanese draughtsmen and printmakers unselfconsciously accepted the nature of their medium by allowing their works to take on a characteristic flatness. As might be said for many prints, the paper surface was a stage for imagery rather than an impediment to fiction that had to be overcome. Playing freely on such characteristics of their medium, the Japanese created an original reflection of their world in which pleasure derived from the aesthetic experience of the image. In addition, as with the wrestler, the subjects were often themselves taken from realms devoted to pleasure or entertainment. The many prints of courtesans fall into this category.

In a painting such as the *Victorine as an Espada* (illus. 22) or *The Fifer Boy* (illus. 43), Manet has assimilated many of the characteristics of Japanese art. The straightforward frontality of the latter, its bold colours, strong outlines (particularly those emphasized by the stripes of the trousers), and its flatness are all hallmarks of the effect. In addition, the careful observer will note some features whose interference with an illusionistic interpretation of the images stress the degree to which Manet's conception of art is untraditional. For example, the Espada's pink cape is a conglomeration of thick brushstrokes, floating like a heap of brilliant colour on the painting's surface. In the *Fifer Boy*, a similar effect is produced by less crude devices. At the place where the right leg of the boy's

22 *Victorine as an Espada*, 1862, oil on canvas. Metropolitan Museum of Art, New York

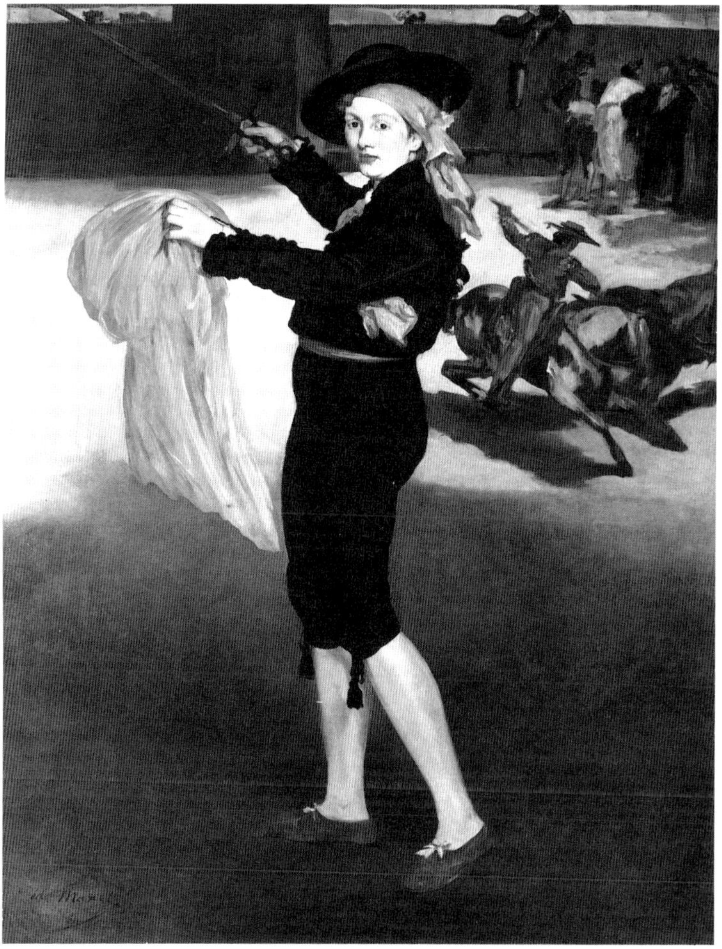

trousers overlaps his spats, the white paint representing the spats has in fact been laid over the red. Behind the foot is a brushstroke that continues its diagonal. At first glance this form appears illusionistically related (a shadow, perhaps), until one discovers that it has no meaning other than its status as a trace of the act of painting. In it we discover a sign of nothing but itself as a material event of painting; by extension it discloses the system of representation of Manet's work and reinforces its destruction of illusionism. The title, 'The Fifer Boy', identifies not a figure from reality but a physical sign, for which the figure that was its referent now seems no more than a pretext.

Manet's signature is a further instance of this kind of defigurative pun. Traditionally it is the only element exempt from the obligation to contribute to illusion: it is generally inscribed in a way that acknowledges the artwork as flat. In the *Fifer Boy* there is a very small, but quite distinctly lettered, signature at the lower-right edge of the painting (cropped from most reproductions); but this signature seems to cast a shadow upward, where another, less distinctly formed, but considerably larger and more visible, echo is painted at a slant. This larger group of markings is what generally passes for the signature in this painting; yet rather than being painted on what appears to be the flat surface, it creates a feeling of recession within the otherwise spatially indeterminate background. In naming himself through signature(s) at the frontier between figuration and defiguration, Manet takes possession of the work, wresting the boy from the reality (or Realism) with which, especially as a figure from modern life, he tends to be confounded.

Signature/inscription, or signature/shadow – which one names the real Manet? Which performs the work of signifying the painter's self? Which authorizes the painting as Manet's work? We again confront the perpetual tension between original and representation, yet, in that confrontation, neither version gains priority; if anything the distinction emerges as highly problematic. And in the fifer boy's eyes we encounter a related effect: realistic enough to fix our own eyes irresistibly upon it, the painted gaze reminds us that for the person watching us we are but a representation, too. The pupils themselves bear traces of the hand, and, as we return their gaze, they seem to insist on the duality of vision, on the paradox of seeing as a transaction or exchange, involving both distancing and possession. Detached from any sense of their surroundings, of a context, whether social or simply a location, figures such as these seem excerpted from life and projected into a world in which visuality is the only value. Paralleling the effects provoked by Victorine's gaze in the *Déjeuner* and the *Olympia*, the defamiliarization their isolation suggests evokes a feeling of estrangement from once comfortable assumptions about the world. Victims of the gaze, these figures are also its heroes and heroines, exposing at their own expense the process of seeing in which they themselves are engaged. Their vacancy is the attribute of their visual purpose; their silence declares their status as representation and their autonomy as visual signs.

23 Katsushika Hokusai, *Wild Horses*, *c.* 1833, colour woodblock print. Museum of Fine Arts, Boston

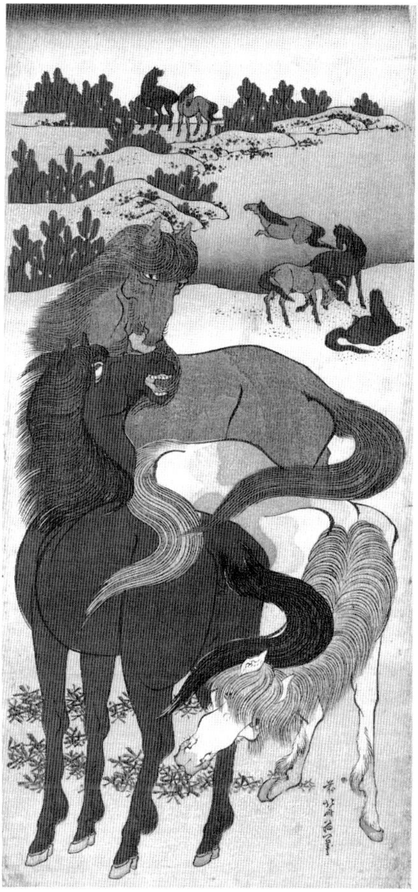

Anti-illusionistic puns such as those in the *Fifer Boy* can be found in Japanese prints, as in the overlapping tails and bodies of Hokusai's *Horses* (illus. 23). Their psychological effect is to declare and revel in the artwork as artifice, to confirm its distance from nature as the condition of our immediate experience of it. That experience is governed by aesthetic and subjective, rather than naturalist, principles. It is that distinction which permits the open-minded viewer to enjoy the beauty of the way an otherwise ordinary, even vulgar, object is painted. The possibility of figuration – a process through which the imagination engages with physical means – is experienced through those passages in which figuration is incomplete. The material basis of art is thus the key to its poetic possibilities. For example, still-life makes art out of common objects by concentrating attention on their

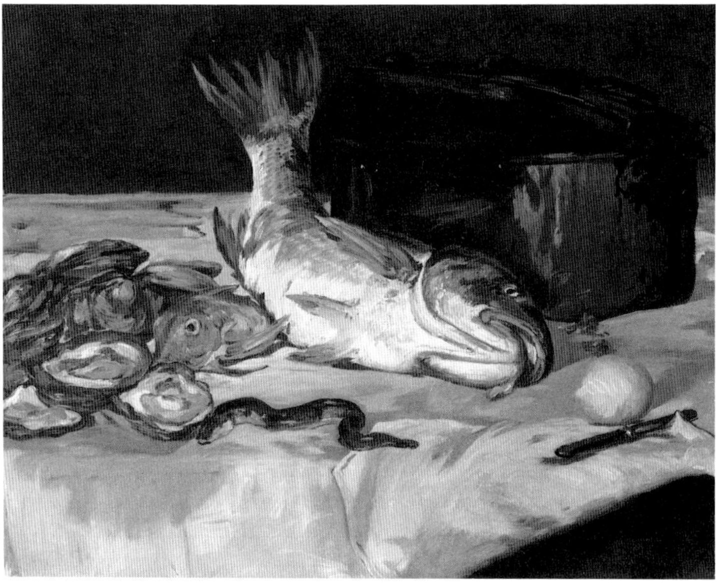

24 *Still-life with Fish*, 1864, oil on canvas. Art Institute of Chicago

artistic representation – their arrangement and execution – as opposed to their natural existence. It may well turn out that such representations have the power to endow forms with new meanings that reflect back on their originals in nature, but there again, it is through the difference from the form perceived in its represented state, as opposed to a natural encounter with it, that such meanings are conveyed. A bunch of asparagus (illus. 48), a decidedly homely vegetable hardly known for being among the noble objects of art, has become the vehicle for a generous and passionate display of virtuoso talent. That we can regard the picture as beautiful without necessarily conferring that attribute on asparagus testifies to Manet's grounding of aesthetic experience in representation, in the figuration/defiguration tension rather than in the object being represented. Similarly, Manet's *Still-life with Fish* (illus. 24) is on one level merely a mound of produce on a kitchen table, a prelude to gustatory pleasures; but on another level it is a vehicle for the visual delectation associated with the pictorial properties of the image, as opposed to the referent itself. The knife and lemon, again allusions to Dutch still-life, are clues to the image's status as a representation located within a tradition. Aesthetic pleasure and understanding thus depend on recognizing the difference between the representation and the actual object. Those properties inherent in representation are, according to that paradigm, what therefore constitute art. Manet thus creates distance from reality without relying on the weary fiction of an ideal world superior to it, while he embeds us in it through an immediate experience of its forms created by the physicality of their representation.

Seen from this point of view, there are clear parallels between Manet's art and the ideas of another poet friend of his, Stéphane Mallarmé, who succeeded Zola as Manet's advocate, and whose portrait Manet painted in 1876 (illus. 44). (We shall engage in a more extended discussion of Manet and Mallarmé in chapter Three.) Indeed, the portrait itself seems as clear an expression of Manet's evolving ideas as any other painting by the master, for it exhibits all the fugitive delicacy and suggestive deftness that, in Mallarmé's poems, reveal a preoccupation with the manipulation of linguistic signs as the terrain of artistic practice. The painter has presented his friend in a moment of contemplation and psychological remove. The cigar smoke, which wafts in the area of the poet's book and his broadly painted hand, suggests the fleeting character of reverie, as does the background, where the wallpaper pattern is sufficiently generalized to verge on intangibility (a word Mallarmé used to characterize his poetry). Thus, the persona Manet presented to his friends of the Batignolles was of a diffident and witty aesthete, one for whom portraits as well as historical and political themes could serve as vehicles for the artistic self.

THE APOLITICAL AND ENNUI

Another instance of Manet's interest in Goya can be found in the painting to which the artist himself, in a personal inventory, assigned the greatest worth. The *Execution of Emperor Maximilian* (illus. 25), painted in 1867, the year before the Zola portrait, is almost unique in Manet's *œuvre* because it is one of the few oil paintings to deal overtly with history and politics, and it is more complex than any of the others that do. Manet was of course familiar with the traditional hierarchy of the genres of subject-matter that still dominated the Salon mentality. The highest rank, with the most noble themes, was historical, while landscape, portraiture and still-life were considered far less ambitious. Presumably more dependent

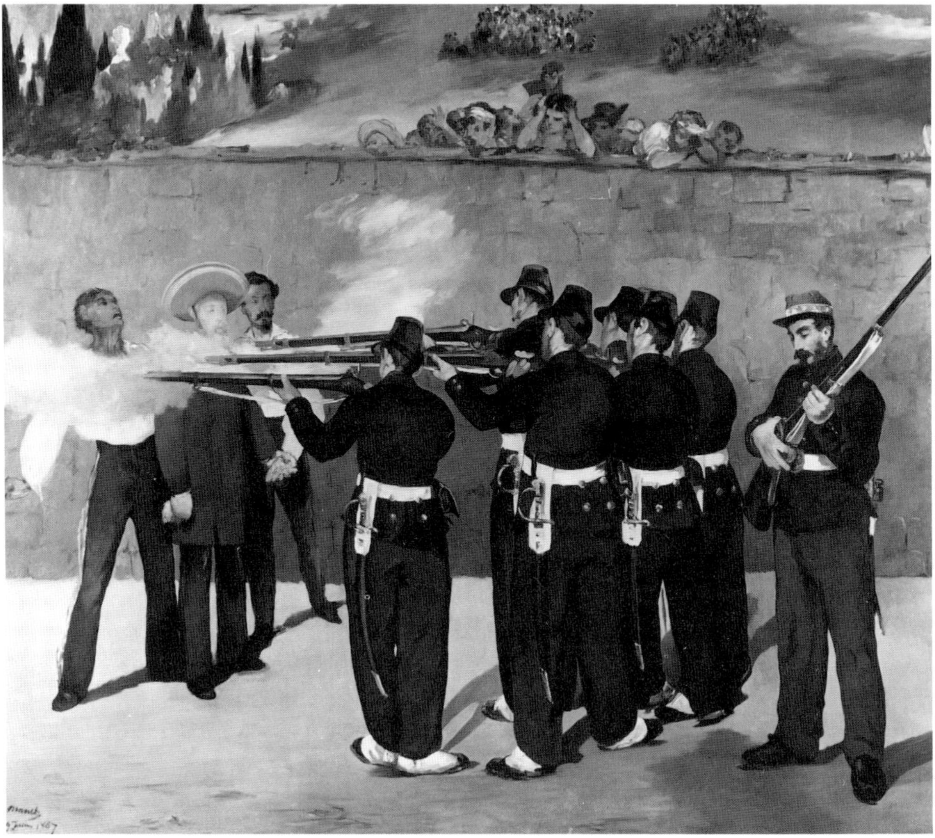

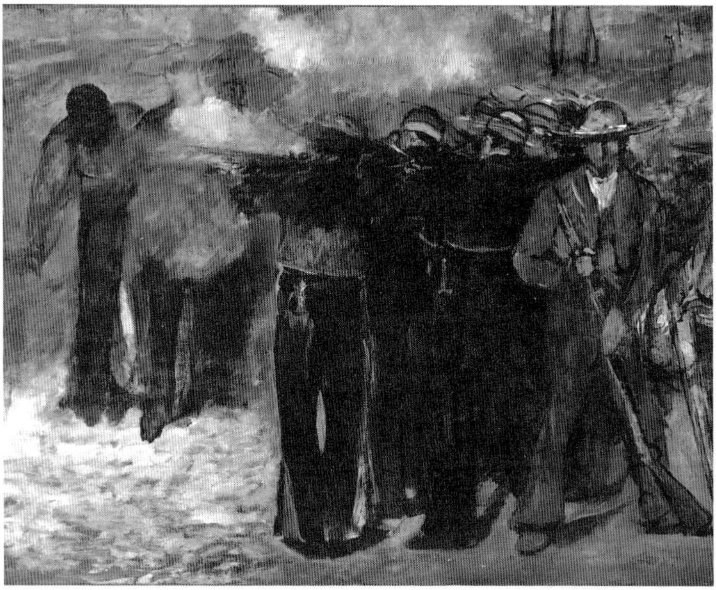

25 *The Execution of Emperor Maximilian*, 1868, oil on canvas. Städtische Kunsthalle, Mannheim

26 Compositional sketch for *The Execution of Emperor Maximilian*, 1867, oil on canvas. Museum of Fine Arts, Boston

27 Francisco de Goya, *The Executions of 3 May 1808*, 1814, oil on canvas. Museo del Prado, Madrid

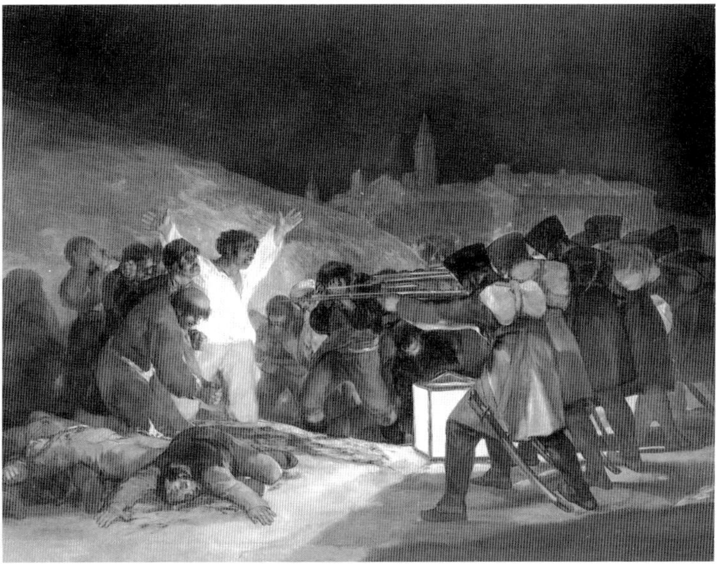

on observation of reality than on imagination, the latter were deemed less creative. At the very least, Manet chose to play off such notions, as he did so often with hallowed traditions. (He also produced a couple of paintings depicting Christ, again reworking sources from the past.) The *Maximilian*'s status as a history painting, then, is precisely what made it both an important exercise for an ambitious painter and a valued achievement. A large sketch (illus. 26) shows the general outlines of the composition before Manet saw the photographs of the firing squad that gave him specific information about height and uniform. The sketch clearly shows Manet's debt to Goya's *Executions of 3 May 1808* (illus. 27), so that, once again, his reinterpretation of a source is a key to his accomplishment. Whereas Goya used facial expressions, dramatic body postures and the play of light to create distinctions between guilt and innocence, between brute and martyr, Manet seems studiously to have avoided imposing his own moral or political point of view. His painting has the look of a dispassionate, matter-of-fact journalistic account, created by unexcited gestures, awkward or slack poses, and the look of boredom among the spectators leaning over the wall.

While Manet's strategies thus imply, on the one hand at least, this posture of neutrality or indifference – of moral distance – his ostentatious preoccupation with Goya is ultimately the opposite of indifference. The point is that for

Manet the artist's presence here attains to a visual and artistic order rather than to an openly moral, didactic one. Maximilian, Archduke of Austria and the Emperor of Mexico, had ruled the latter since 1863 with the military support of European allies, notably France. When the French withdrew their acquiescence the regime collapsed, and he was dragged to a summary justice in 1867, along with generals Miramón and Mejía. Like many Frenchmen, some of whom were outraged at Maximilian's execution, Manet probably held Napoleon III's Government accountable for the loss, and indeed his painting may subtly implicate the French by giving the rebels' footgear and uniforms a French aspect. However, the picture's non-narrative structure, with little display of drama, refrains from inducing an overt emotional bias. Manet preferred, rather, to play on the sense of the soldiers' impassivity and on the deaths of their victims as foregone conclusions. These features themselves might provide a shocking commentary on the cheapness of lives ensnared in an international power struggle. But in addition, it seems as if artistic honesty required Manet's emotional distance from the subject-matter – as if he had a moral responsibility to 'unaltered visual truth' (assuming for the moment that such a thing is possible), that would allow the viewer to make an independent judgement based solely on 'visual facts'. The artist's position, whatever his own personal beliefs, is made to appear external.

So in the case of this highly charged theme, Manet's political diffidence and his assertion of the aesthetic are so trenchant as to verge on the polemical, with far-ranging consequences and implications. The group of spectators leaning over the wall in the background provides a clue to this insight. They are based on bullfight etchings by Goya, where boredom and detachment testify to the perfectly predictable outcome of the event. Manet's interest in bullfights had resulted in an attempted composition on the theme even before his trip to Spain, perhaps because its spectacle exists primarily for its aesthetic – for a formal display bordering on ritual. Indeed, Manet's *Matador* (Metropolitan Museum of Art) of 1866–7 shows the victor doffing his hat, acknowledging his status as performer (as is the artist) in a show calculated to please the crowd for its execution, not for its underlying meaning. The political (not aesthetic) execution of Maximilian can be regarded as a spectacle equally empty at its core, yet the existence of which

28 *The Escape of Rochefort*, 1880–81, oil on canvas. Kunsthaus, Zurich

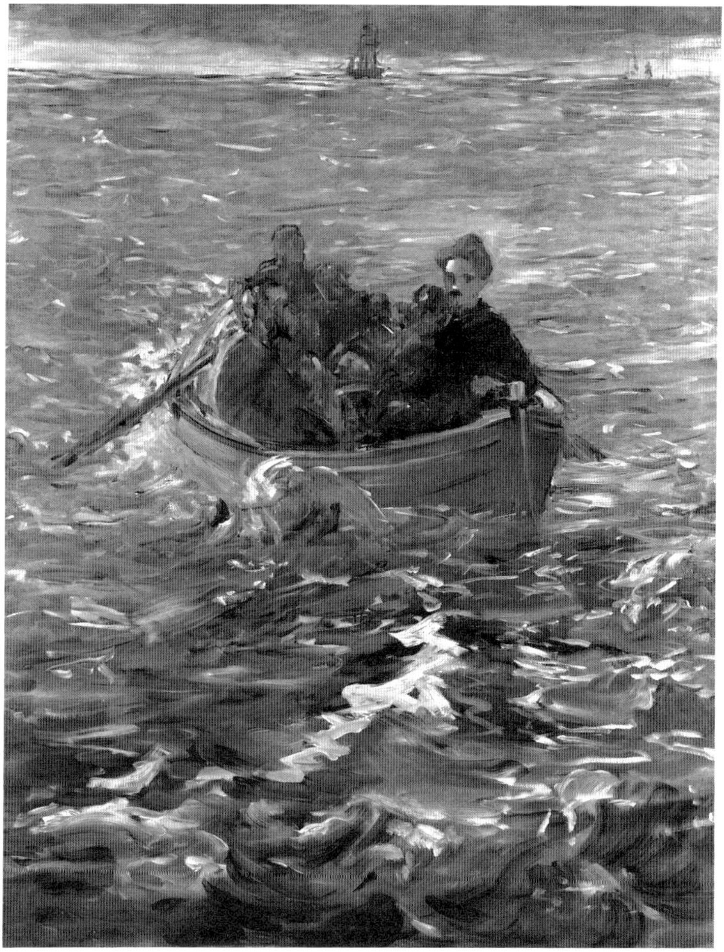

satisfies an urge for catharsis that is more a matter of form than it is politically meaningful by itself. Hence, it is the aesthetic execution rather than the political one that is the artist's ostensible object.

In this regard, the *Maximilian* calls to mind two other interrelated political paintings, in which the relationship to form is similar. In both the *Battle of the 'Kearsarge' and 'Alabama'* (1864; Philadelphia Museum of Art) and the *Escape of Rochefort* (1880–81; illus. 28), newsworthy events likely to inspire interest at the Salon have been recast into the very different genre of the seascape. In both paintings, but especially in the latter, Manet's flattening of perspective and broad brushwork concentrate attention on the water and the process of its representation rather than on the presumed narrative. Henri Rochefort had been a radical journalist and a republican member of the Paris Commune. He was deported to a penal colony in New Caledonia in 1873, from which he escaped the following year. Manet's painting was occasioned by the amnesty that brought Rochefort's return to Paris in 1880. The *Escape of Rochefort* is thus a recollection of an incident of six years earlier rather than a response to a current event, although it was still that incident that made Rochefort most notorious. Muted by dramatic aesthetic effects, human drama here seems anaesthetized. Rochefort's ordeal seems a lonely one with tragic overtones, especially when one thinks of the painting's more extroverted ancestors, such as Géricault's *Raft of the 'Medusa'*, Delacroix's *Dante and Virgil* (which Manet had copied), or the latter's *Shipwreck of the 'Don Juan'*. (These effects are even greater in a second version of the *Escape of Rochefort* in a New York private collection.) Manet's political commentary, to the extent that any exists here or in the *Maximilian*, thus suggests powerlessness and distance rather than militancy and engagement.

Merely treating the topic of Maximilian's execution had made Manet's project suspect to the Government of the Second Empire, which pressured him to withhold the painting from the Salon of 1867. It reminded people of issues that the Government had hoped would be forgotten. The *Rochefort* would have been a similarly embarrassing subject had Manet painted it in 1874, but he did not begin it until the republicans, whom he supported, had taken over the Government in 1879, leading to Rochefort's triumphant return the following year. In the light of official attitudes and censorship, then, treating such themes at all can be considered controversial and presumably partisan, and Manet's need to be circumspect is understandable. Yet, it can also be argued that Manet's posture was merely the consequence for contemporary history painting of the same principle that underlies the *Déjeuner sur l'herbe*. Manet's supression of narrative and his avoidance of the traditional expression of emotions was a striking departure from his predecessors in the history genre. Presenting himself as a dispassionately observing eye, as an artist cum *flâneur*, whose only evident interest was in representing visual experience, in the end constituted Manet's distinctive presence and unique artistic character. It may be that Manet's emphasis on visual experience and his appeal to the artistic ultimately function as a form of political position.

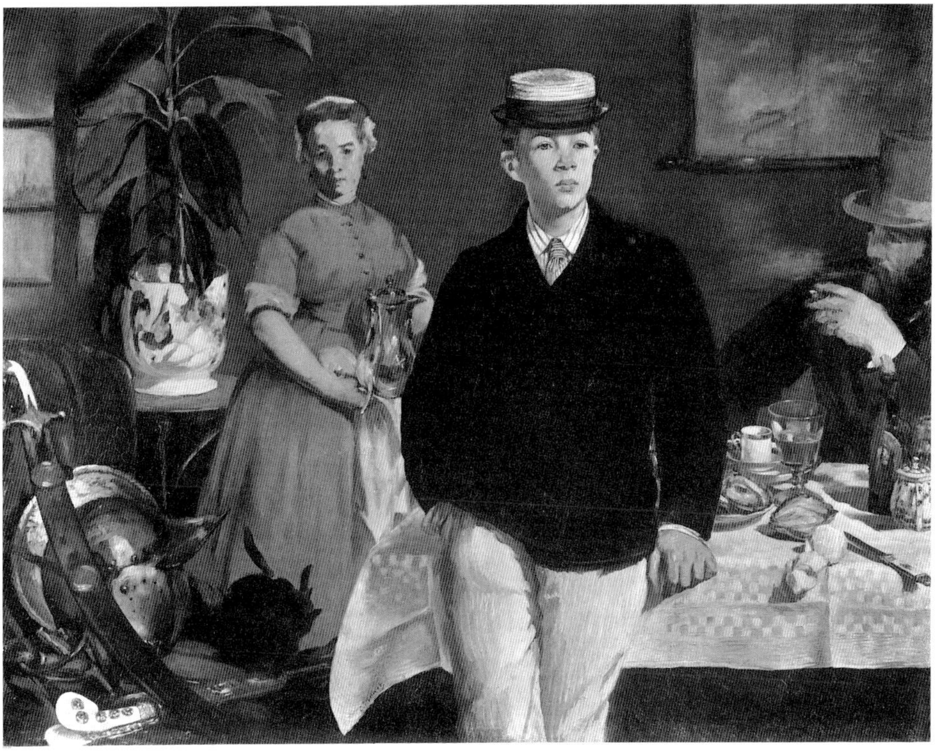

29 *Luncheon in the Studio*, 1868, oil on canvas. Neue Pinakothek, Bayerische Staatsgemäldesammlungen, Munich

But it is a posture in which the dirty world of politics itself, at least as defined by the Second Empire, was rejected. For, especially in the Maximilian affair, it was a politics of impotence and heartlessness. Manet's attitude would then be similar (though perhaps less extreme) to that of Baudelaire's artful dandy, whose philosophy of detachment and disdain was a defence, however vicarious, against the rising tide of ineptitude and banality in public life, and so for whom the private and the aesthetic were the only reasonable refuge and the only solid ground. It is an apolitical politics, with the ironic outlook of the modern solitary at its root.[31]

The apparent emotional emptiness exhibited by the *Execution of Emperor Maximilian* emerges more clearly as an expression of this modern consciousness of alienation and, paradoxically (perhaps dialectically), as a passionate assertion of self in Manet's later work. Two immediately subsequent paintings, the *Luncheon in the Studio* (illus. 29) and the better-known *Balcony* (illus. 30), offer a fascinating indication of that direction. In both, empty or melancholic gazes are keys to what we might still call 'meaning', while at the same time they

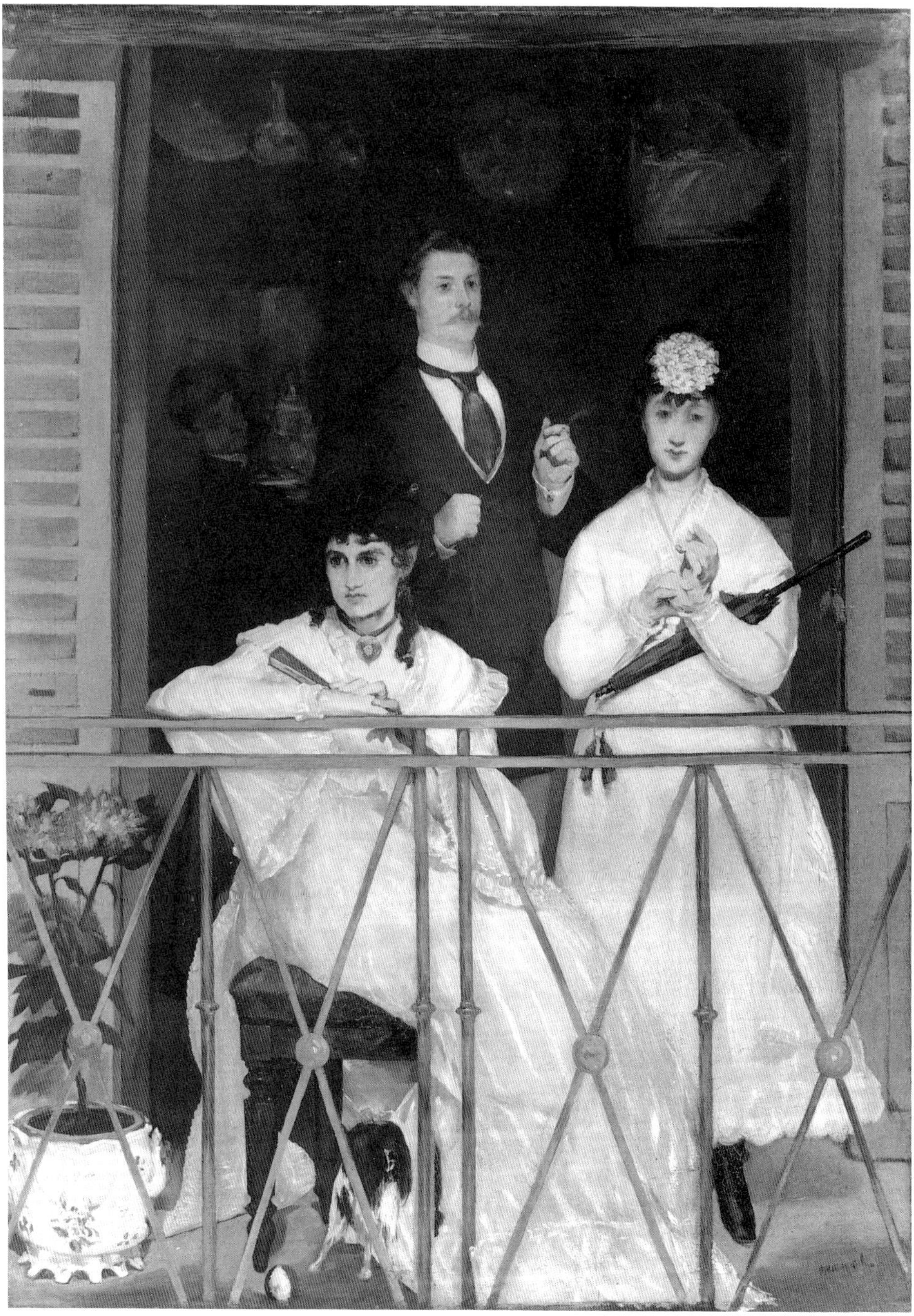

30 *The Balcony*, 1868–9, oil on canvas. Musée d'Orsay, Paris

seem to declare its absence, that is, the absence of themes of human interaction traditionally sought in art. They allude to the solitude of the voyeur rooted in the paradox of visual perception, locked-in by the inevitable transactions of seeing. The *Luncheon* is a portrait of Léon Leenhoff (presumed to be Manet's son), in which the boy's distant gaze recalls those in portraits by Manet's friend Degas. Léon, in fact, had just begun working for Degas's banker father as a runner. Degas's large *Bellelli Family* (illus. 31), began in 1858, was shown at the Salon of 1867. The gazes of the Bellellis tell the story of stressful relationships among themselves, even though, indeed, quite because none of the eyes actually meet. By contrast, the *Luncheon* follows the path opened by the *Maximilian*, in which the artist frees visual appearances from overt emotional connotation, ostensibly concerning himself more with the aesthetics of structure and art-historical tradition, though the underlying theme may finally be that of ennui.

Indeed, in the *Luncheon* Manet is still deeply involved with the art of the past. Its allusions to Holland (the still-life on the table) and Spain (the set of arms to the left) are so obvious they create a system of references to artistic process and identity that completely dominate its concessions to naturalism. It seems to declare the calculating processes of composition and perception – again, of the active eye's presence in representa-

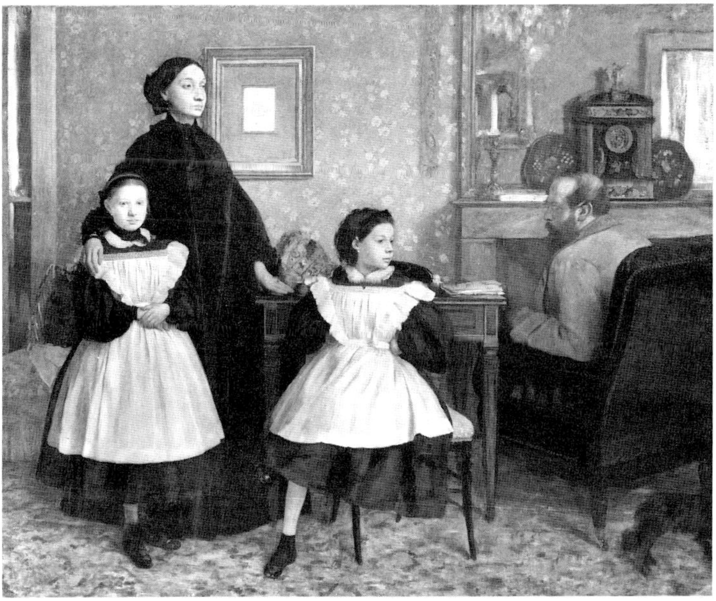

31 Edgar Degas, *The Bellelli Family*, c. 1860, oil on canvas. Musée d'Orsay, Paris

tion. That declaration is cast as a retrospective-like display of Manet's sources and processes up to this particular time. In this studio setting, the subject of the painting, Léon, his body cut off at the knees, seems pressed toward us by the table as the object of artistic scrutiny. The other characters bear witness to the act of vision, which comes through as interiorized, almost an act of reverie, with time suspended. Manet's cigar-smoking friend Auguste Rousselin casually passes the time Manet takes, while the servant makes a direct link to the artist/viewer. The latter figure's role is curious, for although Léon is presumably the main object of our attention, the servant's eyes are the ones reminding us, in the naturalist interpretation, of our exteriority. This displacement of the gaze looks forward to the *Bar at the Folies-Bergère*, as do other aspects of the painting, such as its centred, horizontal composition and its still-life.

The *Balcony* looks to past art, too: like the *Maximilian*, its general composition derives from Goya, whose *Majas on a Balcony* Manet undoubtedly knew. However, unlike the *Luncheon*, the balance between references to past art and the present has shifted definitively toward naturalism. Rather than Goya-esque courtesans, Manet has represented three of his young friends. Standing are the Parisian landscape painter Antoine Guillemet and the violinist Fanny Claus; seated in the foreground is Berthe Morisot, with whom Manet developed an intimate personal and artistic friendship. (The boy in the background with a tray is Léon Leenhoff.) The dog, the ball and the potted plant suggest a relaxed, open-air setting; yet the iron balcony tautly emphasizes the composition's character as a patterned grid of formal design. Indeed, the figures are carefully posed and balanced within the confining frame of the stark green shutters; and each exists in a completely separate psychological world. They are like mannequins juxtaposed, as in the *Old Musician*; despite their identifiable setting, they seem as decontextualized as the free-floating subject in the *Fifer Boy*. Recalling the *Luncheon in the Studio*, the attitudes of the figures in the *Balcony* undoubtedly reflect the seemingly endless hours of posing Manet required to get his painting right – many of his sitters commented on the boredom and fatigue his laboriousness produced. Yet it is hard to understand why Manet would want to reproduce such expressions in portraits of his friends, unless, in the absence of

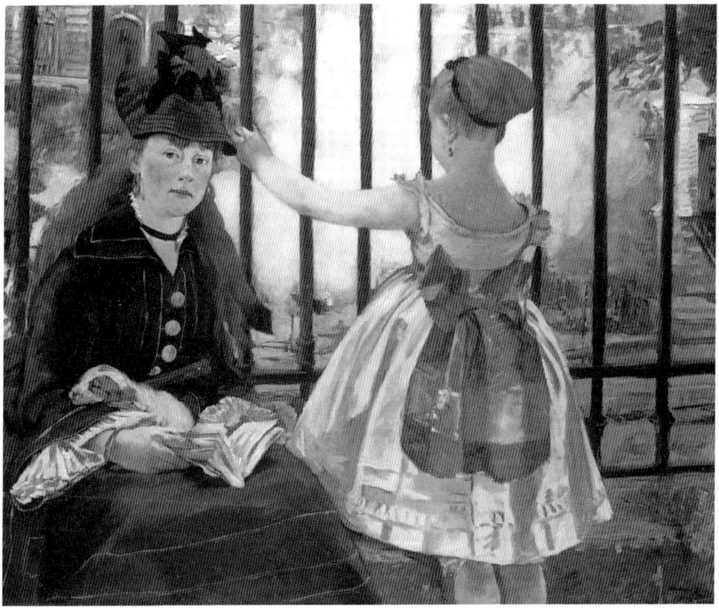

32 *La Gare Saint-Lazare*, 1872–3, oil on canvas. National Gallery of Art, Washington, DC

narrative readings, they are the honest reflections of the state and performance of being seen – as if (some critics noted) he regarded them simply as the objects of a still-life.

A slightly later painting, *La Gare Saint-Lazare* of 1872–3 (illus. 32), is a related image of urban experience taken directly from bourgeois life, though it differs from works of the previous years in being less involved with past art. A young governess (again posed by Victorine Meurent) looks up from her book toward (but not quite *at*) a viewer who seems to have happened past her quite by accident. Her ward, perhaps the daughter of Manet's banker friend Alphonse Hirsch, gazes out on a cloud of steam rising up from the rail station. As in *The Balcony*, these two figures seem lost in totally separate psychological states side by side, within the quintessentially modern setting of industry and the street. The painting is a study in contrasts; its effect hovers between an expression of beneficence – leisure on a warm day – and tedium. Equally ambiguous are the effects of the painting's most prominent geometric feature, the iron railing. The bars press forward claustrophobically. They also function as a kind of screen, a parallel to art itself, through which the aesthetics of modernity are mediated and distanced. As in *The Balcony*, their repetitive, flattening pattern operates like an up-ended musical staff – a grid against which colour tonalities and rhythms of composition are selfconsciously plotted. It is true that comparisons between the abstractness of music and the formal possibilities within painting were made by Delacroix and Baudelaire, and were significantly revived from the 1870s onward.[32] However, the point is not so much that Manet had musicality in mind, but that he was giving his compositional elements the autonomy associated with a more abstract art form.

During the 1870s Manet did a number of compositions featuring couples in which psychological distance is a prominent aspect of the impact. Both *Boating* (illus. 51) and *In the Conservatory* (illus. 33) partake fully of what we recognize as Impressionism through the ostensible naturalism, the fashionable, leisure-charged setting, the brilliant colour and loose brushwork. Moreover, the flattening, which is especially evident in the painting of the woman in the foreground of *Boating*, is typical of paintings of just a few years earlier by Claude Monet (for example, *The River*, 1868, Art Institute of Chicago), whom Manet knew well by this time. Yet, unlike the Impressionists, whose preoccupation with the visual presents itself as ostensibly innocent and uncomplicated, Manet was still mulling over issues associated with the narrative traditions he worked to engage with and then transcend. For Manet knew that juxtaposing two figures inevitably raises the question of a relationship between them.

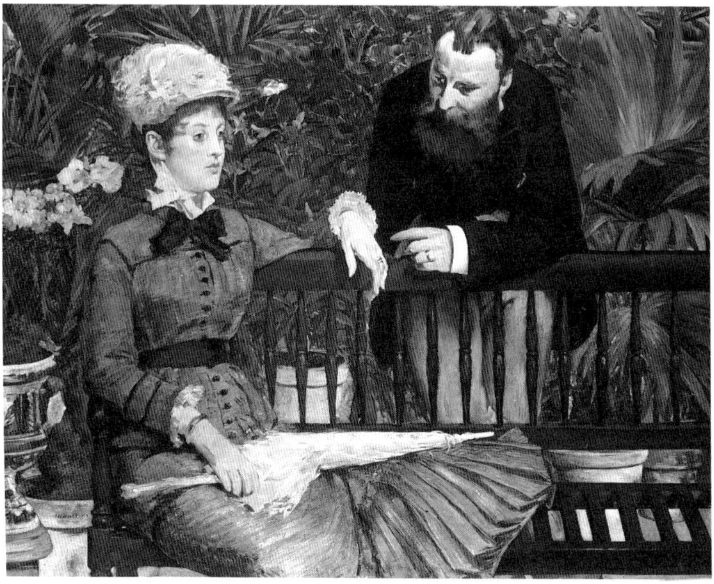

33 *In the Conservatory*, 1879, oil on canvas. Nationalgalerie, Berlin

But he has given no clues to their thoughts: as in *The Execution of Maximilian*, he has created the sensation of detachment, even estrangement. In *Boating*, the woman's mind seems as suspended and adrift as does the sailboat.

Of course, on one level this strategy is that of the artist who, as Zola said, paints 'neither story nor sentiment'. The picture's denial of narrative expectations is consistent with the polemical position Manet took toward history painting from the early part of his career, from the *Déjeuner* to the *Execution of Maximilian* and in the seascapes with historical themes for which the water served as distancing and aestheticizing foils. The artist's concentration of our attention on visuality here is amply accomplished through dazzling and seductive passages, of which the hypnotically shimmering blues of *Boating* are but the most extraordinary example. On the other hand, it is impossible not to respond to the emotional blankness of the figures as an aspect of the subject-matter. And within the context of such aesthetic beauties as the images generously supply, this is disconcerting. One may justifiably ask whether their state of mind is an attribute of what remains in the composition in the absence of narrative, that is, of the element that traditionally supplied meaning, and whether that remove is an expression of ennui. Manet's painting raises the inevitable, yet undecidable, question of the connection in real life between alienation and aesthetics in modern leisure – is leisure necessary as compensation for solitude or is leisure solitude's underlying condition?

REFLECTIONS OF THE I/EYE

If Manet's art has captured something of the modern consciousness, it can only have done so because, untheoretical as he was, and whatever his intentions or awareness of such matters, that consciousness was Manet's own. His reserve toward the representation of emotion and his immersion in the aesthetic side of social life can be taken as examples of modern detachment paralleling that of the protagonists in so many of his works. There is a match between Manet and these figures: they seem to exemplify a way of being Manet himself continually enacted through the exploration of the visual embodied by his artistic practice. So the power of such pictures may lie in the degree to which their realism is social as

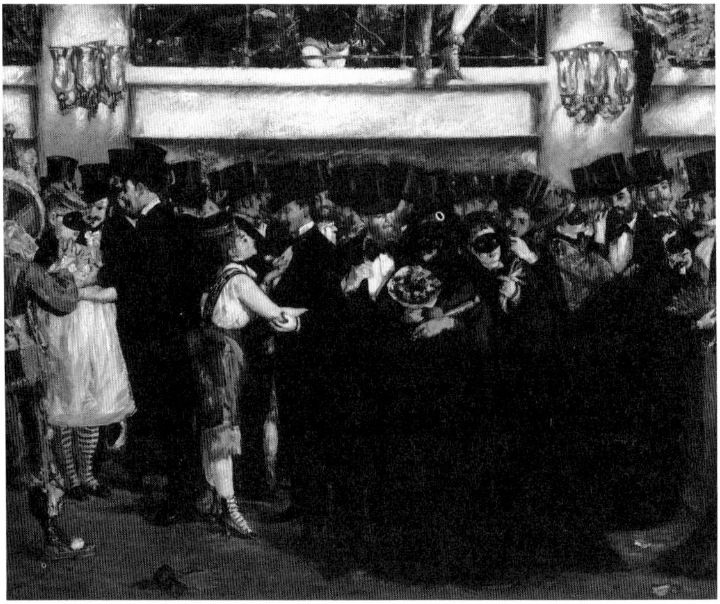

34 *A Masked Ball at the Opéra*, 1873–4, oil on canvas. National Gallery of Art, Washington, DC

well as visual. If a consequence of eliminating narrative content from his painting is to focus attention, as Zola put it, on his temperament, Manet has inscribed the expression of his personality within both the diffident conventions of his class and the vulnerability of us all. The visuality he represents (i.e., both reveals to us and embodies to himself) includes the social dimension of the aesthetic experience – in response to our earlier question, a dialectics of alienation in which the aesthetic, as the form of leisure peculiar to a certain class, is both condition and response.

The social setting of Manet's imagery is perhaps most significant in his last major work, *A Bar at the Folies-Bergère* (illus. 45), which was painted in 1881–2. Its careful construction and monumentality recall the works of the 1860s, but the composition is also the culmination of a series of paintings of cafés and other scenes of urban leisure stemming from the 1870s. For example, *A Masked Ball at the Opéra* (illus. 34) presents a crowd in an elegant setting. The cropped figures on the balcony above are reminiscent of Degas; it thus anticipates a minor feature of the *Bar at the Folies-Bergère*, the feet of the trapeze artist in the upper-left corner. Moreover, the painting's play on costumes and masks, although it is only the women who wear them (signalling, no doubt, their availability), alludes to plates from Goya's *Caprichos*. It suggests the illusions of theatre and the fragility of outward appearances – the complex relation between representation and reality, a theme the *Folies-Bergère* would further explore. With its several portraits of Manet's friends, the *Masked Ball* looks back also to the *Concert in the Tuileries*; like this predecessor, it defines a social class through cultural activities. One wonders whether the Polichinelle, who is half in and half out of the picture, is an image of the artist, who gave himself a similar position in the earlier work.

Closer in theme to the *Bar at the Folies-Bergère*, though less complex, are the group that includes the exquisite *Prune* of 1878 (illus. 35), the *Déjeuner chez le Père Lathuille* (1879; Musée des Beaux-Arts, Tournai), or the *Coin de Café-Concert* of the same year (National Gallery, London), the last a finished fragment of a larger composition depicting the Café-Concert de Reichshoffen. These works remind us of the many hours

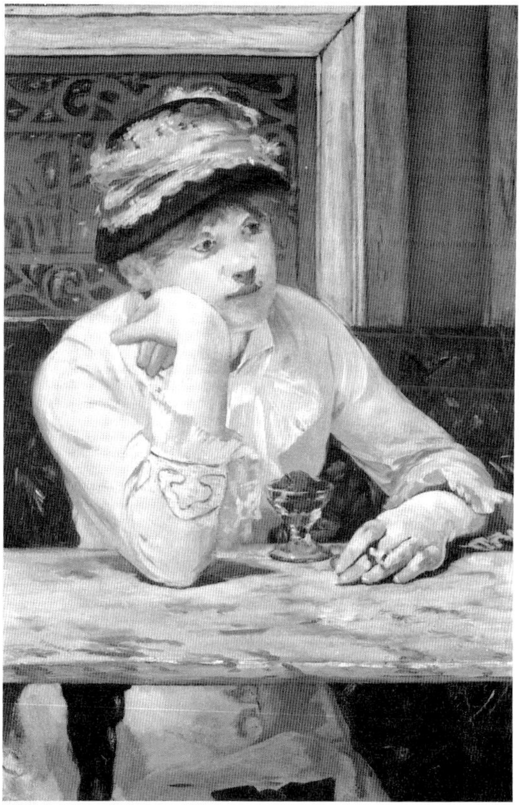

35 *The Prune*, c. 1878, oil on canvas National Gallery of Art, Washington, DC

Manet spent with friends like Degas, Monet, Duret and others in places like the Café Guerbois, La Nouvelle-Athènes and the Reichshoffen. Their loose facture and the expressions of their figures convey the diversity of moods and activities associated with cafés. In such respects, the paintings are among Manet's closest to the Impressionist ethos of spontaneity and on-the-spot observation. They go a step further than the portraits of Astruc, Zola and Duret, who were members of the group that met in the cafés, by making the social life of the café itself their theme. And Manet portrayed that subject in the painterly style developed within that milieu – a style that had virtually become its emblem.

36 *Nana*, 1877, oil on canvas. Hamburg, Kunsthalle

At the same time, Manet did a number of paintings that involve mirrors and reflections, the feature that is so central to the *Bar at the Folies-Bergère*. *In the Mirror* (1876–7; Guggenheim Museum, New York) is a ravishingly luminous, broadly painted work that transposes the erotic tradition of the *toilette* into the pictorial vocabulary of Impressionist modernity and evokes Baudelaire's theme of women's attention to artifice. The abstraction of the loosely painted mirror imagery might suggest how reflections themselves are always interpretations. *Nana* (illus. 36), painted in 1877, is a far more studied version of a related theme, which Manet's title for the work links to a character who features in Zola's Rougon-Macquart series (particularly in *L'Assommoir* of 1877 rather than *Nana*, which was not published until a year or so later, although the painting does not illustrate any particular scene). A more relaxed version of the courtesan than his earlier *Olympia*, the *Nana* continues the play of gazes found in his most highly thought-out pictures. Nana stands before a looking-glass that subjects her to her own scrutiny, while she embellishes her appeal as object of sight and desire. The exotic bird painted on the wall above the escort's head is from the wallpaper of Manet's atelier. Although it appears in a few other works, here it is certainly a humorous allusion both to Nana's social status (she is a *grue*, a crane, that is, a woman of free morals) and to the image she evokes in her escort's mind. She is framed by the glass and the escort, to both of whose gazes, so to speak, she aspires. As in so many paintings, Manet has used objects and the background to emphasize symmetry and flatness that almost theatrically enhance our sense both of the interplay of gazes and the artifice of art – of reality and of

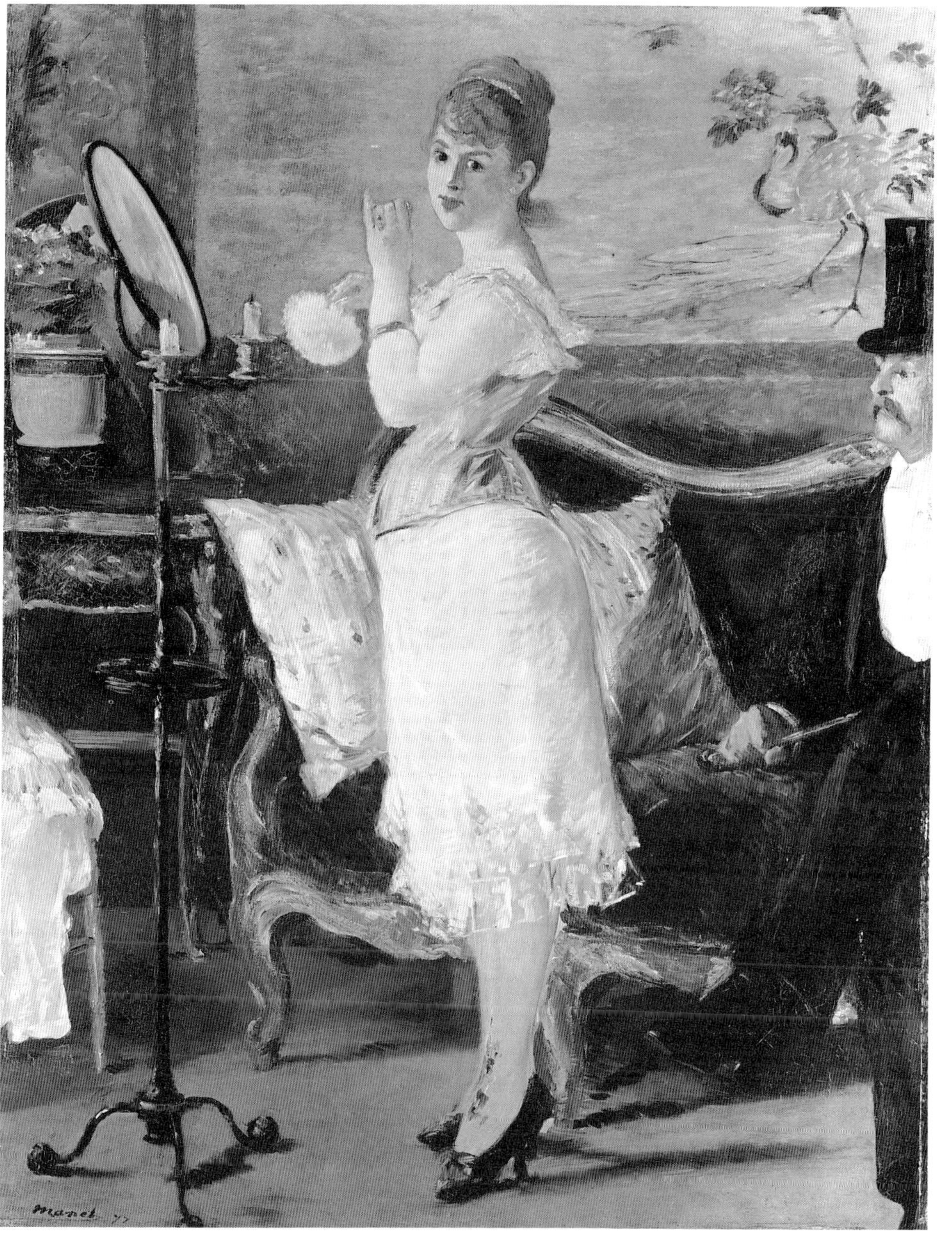
manet 77

maquillage (cosmetics), as Baudelaire would say. A conscious actress in this 'narrative' of the eye, Nana looks out toward the viewer in a way that, compared to Manet's other works, is so conventional it seems parodic.

Other compositions of the late 1870s in which Manet uses mirrors include two self-portraits, virtually the only examples in this genre he produced following his marginal appearance in the *Concert in the Tuileries*. Together they present a dual persona: one, the man of the world, elegantly dressed, standing confidently with one leg forward (this work is in the Bridgestone Museum, Tokyo); the other (illus. 1), the diffident artist with his palette in a presentation highly reminiscent (in reverse) of Velázquez in *Las Meniñas*. Of course, we see no mirror in either of these paintings; but the mirror is, after all, the traditional device used by artists to observe themselves while painting, particularly in the case of a head-and-shoulders self-portrait. The mirror is also associated with Velázquez: it appears in *The Rokeby Venus* as well as in *Las Meniñas*. It is the artist's means of access to his own visuality, an aspect of himself as object; while it is also his reflection of himself in the act of seeing, which he performs as subject. As such, Manet's self-portraits look back to the paintings of Victorine while, no less than the other more obviously related works, they set the stage for the *Bar at the Folies-Bergère*. For the client reflected in the mirror of the bar is a self-portrait of sorts: though not resembling Manet, or anyone else in particular, the question (or uncertainty) of this customer's identity is crucial to the painting's effect.

Typical of the dualities in Manet's art, the mirror in the *Bar at the Folies-Bergère* both deepens and flattens space. We meet a barmaid head on, whose counter is arrayed with one of the most scintillating still-lifes in all of nineteenth-century art. Brilliantly coloured and broadly brushed bottles of aperitif, champagne, cordial and English beer are aligned with fruit, crystal and flowers as an unmatched foretaste of the sensual pleasures offered in a major establishment for entertaining the well-off and the aspiring. Who knows whether the barmaid herself, whose gaze almost avoids the viewer's, might also be an available commodity? In any case, her wooden posture makes her seem a still-life object as well. In the reflection we can make out the vast interior that is filled with light, smoke, spectacle and fashionably dressed men and women. If, for the

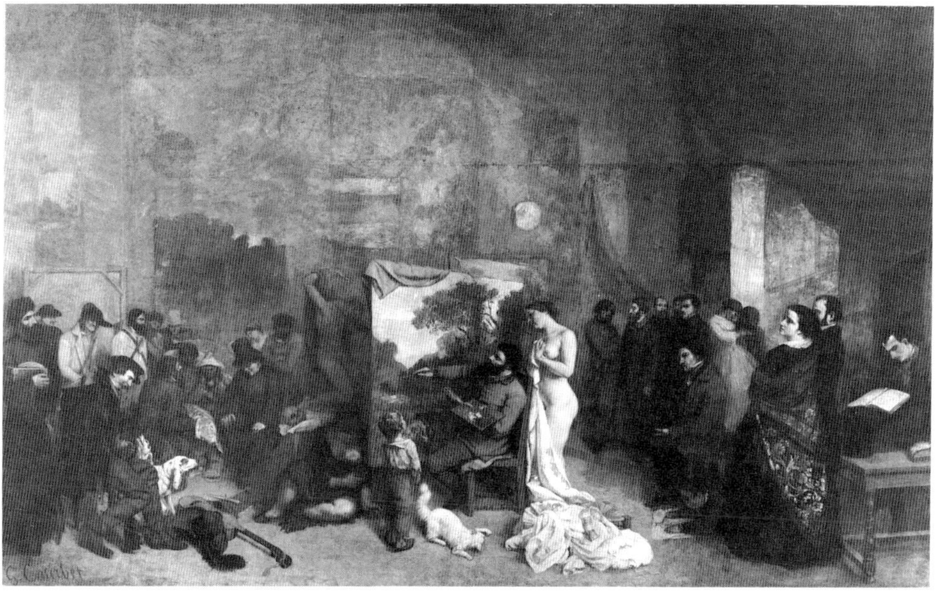

37 Gustave Courbet, *The Studio of the Painter*, 1855, oil on canvas. Musée d'Orsay, Paris

sake of argument, we compare the figure with the barmaid to Courbet with his model at the centre of the *Studio of the Painter* (illus. 37), (the painting through which Courbet proclaimed his artistic achievement), we may say that the *Bar at the Folies-Bergère* similarly embodies Manet's artistic achievement. If the mirror is like the canvas on which Courbet works – there is a long tradition of the mirror as a symbol of art itself – then Manet's art mirrors modern life, and the duality of vision is its key. For here more than in any other work, the two poles of Manet's art are juxtaposed. And both – a pattern of gazes and an array of still-life, fixity and dispersion, realism and aestheticism – are encompassed by the painted and textured mirror.

Indeed, the mirror was at the centre of responses to the picture by Manet's contemporaries, for one could hardly fail to notice how its reflection defies physical possibility. But the psychological effects of this optical anomaly are fully consistent with the rest of his art, particularly the later work. Even though the barmaid does not look directly at the viewer of the painting, she so strongly centres the composition that there is a clear sense of a viewer's position directly in front of her. Yet the mirror reflects objects on the counter as if the viewer were standing considerably to the right. Only from such a position could he see the reflection of the barmaid's back and of the customer she is waiting on. In a study for the painting (illus.

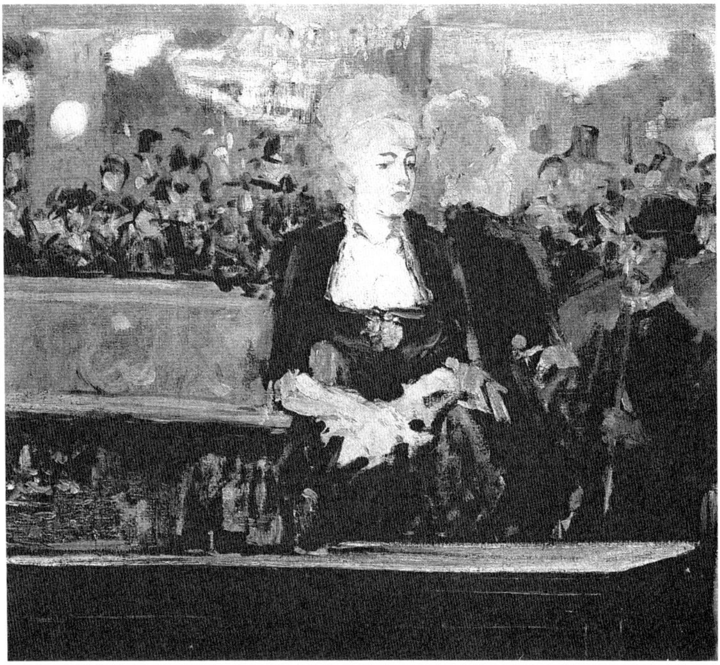

38 Study for *A Bar at the Folies-Bergère*, 1881, oil on canvas. F.F.R. Koenigs Collection, Bennekom

38), it is much easier for the viewer to imagine such a viewpoint. The finished work deliberately places the reflection in tension with normative viewing. Its effect is therefore tied to the ambiguous identity of self and other: standing directly before the painting, the viewer appears to observe himself (the figure opposite the barmaid in the mirror) from a position other than the one he physically occupies. He takes both positions, the one external, the other within. In viewing itself as other, the self can experience itself as body and object rather than as consciousness and subject. As in the *Déjeuner* and the *Olympia*, the consciousness of seeing coexists with that of being seen. The mirror calls attention to the subjectivity of seeing, for two viewers gazing at an object see the same object, whereas two viewers gazing at it through a mirror see different reflections.

It might be said that the *Bar at the Folies-Bergère* has presented the aesthetic of the detached gaze as a surgical operation, in which the eye has been removed (speaking figuratively) from its location in the body. The artist's manipulative hand thus intrudes here even more decisively than when it arranges still-life. Yet, at the same time, the eye is lodged in the world by its presence in the body that is seen in the reflection. In so severing vision from bodily functions such as desire and emotionality, Manet posits an art of pure aesthetic vision, in which a phantom-like viewer seems to transcend the material state of the one represented in the picture. The question of which interpretation corresponds to reality is unanswerable: we must accept both. One thinks of Baudelaire's and Mallarmé's taste for the intangible. (One wonders if Manet knew the disembodied eyes and detached heads that his contemporary Odilon Redon used in a more literally allegorical way as symbols of creative thought or vision.) In Manet, it seems as if the displaced eye concentrates us wholly on the signs of art, such as the artist's compositional counterpoint of alternating forms and rhythmic repetition, or his treatment of surfaces – especially textural ones, where the chandeliers are reflected in the mirror – or on the still-lifes. With an irony paralleling the mirror's perspectival peculiarity, these surface effects dispel the all too easy parallel between reflection and realistic deep space: they immerse the eye in painterly episodes across the two-dimensional support. It is tempting to infer that the consciousness created by Manet's art is that of the selfconsciousness of modernity, in which 'inner' life hovers between the anguished emptiness of solitude and an exquisite revelry in the aesthetic, in which the essence of vision is self-reflexive – it combines the experience of both the voyeur and the viewed. One may see intimately, without interpersonal exchange, such that seeing is privately aesthetic and removed, and yet one knows oneself to be the object of another's gaze. Mirror reflection, reflexivity and mental reflection coincide.

It may be fitting to return to an earlier painting by Manet for clues to the continuity of his art. The *Dead Toreador* (illus. 46) was cut from a larger composition called *Episode from a Bullfight*; Manet must on some level have viewed the fragment as the more satisfactory version, both compositionally and psychologically confronting us with its single poignant and inescapable fact – the stillness, yet physical beauty of the corpse. As was common in his works of the 1860s, Manet played off a source from past art: a picture (then attributed to Velázquez) of a dead soldier, which at that time was in a well-known collection. But he defied conventional expectations, having emptied the painting of those elements of dramatic and emotional commentary that, for the viewer reared on

Romantic painting, may be said once to have constituted the poetry of art. However, it is not enough to say that by emptying his painting of these elements Manet eliminated artifice in favour of realism. On the contrary, while that may be the psychological impact, so that the toreador's death looms as brutally immediate and stark, the vacuum left by what was a real surgical operation – the cutting of the painting, leaving nothing but the non-narrative fragment – is gradually filled by one's perception of the signs of art. This process again demonstrates how vision both appropriates and distances. Free of overt narrative purpose, compositional and stylistic processes are visible in themselves as elements of representation. The emotional chasm is filled by the aesthetic, by the effects of deft handling and deliberate brushstrokes that stand for the shimmer of silk, the polish of leather or a trickle of blood. The beauties of representation are the signs of seeing that become the visual poetry of art. And it seems a poetry rooted in, even dependent on, silence. The manual replaces the verbal; the body subsumes the mind. The eye (the I), its presence denoted by the markings of the hand, immerses itself in the physicality of the work, revelling in a self-recognition of bodily presence that is the obverse of solitude and alienation. Thus, the materiality of Manet's painting is more than a metaphor for the operation of the act of artistic vision: it actualizes that act. As such, it signals the spectacle of consciousness contemplating itself – a corporeal self that is defined, it seems, by the paradox of discovering its own absence and by the uncertainty produced by suspicion that its reality is inseparable from representation.

2 Uncertainties of the Word

Henri Fantin-Latour made two group portraits that help to define the artistic generation to which his friend Manet belonged. In spite of what I have called Manet's elimination of the literary in his paintings, his entourage included numerous writers. In the *Homage to Delacroix* (illus. 39), which was shown at the Salon of 1864, and in *An Atelier of the Batignolles Quarter* (Musée d'Orsay, Paris) of 1870, the painters depicted by Fantin-Latour are prominently accompanied by critics. In the earlier work, chief among the painters posing with the famous *Self-portrait* of Delacroix is Manet. Delacroix had died the previous year; both Manet and Baudelaire had attended the funeral. Manet (who stands immediately to our right of the *Self-portrait*) is accompanied by (from left to right) the now forgotten painter Louis Cordier, the art critic Edmond Duranty, the Realist painter Alphonse Legros (whom Baudelaire would review along with Manet), Fantin-Latour himself, James McNeill Whistler (who offers flowers), the Realist critic and writer Jules Champfleury, the painter and etcher Félix Braquemond, Charles Baudelaire and Manet's sometime studio-mate, Alfred de Balleroy. For the most part these were the same people who visited Manet's atelier in 1861 to show

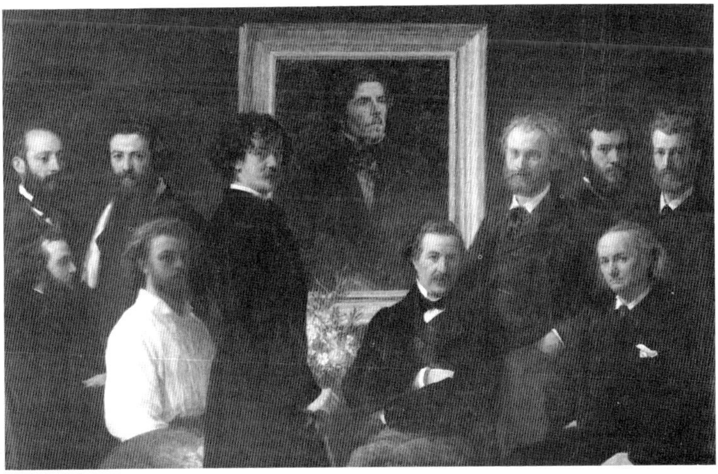

39 Henri Fantin-Latour, *Homage to Delacroix*, 1864, oil on canvas. Musée d'Orsay, Paris

their admiration for *The Guitar Player*. The painters informally constituted a younger Realist school, although the writers had begun their careers earlier; Champfleury in particular is generally associated with Courbet, but had broken with him by this time. Here, of course, the relationship between Manet's generation and that of Delacroix was the main issue. While there are a number of specific connections, stylistic and otherwise, between Manet and Delacroix, this is not the place to rehearse them. Suffice it to say that, in paying homage to Delacroix, Manet and his friends look back beyond the more immediate, undeniable and powerful example of Courbet, whose absence is indeed conspicuous. We shall see that the Realism Courbet represented was under attack from those critics who called it 'unpoetic', a point of view with which Baudelaire, for one, agreed. So in Fantin-Latour's *Delacroix*, the new generation and its allied critics honoured a painter who had maintained a link with the literary and the poetic.

In Fantin-Latour's *Atelier of the Batignolles Quarter*, we see the Impressionist school as it was beginning to coalesce, and, again, writers have a prominent place. Now Manet is clearly the leader, shown at the canvas portraying his friend the critic and poet Zacharie Astruc, accompanied by, among others, Zola, Auguste Renoir and Claude Monet. That Astruc, who was profoundly indebted to Baudelaire, was the sitter for Manet suggests the centrality of such cross-disciplinary relationships and, again, their link to Romanticism. For Fantin-Latour, then, Manet's painting was inseparable from a generation of art writers despite the way it challenged them, as we shall see. And however Realist Manet's art may at first glance have seemed, personal subjectivity was also highly featured in the milieu Fantin-Latour adduced.

Indeed, Manet's art has always meant different things to different people: its paradoxes help explain a diversity of views, but paradox is also inherent in individual views themselves. Manet is most often associated with three great writers, Baudelaire, Zola and Mallarmé, all of whom to varying degrees practiced art criticism. Manet's personal relationship to each was very different, and each estimated Manet according to their individual literary interests. Moreover, each in turn responded vigorously to his predecessor's views on Manet, and dealt with the issues the other had raised. Of course, the differences between these writers are fascinating; yet we should keep in mind the common ground they shared. For even the most 'Realist' mid-nineteenth-century theory took subjectivity of vision as a given; hence our critics agreed on the dialectic of naturalism and subjectivity through which Manet engaged and created his painted world. In addition, each was sensitive to connections between the artist and society. But from these shared premises, each evolved a particular interpretation of Manet's painting. They help us understand that the appeal of an art of personal artistic vision lies in its accessibility through the diverse personal visions of its beholders, rather than through its expression of a definitive or didactic content. Viewing Manet through their eyes thus suggests the pluralistic possibilities of an art that concentrates on vision and visuality, a pluralism as determined by their different critical discourses as by Manet's own multivalency.

Yet while criticism tried to establish parameters for discussions of Manet's painting, it did at the same time reveal the inadequacy of its own conventional vocabulary, its incapacity for defining precise meaning. The performative and confrontationally visual impact of his style, and of what would come to be seen as his individualistic approach to figure painting – as if it were still-life – forced critics, who were none the less impressed, to search for new criteria. Their first efforts dwelt on Manet's art as an expression of his biography and/or biology, focusing more on the artist as its content than on the subject-matter the artist had chosen. In this sense, the art criticism of Manet's time confirms the idea that his painting embodies the artist's presence in the world, although at this point that presence was defined as his persona rather than his perceptual participation and semiotic operation. In responding primarily to Manet as a social phenomenon to be defined through the particularity of his 'performance' of the act of painting, however, criticism did at least transcend the conventional dichotomy between objectivity and its opposite. That was to be a first step toward recognition of the inseparability of perception from the means and process of its representation.

To defend an artist as original says little about his work except that it is in some way different from what preceded it. As such, originality itself is rarely a strong defence, for it is born more of admiration for audacity and perseverance than necessarily of understanding. The fact that originality was the characteristic most frequently attributed to Manet seems unremarkable to us today, for when looking back we tend to see it as an absolute value, one advancing art-historical progress. But that in Manet's own time it was one of the few aspects of his art on which there was general agreement is surprising. The period was rich in theoretical discussion and there was an abundance of available positions and explanations. Yet none of them in particular seemed sufficiently encompassing or convincing, and Manet himself gave little or no hint of where he stood. In briefly exploring these possibilities, we shall discover that discussion of Manet's art quickly led to unresolvable philosophical questions about human perception. The fall-back to originality as a basis for critical consensus, then, provided the surest footing for a positive view of him by shifting criteria away from issues of perception to those involving the painter as acting subject.

When Manet was an art student during the 1850s, Realism and Gustave Courbet dominated artistic discussion. Realist theory itself emerged primarily as a response to the Realists' negative press. The opponents of Realism believed its artists refused or failed to seek the beautiful: they felt Realism was an art of the physical world so transparently and uncreatively represented that it ignored art's poetic aspiration to rise above nature. Since it was generally believed that beauty resided in aspects and realms beyond the material world, Realists seemed to have limited themselves to the ugly. Realist theory, then, was implicitly charged with explaining that there was indeed creativity in Realism. It did so by identifying it with the subjectivity of all seeing. Consequently, what the Realists themselves objected to in other art was not subjectivity but insincerity, the opposite of authenticity. As Fernand Desnoyers wrote in *L'Artiste* (1855): 'Realism is the true painting of objects. There is no *true* painting without colour, spirit, life or animation, physiognomy or feeling'. He argued that 'the word "realist" has simply been used to distinguish the sincere and clairvoyant artist from the one who . . . continues to see through tinted glasses'. As to the poetic enterprise of art: 'We deny to no one the right to like what is false or ridiculous and to call it ideal or poetry. . . . But everyone abuses poetry. . . . It is sprouting between all the paving stones in Paris'.[33] Even Courbet, who claimed you cannot paint what you cannot see, acknowledged both the notion of idealism and the subjectivity of artistic expression. His famous 'Realist Manifesto', published as an introduction to the brochure of his 1855 exhibition centring on the *Studio of the Painter*, presented the artist's aim as both the representation of man in his appearance and his epoch *and* the expression of the painter's individuality.

Desnoyers's 'tinted glasses' stood for an extraneous, usually academic or romantic, overlay on visual perception. He did not deny the role of honest subjectivity that was part of a natural process. On the contrary, Realism's protest against falsehood would always be coupled with advocacy of individual expression. In his short-lived journal *Le Réalisme* (1856), Edmond Duranty noted that 'Realism is the reasonable protest of sincerity and hard work against charlatanism and laziness . . . in order to wake up people's minds and return them to a love of truth'. To speak of Realism as a school was a contradiction, for Realism 'signifies the frank and complete expression of individuality; it is an attack upon convention, imitation, any kind of school. A Realist is entirely independent of his neighbour, he renders sensations he feels when contemplating things, according to his nature, his temperament'.[34] In short, Realism's very independence from convention was a form of protest against convention. In an essay with the portentious title 'Philosophy of the Salon of 1857', Jules-Antoine Castagnary was even more far-reaching:

> Visual art can be neither a copy nor even a partial reproduction of nature, but rather an eminently subjective product . . . expressing a purely personal conception. Nature, the raw material of art, merely provides the artist with imagery for representations. From it, through an entirely mental and psychological process, he derives . . . beauty; for beauty, as an idea, can only exist in the artist's conception. . . . Above all, art is an expression of the human self solicited by the external world; . . . it is one of the highest acts of human consciousness. . . .[35]

Desnoyers had defined Realist subjectivity in terms of temperament – the individual's natural way of feeling; similarly, Castagnary placed the justification for Realism – its honesty or sincerity – on the familiar ground of Romantic self-expression. So a common theme of the Realist defence was that it was not a mechanistic or unimaginative style, because such a process was innately impossible to the human perceiver.

Ironically, when in the following decades the loose technique of the Impressionists clearly displayed the artist's subjective and individualistic approach, it came under attack as a shoddy and imperfect vehicle for accurate representation. The underlying theme of criticism of both Realism and Impressionism was therefore that artists were not doing enough, in the former case spiritually, in the latter technically, to transform nature into art. However, the simplest and most frequent justifications of Impressionism addressed the issue of accuracy and relied on naturalist grounds. For example, to explain Impressionist lighting effects, Duranty claimed that 'everyone has crossed through countryside in the summer and has been able to see how foothill, meadow, and field dissolve, so to speak, in a single brilliant reflection from the sky'.[36] And Théodore Duret lamented over the way the 'poor Impressionist vainly asserts his complete honesty, declares that he only reproduces what he sees, that he remains faithful to nature. But the public and the critics condemn him. They don't bother to find out whether the canvas corresponds to what the painter has actually observed'.[37] Narrow interpretations of Impressionism follow similar lines. If one would look at nature honestly oneself, one would realize the naturalist truth of Impressionist paintings. The Impressionists would no longer appear defiant or derelict; their paintings would vouch for the honesty and sincerity of their acts of vision, not in spite of their technique but by means of their technique.

But in the 1870s, neither Duranty nor Duret were misled by their own apparently facile arguments; nor should we be now. Neither really claimed that Impressionism was objective, merely that it was authentic – that is, based on direct experiences of nature. Both recognized and accepted its subjective element, which Manet's leadership so highlighted through its originality. Indeed, for purposes of contrast with Impressionism, the burden of objectivity was transferred to

Realism. That is, as Impressionism emerged as a better expression of the subjectivist defence underlying Realist theories, reservations about the lack of creativity of Realism itself resurfaced. For example, in *Les Peintres français* (1867), Duret compared Manet favourably to Courbet because the older painter seemed to work only with the eye, neglecting both imagination and emotion, that is, 'all that constitutes poetry in art'. Duret meant that Courbet painted mechanically, that he saw 'only the body of objects, only the tangible side of things'. So he insisted that Courbet's style was unpoetic, despite the evidence we can easily find in it of paint handling and 'rustic' personality.

On the other hand, Duret's explanation of Manet's style sounds much like what he might have written about Delacroix: Manet was vigorous and original; his work contained a 'true feeling for colour', his only flaw being that he was in such a rush that he was technically immature (a charge that had also been levelled against the young Delacroix).[38] Contrasting Manet to Realism in 1870, Duret distinguished between painters who want to 'fix a faithful reproduction [of things] upon the canvas' and Manet, who, 'having a powerful vision of things, and experiencing a personal impression at their appearance, manages to *fix his vision upon the canvas*, in such a way as to convey his personal impression'. Duret seems to be saying that Courbet tried to put things themselves (actually signs transparent enough to preserve the illusion of things) on the canvas, whereas Manet's representations were visions – personal signs for things, in the sense that they bore the mark of the participation of his consciousness in their creation. For him, the use of signs that retained traces of the individual was poetic; the use of what appeared to be mere things themselves was not. It is as if he made a distinction between the tactile and the optical, suggesting that the former, as an attribute of the object, corresponded to what Baudelaire would denigrate as positivist, the world represented as if the viewer did not exist, whereas the latter was informed by the artist's imagination. We realize of course that Manet himself played on the tactile – but as a property of his medium – to impress signs with his performance in the process of their creation. So what Duret meant was that Courbet was sticking simply to the object and that objects are physical, whereas Manet was displaying the self's consciousness of the object. In the case of vision so defined, the artist's presence would be inherent in the object. Note that Duret used the word 'impression' in the context of feeling rather than transcription: 'We pay no attention to a painting that is only for the eye; we only look at a painting in order to *feel* it, to *experience* through its appearance an *impression* or *emotion*.'[39] Here, Duret distinguished between the eye as a mechanically functioning organ, which could theoretically conceive an image dissociated from mind and emotion, and its artistic functioning, which is defined by the feelings it expresses through imagery. Duret was seized by the subjective in Manet's work, by his sense of a personality emanating from it rather than the mere effect of physical properties deprived of other connotations. Recalling our earlier terminology, we could say Duret sought to *experience* art as *performative* – as altering our consciousness of the object world and transgressing its conventions – in preference to a *reading* of art as *descriptive* or *constative*, which would merely confirm the existing status of its objects.

In a phrase anticipating Zola, Duranty, as early as his article on Realism in 1856, had held that the artist 'renders the sensation he experiences before things, according to his nature and his temperament'.[40] In *La Nouvelle Peinture* of twenty years later (hence, after Zola's writings), he affirmed the origins of Impressionism in the Realism he had so defined, thus legitimizing his earlier claims on the basis of the later style. But at the same time, Duranty characterized the Impressionists' specific discoveries scientifically, as relating to prismatic division and recombination of light. When including Manet within the group, however, he made the artist's right to freedom of perception the underlying issue. Manet was at the forefront of that particular battle: '[Manet] seized the leadership of the movement . . . repeated the most audacious affirmations, conducted the most tenacious struggle, opened not only a glimmer, but wide windows . . . onto plein-air and true sunlight.'[41]

So no one accused Manet of an objective or uncreative view of the world. But praise for his originality helped his detractors define their opposition. They dwelt insistently on two aspects of his painting: its offensive subject-matter and its crude or inadequate technique. And they were indignant that such flaws could be justified by so-called originality. Ernest Chesneau, a frequent writer on the arts who at first had shown some sympathy for Manet, summed up these arguments in a passage on the *Olympia*. Chesneau had admired the still-lifes and flower pieces Manet was exhibiting at Martinet's gallery. He tried to explain those efforts by a quasi-scientific theory that echoed justifications of Impressionism: '[Manet] wants to limit painting to the strictly faithful representation of natural tones in diffuse light' – as if to say that here at least were intentions one could understand. But when Chesneau saw Manet's attempts at figure painting, the deficiencies he apprehended in painterly technique became unbearable: 'The grotesqueness of Manet's exhibits has two causes: first, an almost childish ignorance of the basics of drawing, and then a preference for the most inconceivable vulgarity.' Insensitive to the subject's Baudelairian irony, Chesneau attributed public ridicule of the *Olympia* to the pretentiousness of trying to make a serious picture out of a 'créature *cocasse*', whose hand he said Manet had given the shape of a toad. While originality was of value in itself, Chesneau believed Manet's failure resulted from trying too hard to be unconventional. Of course, he equated the morals of Manet's figure with Manet's artistic morality. The main issue for him was that originality alone was not enough to justify complete disregard for standards of technique and decorum that were part of social convention.[42]

Thus the tension between subjectivity and objectivity that lay at the heart of contemporary discussion of Realism and Impressionism was central to the debate over Manet. But even among Manet's supporters agreement was hard to find. Duret stressed differences between Impressionism and Realism: Manet's stubbornly original vision had initiated the new phase. In 1863 Desnoyers wrote that Manet's *Guitar Player* displayed a strange new manner, one half-way between the Romantics and the Realists.[43] Surely he too alluded to a Realism that maintained its poetic value through subjectivity, which he still associated with Romanticism. For Duranty, who stressed continuity with Realism, that subjectivity was tied to the continuing struggle with tradition, in which Manet was a leader. Impressionist 'objectivity', though certainly a misnomer, was the right to see things honestly and naturally, as justified by premises considered scientific at the time. In any case, the argument of originality really obviated these issues. For these critics focus on sensuous rather than verbal content; they feature Manet's action rather than his ideas. Hence, their concept of art responds to what I have labelled 'performative', that is, to an artistic language consisting of 'painting acts' (the pictorial equivalent of 'speech acts'), unmediated by other discourse in their transformative effect on our perception of the world. If such a concept underlies critical attitudes towards Manet's painting, then, paradoxically, it also implies considerable limits to the kind of explanations that had been the stock-in-trade of criticism. A new form of criticism would have to emerge to deal with art as performative act rather than discursive text.

To be sure, the notion of Manet's art as performative connects directly with the idea of temperament, which for Baudelaire and Zola became the central concept in their discussion of Manet. The word 'temperament', which simultaneously alludes to the artist as active producer of art-language acts and to the personal perception-based content of his representations, was already shared by most critics of the day. But like so many general concepts or criteria, it had different connotations for them, as we shall clearly see even in Baudelaire and Zola. For the former, it was an abstract concept linked to intellectual and emotional imagination, through which the artist expressed his humanity. For the latter, who accepted the trend toward positivism that Baudelaire despised, it was to be grounded in an objective physicality qualified by biological and environmental factors. Going further, Mallarmé dealt with temperament by in some sense obviating it through the claim of Manet's impersonality. He meant that Manet's immersion in the world gave him a universal, trans-individual (or Hegelian 'absolute') personality. Yet since for Mallarmé impersonality was itself an index of Manet's originality, he too returned to that underlying value. For both Baudelaire and Zola, the eye was the extension of an inner self distinguishable from external reality and capable of leaving its imprint on it. Though neither supported 'pure' Realism, both shared its paradigm of art as an enactment of the world made by an omniscient eye, and they tried to explain Manet's powerful effect on his audience through temperament. While Realism as a style was thus defined and defended by subjectivity, that very definition was beholden to the dubious paradigm of objective representation as its opposite. Mallarmé recognized that paradox and placed it at the centre of an interpretation of Manet's painting in which, given human immersion in and identity with reality, his art achieved an affirmation of both the objective physical world and the creative human element as part of it.

BAUDELAIRE AND TEMPERAMENT

The source of a new approach to criticism is already found in Baudelaire's writings on Delacroix, in which the poet eschewed preoccupation with narrative, so typical of other criticism, in order to concentrate on psychological responses to pictorial expression. This theory contains in embryonic form the notion of painting as performative, since it focuses on how artistic language acts on the viewer. We know through correspondence and third-party testimony that Manet and Baudelaire were close, and we have seen how many attitudes the painter and the poet seem to have shared. Yet, even so, there is scant evidence for Baudelaire's opinion of Manet's painting or for estimating the extent to which he found his approach to Delacroix relevant for Manet. Only once did he mention Manet in an article; other clues are gleaned mainly from a few letters.

Of course there are some practical explanations for Baudelaire's relative silence: he had little experience of Manet's public exhibitions beyond the early years, during which the painter attracted only slight attention. After all, the poet had left for Belgium in 1864, and he died in 1867. So rather than ask why Baudelaire did not do more to defend Manet, it may be more useful to ask on what grounds he supported him when he did. It seems at least that later writers perceived an affinity between the two, since they felt obliged to discuss it or refute it. Zola, for example, denied Manet's painting contained ideas of any sort, especially not ones Baudelairian. Antonin Proust claimed that rather than Manet having been influenced by Baudelaire, the reverse had been the case.[44] Even if both were right, they do not exclude the more basic sympathy, which lies in a conception of art as the expression of a personality.

There are several clues that Baudelaire did indeed view Manet in positive terms relating to the kind of critical principles he had established over the years. He mentioned Manet favourably, however briefly, in the article 'Peintres et Aquafortistes' of September 1862: 'M. Manet is the author of the *Guitarist*, which provoked a lively sensation at the last

Salon. At the next Salon, we shall see several paintings imbued with such a strong Spanish flavour that one might think the Spanish spirit has taken refuge in France.' Baudelaire went on to praise Manet and Alphonse Legros for uniting 'with a definite taste for reality, modern reality – which is already a good symptom – that imagination, vital, ample, sensitive and audacious, without which, we must say, all the best faculties are but servants without masters, agents without a government'.[45] It is true that the links Baudelaire made with Spain cite the obvious, with little probing for Manet's underlying motivations. However, when two years later Théophile Thoré accused Manet of producing pastiches of Spanish works, Baudelaire wrote a letter of vigorous defence. Citing his own affinities with Edgar Allan Poe, Baudelaire called parallels between Manet and the Spaniards a kindredness of spirit.[46] Still, Baudelaire's other words, though predictable, even a trifle perfunctory, may be more informative. For they directly and flatteringly associate Manet with the central concept in the Baudelairian theory of art – the 'government of the imagination'.

In another public gesture of support, or of affinity at least, Baudelaire sent Manet a quatrain to accompany the etching of *Lola de Valence* shown at the Salon des Refusés of 1863. (He had seen the painting at Martinet's earlier that year.) Manet attached Baudelaire's poem to the painting, where it remained on display for the rest of the exhibition:

Entre tant de beautés que partout on peut voir,
Je comprends bien, amis, que le désir balance;
Mais on voit scintiller en Lola de Valence
Le charme inattendu d'un bijou rose et noir.

Among so many beauties visible to the eye
I can well understand, friends, that desire is tempted;
For in Lola de Valence we see brightly shining
The unexpected charm of a pink and black jewel.

When the poem was published in *Les Epaves* (1866), an editorial note (probably written by Baudelaire himself) denied the obscene connotation of a 'pink and black jewel'. Ironic or not, the disclaimer brought out the sort of reference that surely contributed to Manet's reputation as a deliberate provocateur. In sending Manet the poem – even though it was a joke – Baudelaire obviously concurred in associating his own and Manet's tastes. Though Manet may have used the poem solely for notoriety, the *Lola de Valence*, painted in 1862, together with the *Olympia*, show him positioning himself within a known literary milieu. Baudelaire had been taken to trial in 1857 for indecent writings, with the result that several poems from *Les Fleurs du mal* were suppressed. But that was eight years before Manet exhibited the *Olympia* at the Salon, and Manet was surprised by the extent of its controversiality. What may not have occurred to him was that, for most people, painting was too concrete an art for certain kinds of Baudelairian fantasy.

A closer glimpse of Baudelaire's attitude towards Manet can be had from two letters of 1865, written after his departure for Belgium. On 11 May he wrote to Manet:

> So I have to say something about you again. I must try to convince you of what you are worth. What you want is really stupid. *They are making fun of you; the jokes* annoy you; they don't do justice to you, etc., etc. Do you think you are the first to be in such a situation? Are you a greater genius than Chateaubriand or Wagner? They [the public] made fun of them? And so as not to inspire you with too much pride, I will tell you that those men are models, each in his genre, and in a world full of riches, and that you, *you are but the first in the decrepitude of your art*. I hope you won't be too upset by the unceremoniousness with which I treat you. You know my friendship for you.[47]

The word 'decrepitude' is difficult, but thanks to the comparison with Chateaubriand and Wagner, we can take it as a reference not to Manet's personal work but to the art of painting generally. Baudelaire was exasperated by Manet's discouragement after his poor critical reception at the Salon of 1865, at which he had shown the *Olympia*. For him, the gulf between the avant-garde and the conservative mainstream was a sign of paralysis, and he believed Manet would simply have to persevere until his vision eventually prevailed. Baudelaire obviously applauded the powerful impact of Chateaubriand and Wagner for clearing the air for literature and music. He might have cited his own experience in the domain of poetry. While encouraging Manet's effort to do the same for painting, he feared the painter's lack of will. He wanted him to ignore the opinions of others in order just to be himself. He is even slightly patronizing, as if he thought Manet a bit naïve. In a letter to Mme Paul Meurice, Baudelaire said Manet ought to be thankful for the attacks on him: 'Manet has such a brilliant and facile ability that it would be unfortunate if he became discouraged. . . . He will never entirely overcome the flaws in his temperament, but he has *a temperament*; that's the important thing. And he does not seem to suspect that the greater the injustice, the better the situation.'[48] Of course, such encouragement on principle says a great deal about Baudelaire's personal sympathy for Manet. But again, the painter comes out seeming a little obtuse, and Baudelaire a bit impatient. Why couldn't Manet stand the suffering that he, Baudelaire, had endured? Yet his remarks do confirm that the key issue was the relationship to the public created through Manet's persona, that is, his unconventional originality. The 'content' of his art became inseparable from his image as an artist. The *ad hominem* attacks meant that the artist seemed to be present in his works.

So although Baudelaire's writings on Manet are relatively slight gestures, and despite their occasional ambivalence, they do evoke the major themes of his criticism. The core of Baudelaire's theory can be found in the famous passage from the *Salon of 1846*, where he showed how Delacroix sacrificed detailed representation for general impressions:

> Nature, for Eugène Delacroix, is a vast dictionary whose leaves he turns and consults with a searching eye. . . . The effect produced upon the spectator's soul is analogous to the artist's means. . . . Ceaselessly sacrificing detail to the whole, and hesitating to impair the vitality of his thought by the drudgery of a neater and more linear execution, he rejoices in the full use of an inalienable originality, which is his searching intimacy with the subject.[49]

These words were written about Delacroix's *Barque of Dante and Virgil*, in which the painter dealt with the relationship between modern art and tradition. It is one of the few French paintings of which Manet made a copy. In an article following Delacroix's death in 1863, Baudelaire republished lines from his *Salon of 1859*, in which he restated Delacroix's attitude toward nature and then focused on imagination as his artistic essence. It was here that Baudelaire defined the difference between Realism, which he called Positivism, and an art of imagination: 'The *positivist* says: "I want to represent things as they are, or as they would be, supposing that I did not exist". The universe without man. The man of imagination says: "I want to illuminate things with my mind and project their reflection to the minds of others".'[50] For Baudelaire, vision was a creative and projective force through which the artist acted on external reality and through which he endowed the artwork with an active, even performative, presence.

But Baudelaire's definition of Realism as positivist was in fact hypothetical. Even Courbet had asserted the personal aspect of his art when he claimed to be 'not only a painter, but a man as well' in the Realist Manifesto of 1855. And all the defenders of Realism had argued the inevitability of the artist's subjective contribution – Jules Castagnary most forcefully, in his 'Salon de 1857', as we saw earlier, just two years before Baudelaire's attack, and linking it to Romanticism. Constantin Guys, the hero of Baudelaire's essay *The Painter of Modern Life* (1863), achieved a reconciliation between Realism, as an art of forms from contemporary society, and the imaginative art so admired in Delacroix. In his writings on Delacroix, Baudelaire had said the painter was sometimes like a savage; and he often related art to primitive drives. In *The Painter of Modern Life*, he defined genius as 'childhood recovered at will', that is, the artist's ability to enter a state of naïve sensitivity and perception. Later, as we saw in his observations on women and cosmetics, Baudelaire linked art to the human need to rise above base nature, to the instinct to improve oneself and embellish one's surroundings. Countering the Enlightenment claim that all virtue resides in nature, though accepting nature as the condition for representation, Baudelaire located the moral value of art in the transcendence beyond nature it produced through the artist's personal vision and technique.[51] He transposed the struggle between individual man and the world featured so prominently in themes chosen for Romantic literature and art – one thinks of Goethe's *Werther*, Géricault's *Raft of the 'Medusa'*, or Hugo's poem 'Mazeppa' – into the realm of art as the effort of the artist, representing us all, to express his imagination despite the limitations of his medium and despite the banality of reality. Ultimately, Baudelaire envisions the Romantic quest with the artist as its master theme.

Although Baudelaire himself did not write about Manet in the way his ideas suggest he might have done, his concept of art provided a new basis for first approaches to Manet by some of his contemporaries and successors. For instance, in 1863 Manet's friend Zacharie Astruc, a confirmed Baudelairian, exemplified the shift of ground from conventional issues of storytelling and technical skill to matters of artistic presence and temperament:

> Unlike most natural-born talents who lead us first to consider the material practices of their art, [Manet] reveals and imposes himself through his vitality. It is the soul that strikes, the movement and play of physiognomies full of life, action and feeling. . . . He pleases or displeases immediately. . . . Individuality is so strong that it breaks away from technical mechanisms, which give way to allow creativity its full metaphysical and material value. . . . Manet's talent is strikingly decisive: cutting, sombre and powerful, both contained and inflamed, it is especially sensitive to accentuated impressions. His character seeks truth without subtle research, and caring little for show, he is stimulated by whatever nature reveals on the side of passion. Irresistably attracted by the grey colours of the Spanish, he mutes bright tonalities in order to transpose to them a kind of feverishness.[52]

Except for the last sentence, Astruc has said little about Manet's art itself. He is unconcerned with judging technique or naturalism; on the contrary, he takes the irrelevance of such norms as a measure of Manet's originality. Words like 'metaphysical', 'passion' and 'feverish' stress the artist's transcendence of mere representation to the plane of self-expression and action on his audience through artistic form. He almost sounds like Baudelaire on Delacroix. 'Impressions', 'colours' and 'tonalities' are Manet's means. In the only allusion to Manet's subject-matter, the terms 'life, action and feeling' feature their expressive rather than physical aspects; he is not concerned with their referents in reality. Astruc's impression of the vitality and immediacy of Manet's painting and his claim that Manet speaks through the soul rather than through technical subtlety or mechanism directly echo Baudelaire, too. Seeing nature as an external stimulus to the painter's means thus places Manet in the wake of Delacroix. Just as a poem

Astruc had composed on Manet's *Olympia* echoed *Les Fleurs du mal*, here Astruc tried to write criticism with Baudelaire's lyrical enthusiasm, if not entirely equalling his mentor's cogency.

In a very different kind of post-Baudelairian opinion, Jules Claretie claimed that the Impressionists, whom he compared to a 'camp of revolutionaries', had proceeded directly from Baudelaire, and that Manet was their leader.[53] Referring primarily to the modernity and rebelliousness of Impressionism rather than to its pictorial qualities, Claretie nevertheless recognized that certain technical innovations would eventually leave their mark. He was implying that, like Baudelaire, Manet deliberately chose vulgar objects to be transformed through artistic process. Claretie's perception of Manet's relation to Baudelaire is thus coloured more by knowledge of the latter's poetry than of his criticism. Focusing on the personality and technique of rebelliousness was the only way to make sense out of what for most critics were the artist's incomprehensible choices. For Claretie, Baudelaire's name at least placed Manet in an existing context of originality and imagination, however dubious.

Despite the emphasis on temperament and originality that Baudelaire's criticism offered, Baudelaire himself was in certain ways a traditionalist. For his theory can be treated as a reformulation of moral standards to which art had always been held. Answering the Realists' self-righteous claim that an artistic reflection of nature paid homage to truth and sincerity, he saw in so-called 'positivist' art the death knell of imagination and the suppression of those human faculties that, by testifying to human virtue, had always justified the making of art in the first place. Moreover, Baudelaire's art criticism is in some ways less remarkable for its foresight than for its brilliant defence of conservative values. In Delacroix, Baudelaire extolled an artist of a previous generation who seemed through imagination to impose his will on the objects of the world and ultimately on public perception. Guys was a man whose status as an illustrator of contemporary customs (*peintre de mœurs*) linked him to aristocratic taste, which Baudelaire admired for its resistance to the onslaught of democracy. Surely we must recognize the tension in Baudelaire's views? For while he admired the man of the world in Guys, and he extolled Delacroix's 'searching intimacy with the subject', he also eulogized their distance from the world that allowed them to mark it with their personality.

If Baudelaire did have some reservations about Manet (we must keep in mind that he only knew the Manet of the early to mid-1860s), they may in part have had to do with the painter's persistent dialogue with art history and his as yet tentative engagement with modern life, features Baudelaire could attribute to the apparent lack of self-confidence or weakness of character about which he complained. Baudelaire the poet or critic could never be described as a diffident observer. And although Delacroix and Guys possessed certain characteristics of the dandy, Baudelaire's lyrical descriptions of the former's driving creativity or the latter's intoxication with the phenomena of modernity hardly correspond to Manet's frequent look of dispassionate neutrality. Though the painter did indeed have a temperament, Baudelaire had always been more interested in the kind of passion and commitment that Manet seemed to shun. He may have been put off by Manet's silence. For Baudelaire was looking for a painter of modern life who would project on modern subjects the kind of imaginative impulses that had transported him in the work of Delacroix. Those impulses carry us away from reality. The thrust of Manet's art, however, suggests that imagination underlies our perception of the real. It might even be said that Manet used imagination to approach the real. His painting grounds us firmly in reality while exploring and recording the self's contribution to it; all of his figures have the powerful effect of reality, yet they are undeniably his personal creations. Here is where Manet may have been ahead of Baudelaire.

So although Baudelaire helped lay the ground-work for Manet's art, he left Paris and died too soon to properly elaborate their mutual links or explore the impact of Manet's peculiar temperament on his artworks in the way that Zola would. We can only speculate on whether Baudelaire was disconcerted by Manet's Baudelairian themes (too close for comfort) and idiosyncratic technique (subverting those subjects). The fact is that Manet appeared neither as the man of imagination Baudelaire extolled in Delacroix, nor as the positivist Baudelaire disparaged in Courbet. Lacking words equivalent to Manet's art forms, he turned to the artist's personality instead. And even if Baudelaire himself regarded Manet as an irresolute and eccentric hispanicizing Realist, for others reared on Baudelaire's writings, Manet's originality and temperament provided positive grounds for a critical discourse that now focused on the artist himself. And as the artist became the object of criticism, so he ultimately came to be seen as the primary subject – that is, active agent – of art.

ZOLA AND SINCERITY

Emile Zola's view of Manet's art is certainly the most articulate of those we shall consider, and for a long time it has been accepted as the classic interpretation. It owes its success in part to its relative simplicity, at least as compared to Baudelaire's and Mallarmé's far-ranging moral or philosophical theorizing. Zola drew from the realm of science, but rather than simply emphasizing Realism or positivism in Manet's art, he made his own critical premises themselves appear scientific. As such, he could demonstrate the impact of Manet's personality despite its lack of the literary and programmatic elements associated with Romanticism. Indeed, apparently taking the possibility of objective naturalism for granted, Zola otherwise stressed that Manet's programme was merely the sincere expression of personal vision. His conception of Manet's art brought it close to Impressionism, which for Zola balanced the artist's imprint on reality with the imprint of nature on his mind. Though Baudelaire was the most compelling critical voice in the early 1860s, his continuing support of Delacroix and his abandonment of Courbet, and Courbet's brand of Realism, in the early 1850s may have appeared suspiciously old-fashioned. More polemical and simplistic, Zola cultivated a literary position closer to journalism than to poetry. So while indebted to the concept of temperament that Baudelaire had established as a principal term for critical discussion, Zola recast it in the progressive and democratic vocabulary of contemporary science and psychology.

Zola sought to describe a world in which Manet's vision was normative rather than deviant. The criteria he established and his willingness to do so are rooted in his immediately preceding, intellectually formative years. Although the young Zola had visited Manet's atelier in 1865, it was just one of many direct contacts with artists he had in the early 1860s. Their actual friendship developed only after Zola had defended Manet's painting in the press – for which Manet expressed his gratitude both in writing and in painting. The first stage of Zola's development can be gauged by his relationship to his childhood mentor in artistic matters, Paul Cézanne. The two friends had shared an infatuation with Romanticism, but as early as March 1860 Zola wrote to Cézanne, who was still at home in Aix-en-Provence, that one could find 'poetry' in 'realist' subjects as well: 'Everything has its poetry, both the dung-heap and the flowers. . . . Art is one, spiritualist and realist are but words . . .'.[54] Zola's position is like that of Castagnary, whose 'Philosophie du Salon de 1857' might well have been fresh in his mind.

In a long theoretical letter of August 1864 to another artist friend, Antonin Valabrègue, Zola elaborated on Castagnary's argument that nature was but the raw material for art, and that art was ultimately the product of subjectivity. He denied the possibility of true realism, claiming that in art nature was seen through the 'screen' of a man, 'through a temperament, a personality. . . . Exact reality is impossible in an art work. There is a deformation of what exists. There is a lie'.[55] (In the same years, Mallarmé referred to his poems as 'glorious lies'.) Zola had just met Hippolyte Taine while working for the publisher Hachette, and he would soon issue a laudatory review of Taine's *Philosophie de l'art*. For Taine, 'the Screen is one of flesh and bone that reproduces images *materially*'.[56] Zola's conception of the artistic process was guided by that concept, to which his quasi-scientific vocabulary lent weight: 'The artist places himself in direct contact with nature, views it in his manner, is penetrated by it, and then sends back its light rays after refracting and colouring them, like a prism, according to his nature'. The competing artistic schools, Classicism, Romanticism and Realism, were like different screens through which to view reality. Zola preferred the Realists, for although he denied their claims to absolute truth, at least they were 'content to lie just enough to make me feel the presence of a man in their image of creation'.[57]

This conception of artistic vision posits the externality of the eye to nature, with consciousness as a kind of intermediary. Taine's *Philosophie de l'art*, based on courses given at the Ecole des Beaux-Arts in the 1860s, anchored art in historical and social contexts more systematically than had been done before by reducing them to three factors: race, milieu (geographical and social) and historical moment. Taine continued the tradition of using the term 'ideal' to distinguish art (with its poetry) from reality. But rather than assuming its expression through classical form, he identified it simply with the personal and internal conceptions of individual artists: 'Things pass from the real to the ideal when the artist reproduces them with modifications corresponding to his idea.' Taine held that artists perceived characteristics in things that cannot be revealed by merely reproducing things themselves.[58] The ideal was thus the imprint of the idea, which is formed through temperament. Taine's contribution was the psychological notion that ideation transformed reality into a sign for aspects of it that exist within human perception.

This notion of representation as signifying the external world perceived is consistent with Taine's theory of perception, the publication of which in *De L'Intelligence* (1870) came in the year that followed his series of lectures on art. In this influential treatise Taine wrote that 'our external perception of the world is an internal dream in harmony with external objects'. Here he echoed the philosophy of Arthur Schopenhauer, who was known in France by the 1850s and became virtually an obligatory reference by the 1870s. (Even Manet's friend Théodore Duret wrote a short essay on Schopenhauer in 1878.[59]) Taine tied Schopenhauer's oft-repeated notion that 'material nature is a true lie' to physical reality: 'Rather than saying that hallucination is a false external perception, we should say that external perception is a true hallucination.'[60] Proof that sensations are internal could be found in dreams, hypnotism and hallucinations: 'In effect, by its presence alone, a sensation . . . engenders an interior phantom that appears to be the external object.'[61]

A scientific version of Schopenhauer's metaphysical claim could be found in the well-known writings of Hermann von Helmholtz, whose *Optics* was translated into French in 1867. Crucial to his contribution was his notion of the sign. Helmholtz reconciled the dualities of perception by arguing that representations were internally perceived signs of the external world: 'For our consciousness, *sensations* are signs to be interpreted by our intelligence. All sensations taken together in a complex idea constitute the *representation* we make of an object, which we call *perception* as long as it is produced by actual sensations and *memory* when it is the opposite.'[62] Regarding the binocularity of sight, Helmholtz reminded his readers that 'vision shows us the world is not as it *is*, but as it *appears* from our point of view'.[63] A later disciple, using binocularity to illustrate the subjectivity of vision, showed how pushing on one of the eyes alters the mental image.[64] (One thinks of the psychological 'displacement' of the eye in Manet's *Bar at the Folies-Bergère*, in which the eye seems to be in a different location from the body.) In his widely read *Philosophie de Schopenhauer*, Théodule Ribot equated the term 'appearance' with Helmholtz's 'symbol': 'The data given by the senses can be considered no more than *symbols we interpret*; we can conceive no analogy between a perception and the object it represents; the former is simply the mental *sign* of the latter.'[65] Using Helmholtz's terms, Taine had written that 'our visual sensations are nothing but *signs*. Only experience teaches us their meaning, through their association with corresponding muscular and tactile sensations'.[66] These phantoms were fragments of the self, ostensibly detached and opposed to it, but actually the self in another guise.[67] Thus, while all reality could be considered emanations of the self, it was grounded in original physical experience. The body had to be the source of understanding. Representations are but the body in another form.

Although these theories may seem to make artists prisoners of their bodily functions, Zola saw them as liberating. Artists were free to be themselves rather than define their art by schools and conventions. For Taine, according to Zola, artists were both ideal and modern not by their adherence but by their very nature. Another critic agreed. In 1879 Castagnary noted that all artists were inherently naturalist: 'The painter can only express himself by means of forms and colours. . . . He remains thus . . . chained to visible reality.'[68] In his 1868 *Salon* he had explained his naturalism as a liberation: '[Naturalism] says to artists: Be free! Nature and life, which are the basis of all poetry, are all around you. Go out and show us what you have found. We all live on this earth together . . . and see the same things, but your eye is a deeper and clearer mirror . . . a condenser that fixes and makes fugitive sensations tangible.'[69] Far from disparaging poetry, Castagnary saw it as the product of a more deeply perceiving eye, to which art gave a means of material expression. His formula made art the manifestation of that which is merely imminent in reality, waiting to be perceived, that is, transformed into sign.

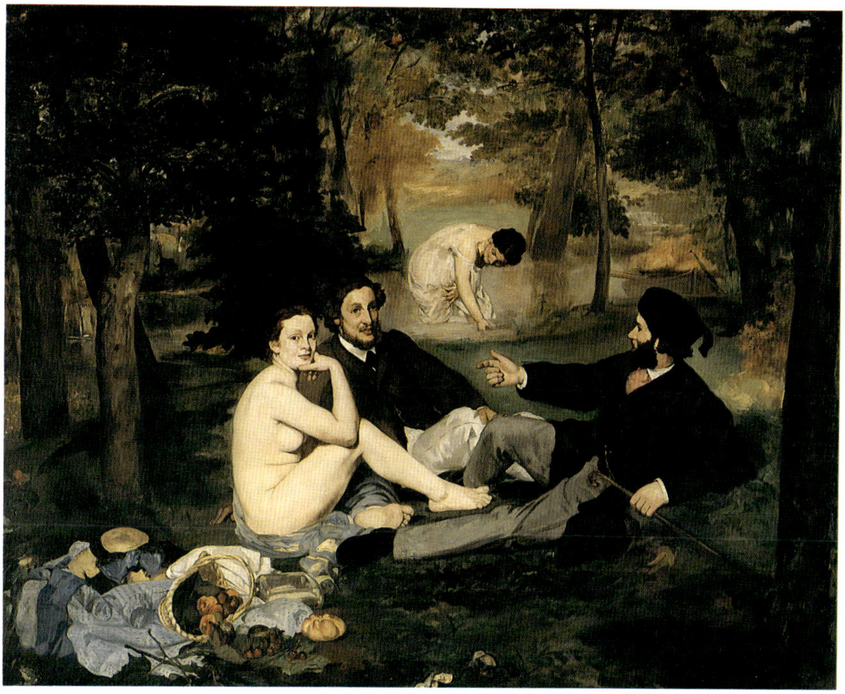

40 *Le Déjeuner sur l'herbe*, 1863, oil on canvas. Musée d'Orsay, Paris

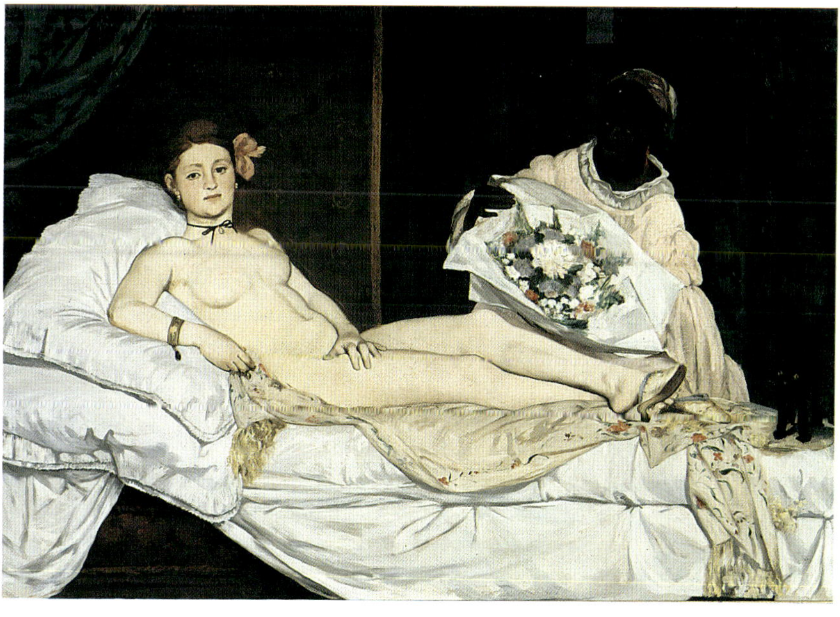

41 *Olympia*, 1863, oil on canvas. Musée d'Orsay, Paris

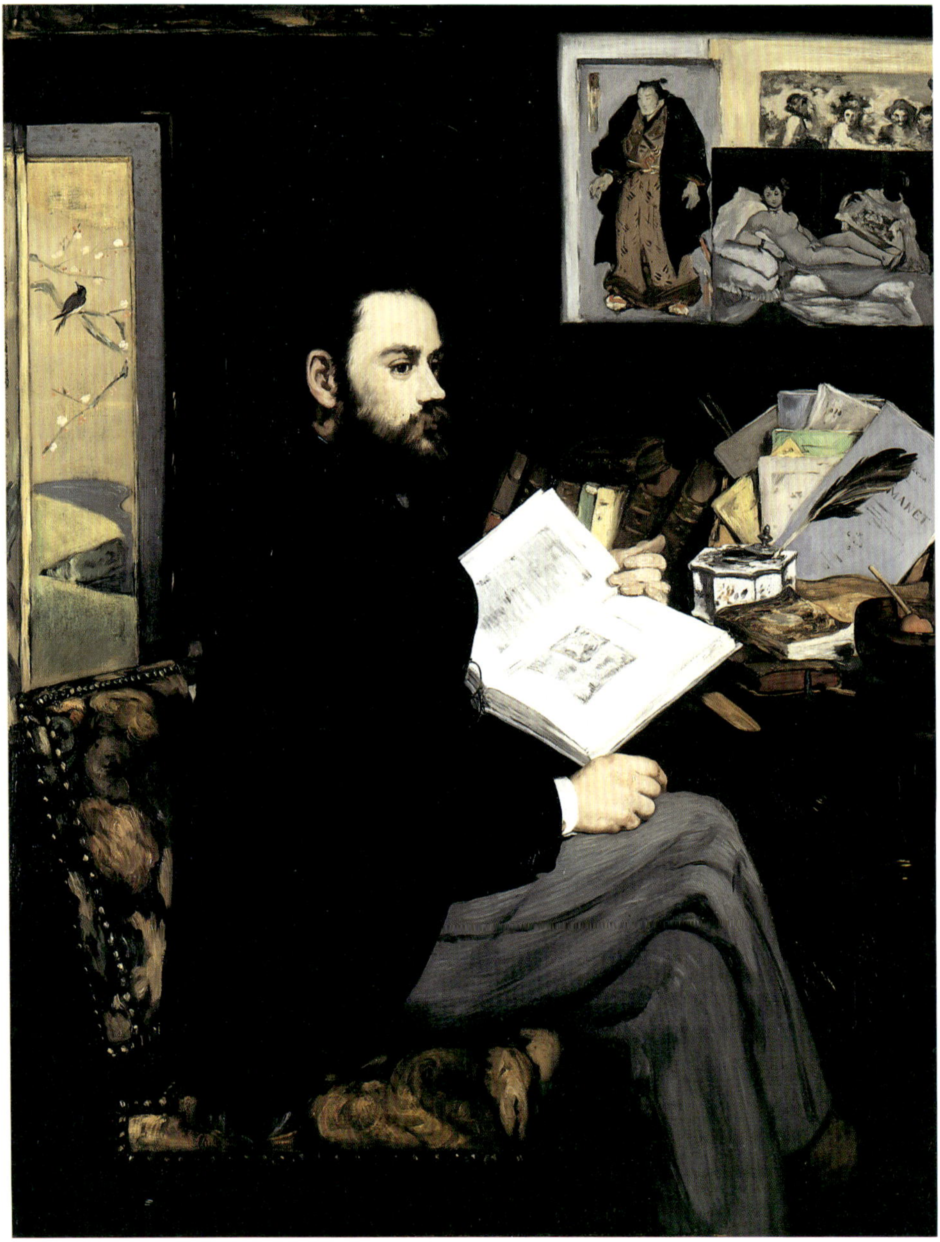

42 *Emile Zola*, 1868, oil on canvas. Musée d'Orsay, Paris

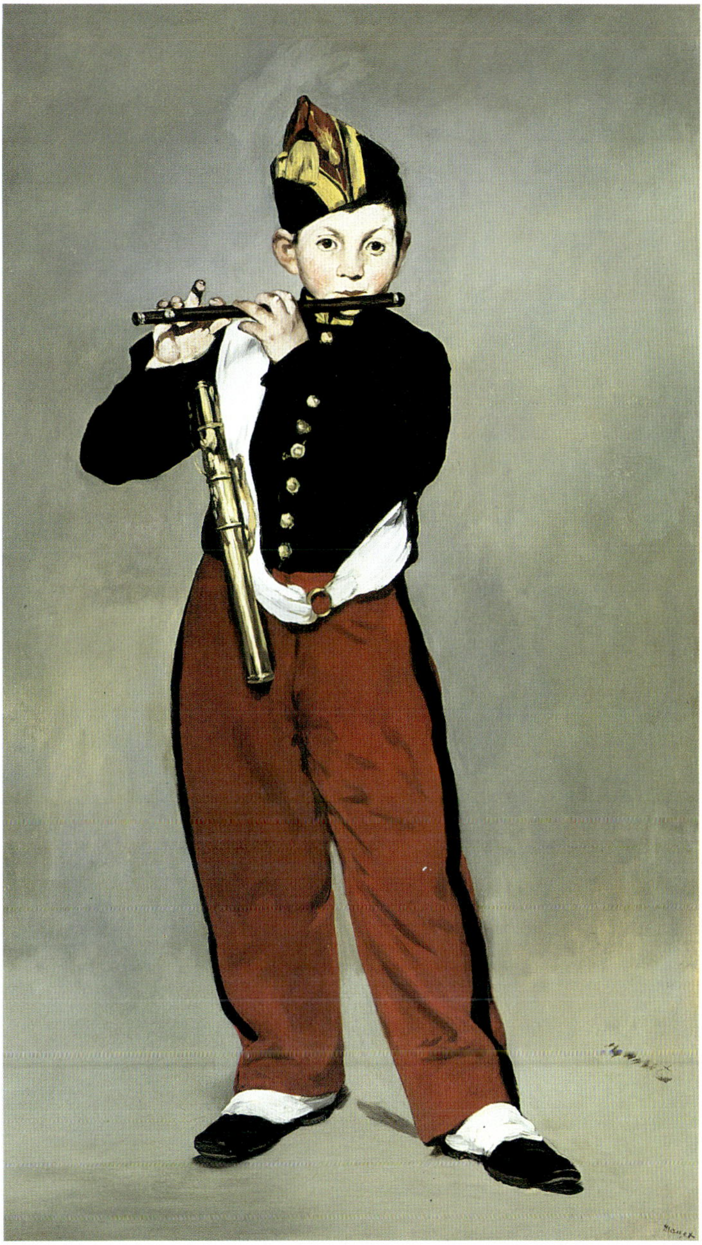

43 *The Fifer Boy*, 1866, oil on canvas. Musée d'Orsay, Paris

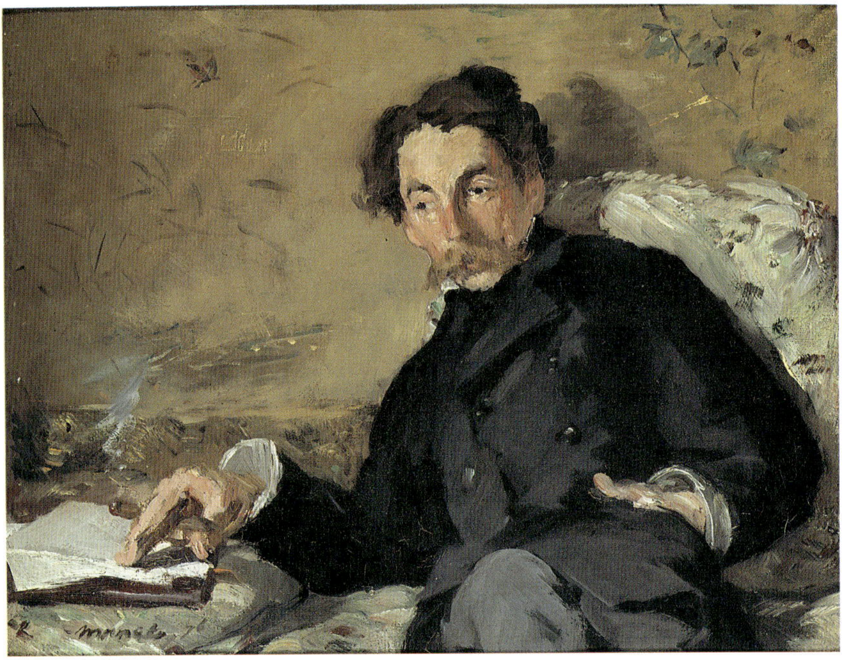

44 *Stéphane Mallarmé*, 1876, oil on canvas. Musée d'Orsay, Paris

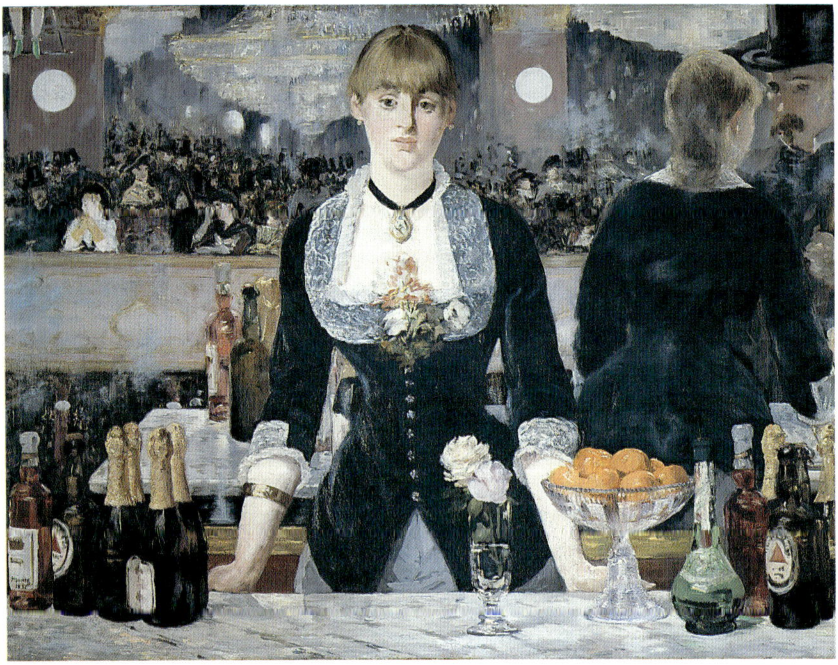

45 *A Bar at the Folies-Bergère*, 1881–2, oil on canvas. Courtauld Galleries, London

This excursus suggests a confluence between philosophy, psychology and optics as the context for Zola's art criticism. Although he would not have known all the writings I have cited, some of which appeared just after his own first articles, Zola belonged to the same community of progressive and scientific thinking. Indeed, even when he did know certain sources, he fully assimilated them to his straightforward, non-specialized vocabulary. He developed a simple criterion – the human presence in art, or temperament, as he would systematically call it. In his first article relating to art, an essay on the social theorist Pierre-Joseph Proudhon's posthumous *On the Principle of Art and its Social Destination* (1865), Zola disputed the validity of any ulterior purpose for painting. Proudhon had defined art as 'an idealized representation of nature with a view to the moral and physical improvement of humanity'. Art was to have a social purpose. Zola's retort was that 'my principle is that the artwork lives thanks solely to originality. I must find a man behind each work, or the work leaves me cold. I frankly sacrifice humanity in favour of the artist. Were I to formulate it, my definition of the artwork would be: "A work of art is a corner of nature seen through a temperament".'[70] Despite Proudhon's radical politics, his definition of art was still rooted in a moralism not unlike that of old-fashioned classicism, whereas Zola defined art by a natural, or in view of Taine, a scientific description.

Zola systematically stripped art of ulterior implications. For example, he avoided the skilful formulation of Castagnary, who, though a disciple of Proudhon, had a far more sophisticated attitude toward art. In his *Salon de 1863* Castagnary had placed the origins of what he called the 'Naturalist School' in 'the depths of modern rationalism'.[71] Naturalism meant that everyone would look at nature as they wished; hence, its democratic, anti-hierarchical attitude would lead in the direction of social justice. Even though he would claim for Manet exactly the attitude Castagnary described, Zola kept those claims apolitical. (Castagnary would himself more or less accept that view of Manet by 1868.) Similar was Zola's reaction to the question of Baudelairian influence on Manet. In his essay of 1867 on the painter, Zola attributed Manet's expression of temperament to 'the unconscious element, the very nature of the painter'. To those who saw parallels to Baudelaire's poetry, Zola's response was that Manet 'has never been foolish enough . . . to put ideas in his painting'.[72]

While Zola sought an artist's personality in Manet's art, his description of how such expression was embodied by the physical work focused on the organ of vision. Thus, subjectivity meant the natural mechanics of the individual eye. In the essay of 1867, which was entitled *A New Manner of Painting: Edouard Manet*, Zola wrote:

> Sensing that he would accomplish nothing by copying the masters, by painting nature seen through individualities other than his own, he quite naively realized one bright morning that there was nothing left but to try looking at nature as it is, without seeing it through the works or opinions of others. As soon as this idea occurred to him, he took any object whatsoever, a being or a thing, placed it in the corner of his studio, and set out to reproduce it on the canvas according to his faculties of vision and comprehension. . . . There was nothing more in it than a particular intelligence, served by organs endowed with a certain character, placed before nature and translating it according to its manner.

Zola frequently repeated phrases such as 'he sees through his eyes [as opposed to those of someone else]' and 'he lets himself be guided by his eyes'. And he claimed that 'the artist's entire personality consists of the manner in which his eye is organized'.[73]

Zola thus gave the concept of temperament, which in Baudelairian terms referred primarily to imagination, an empirical basis in the individual eye's psychological and physiological profile. But that does not mean Zola presented Manet as a Realist. On the contrary, he used science in support of Manet's subjectivity, though of course, it was the kind of organic subjectivity susceptible to scientific analysis – Manet as an organism. As if mindful of Baudelaire's imprecations against Realism, in *Mon Salon* (1866) Zola observed:

> Here is what happens in our time of psychological and physiological analysis. The wind is blowing in the direction of science; we are drawn in spite of ourselves towards the exact study of things. All strong personalities will thus reveal themselves in the direction of truth. The movement of the epoch is certainly realist, or rather positivist. Thus I

am forced to admire men who seem related to one another, related by the times in which they live. . . . I cannot repeat it enough: I am looking for men, not puppets, but men of flesh and bone.[74]

Applying these principles to Manet in 1867, he spoke of him as 'the child of our age':

I see him as a painter-analyst. All our beliefs are being questioned; demanding solid foundations, science has brought us back to the exact observation of fact. And this movement extends beyond the scientific domain; all knowledge, all human works tend to seek firm and definitive principles in nature. . . . Edouard Manet applies this same method to his works. . .analyzing nature with care. I repeat, he is a simple analyst; his labour is of greater interest than the plagiarisms of his contemporaries; art itself tends towards certainty; the artist is the interpreter of what exists, and his works have for me the charm of a precise description made in an original and human language.[75]

Zola's argument is not simply that Manet adopts the approach of the analyst as that which is demanded by his age. He goes further: Manet paints according to characteristics physically and psychologically determined in himself. Those characteristics are signified by the unique traces of the artist's 'labour' or 'original and human language'. The painter thus avoids the insincerity of seeing through another's eyes. Seeing through one's own in the most objective way is the only way for personal language, or poetry, to emerge:

Beauty becomes human life itself, the human element mixing with the fixed element of reality and giving birth to a creation that belongs to humanity. Beauty lives within us, not outside. . . . What interests me, me as a man, is humanity. . . ; what touches me . . . is to find within each [artwork] an artist, a brother, who shows me nature with a new face, with all the power or gentleness of his personality. . . .In a huge room hung with the works of all the painters of the world. . . .I have the same poem in a thousand different languages . . .[76]

Zola seems to echo the 'Hypocrite lecteur, mon semblable, mon frère' of *Les Fleurs du mal.* For surely the notion that beauty lies with the individual rather than in nature is Baudelairian, that is, unless Zola and he now simply share a sufficiently generalized conception. It is in any case a deeply anti-Realist one; and though Zola hardly follows Baudelaire in attributing moral value to self-expression, he still makes sincerity – that old Realist catchword meaning one's own way of seeing – the key to quality in art.

For Zola's purpose is primarily an explication of Manet's art, not a theoretical or moral discourse, as was Baudelaire's. He provides a rationale for the contradictions between the marvellously successful and apparently awkward passages he was hardly the first to observe in Manet's painting. (Even the most open-minded and sophisticated viewers, such as Thoré and Castagnary, noted and were disturbed by them.) Indeed, such contradictions were evidence for what Zola describes as the natural function of seeing that was particular to Manet. They need no other justification, for a natural function is self-explanatory. Describing Manet's painting thus constitutes in itself an analysis of the structure of the painter's eye. In his first article (1866), Zola's terms were general: 'M. Manet's talent is made of simplicity and accuracy. . . . He has taken art from its beginning, that is, from the exact observation of objects.'[77] The article of 1867 makes a considerable elaboration and is more systematic. Zola finds three principal qualities in Manet's vision. What first strikes him 'is an extremely delicate accuracy in the relationships between hues'. He explains that when a painter begins with a value lighter than what he finds in reality, all his colours must be adjusted toward the lighter end. Manet sees according to this 'law of values': 'His paintings are blond and luminous; they have a firm and solid paleness. The light falls white and broad, gently illuminating objects.' Second, Zola notes that the painter

> has been guided by his eyes, which perceive the subject in terms of large areas of interrelated colour. A head posed against a wall is no more than a more or less light spot against a more or less grey background. . . .From this derives a great simplicity, almost without details, an ensemble of accurate and delicate areas of colour which at a few paces give the painting its powerful relief. . . .The entire personality of the artist consists of the manner in which his eye is organized: he sees blond, and he sees by masses.

The third characteristic is 'a slightly dry, but charming gracefulness', which Zola relates to Manet's love of society and of 'the elegance of Salons'. It was here that he spoke of Manet's painting as deriving from the painter's innate, unconscious yet social nature.[78]

Summing up, Zola passed from what he called analysis to a synthesis: '[Manet] speaks a language made of simplicity and accuracy. The new tone he brings is that of blondness filling the canvas with light. The translation he gives us is accurate and simplified, using broad relationships, indicating only the masses.' As if aware of the limits of this view, which he can do no better than describe by repeating the words 'simplicity', 'accuracy' and 'blondness' over and over again, Zola warns us not to look for more:

> I cannot repeat enough that we must forget a thousand things in order to taste this talent. We are no longer concerned with the search for absolute beauty; the artist paints neither story nor soul; composition [i.e. dramatic] does not exist for him, and the task he has set himself is not to represent some idea or some historical act. That is why we must not judge him as a moralist or a writer but as a painter. He treats figure paintings in the same way as in art schools one may treat still-life; I mean that he groups figures before him, somewhat by chance, and that his only concern is then to fix them upon the canvas as he sees them . . . as no more than an accurate and literal translation. He knows neither how to sing nor to philosophize.[79]

In defining Manet's temperament through its limitation to pictorial and visual concerns, Zola believed he was performing an appropriate and objective form of criticism that removed Manet's painting from the hierarchical structures and moralizing criteria associated with history painting. In portraying him as a painter-analyst, Zola made him a child of the scientific age, a kindred spirit to the writer himself, whose criticism had, he believed, an identical foundation. Indeed, having admitted he sought in the artist an *alter ego*, a brother, it is hardly surprising that Zola's vision of Manet corresponded to his vision of himself. Although Zola would have denied projecting his own ideas on the artist, he made no secret of their affinities. He paraded the word 'analysis' as the basis of his critical position every bit as much as he used it to characterize Manet, even though he also claimed his approach was engendered by the nature of Manet's art: 'One must proceed in the same way as the artist himself proceeded: forget the riches of the museums and the requirements of so-called rules, block out the memory of the works of the dead; see only nature face to face; seek in Manet's works no more than a translation of nature.'[80] Criticism should regard paintings simply as visual evidence. 'Our role as critics is to study the languages of temperaments. . . .Philosophers, if necessary will reduce them to formulas. I wish only to analyze the facts, and artworks are but simple facts.'[81] Such words closely parallel Zola's explanations of his own writing. For example, after the tumultuous reception of his murder novel *Thérèse Raquin* (1867), Zola claimed in the preface to the second edition that he was merely the student of temperament: 'I chose characters completely dominated by their nerves and their blood, deprived of free will, pushed to each action of their lives by the fatality of their flesh.' These aims were scientific: 'I have simply done on living bodies the work of analysis which surgeons perform on corpses.'[82]

In encounters with individual works, Zola's process of criticism, anti-historical and determined by the painting's own form, becomes none other than the process of seeing. Zola described painting by look rather than by story. In comparison, even the Baudelairian approach had fallen back on narrative – the grand epic of the heroic imagination versus convention. Zola called his own approach natural, both for viewing nature and for viewing art. He steps back, moves closer, then steps back again. As part of his 'synthetic' characterization (that is, following his 'analysis') of Manet's temperament, he wrote:

> The first impression of a painting by Manet is a bit dry and tart. Then . . . there is a surprisingly elegant stiffness. The eye first sees broadly applied colours. Soon objects define themselves and take their places; after a few seconds, the ensemble emerges, vigorous and solid, and one senses the true charm of contemplating this clear and serious painting, which renders nature with a gentle brutality, so to speak. Approaching the painting more closely, we can see that the *métier* is more delicate than brusque; the artist uses only the brush and does so prudently; rather than a buildup of colours, there is a unified layer.[83]

A similar, even more detailed, description of the critic's experience of seeing is given for individual works, particularly the *Olympia*:

> Lying on her white sheets, Olympia makes a great pale spot [*tache*] against the black background, in which we find the head of the negress bringing in a bouquet and the famous black cat that has so amused the public. At first glance, one distinguishes only two tones in the painting, two violent tones repelling one another. Moreover, the details have disappeared. Look at the girl's head: the lips are two thin pink lines, the eyes are reduced to a few black strokes. Now look at the bouquet, and closely, I ask: touches of yellow, blue and green. Everything is simplified, and if you wish to reconstruct reality, you must move back a few steps. Then something strange happens: every object takes its place, Olympia's head stands out against the background with startling relief, and the bouquet becomes a marvel of brilliance and freshness. The accuracy of the eye and simplicity of the hand have created this miracle; the painter has proceeded like nature itself, by way of clear masses and broad planes of light, and his work has the slightly hardy and austere look of nature.[84]

If there is narrative here, it is the narrative of seeing and the story of the hand. What Zola and Manet share, of course, is the faculty of seeing, on which Zola builds his argument for the naturalism of Manet's sight. For if Manet's painting causes Zola to re-enact the experience of seeing nature, then Manet's process is rooted in the same. Zola's belief in such a re-enactment is supported by the movement of the eye as it scans the canvas surface and by the physical movement of the body through space during the viewing of Manet's work. Acting out at least to that degree, the process of art-making makes the link between hand and eye, touch and sight, body and consciousness, a concretely experienced result of Manet's art. It confirms the performative ability of the artwork to act on, even to displace, the viewer. Considering the painting as an object, ontologically similar to any fact of nature, Zola denies to it the spiritualist values of tradition. There is no escape from its materiality and from the effort of the painter's processes, through which, indeed, each work is critically defined. Zola attributes value to this materiality not as a sign of labour, as would be the case for a craft product, but as a sign of personality. Personality, however, is defined by bodily functions, which Zola as critic-surgeon probes. Artistic self-expression is inevitably their result; in this sense art is grounded in the physical process of its making. For Baudelaire, artistic self-expression had been the sign of virtue and truth. Now grounded in biological and psychological materiality, the expression of temperament testifies to the diversity of nature; originality in art is good because it is (naturally) true. The naturalism attributed to Manet is thus at least in part derived from the view that his creative process follows natural bodily functions. Removing the artist from Baudelaire's heroic battle, Zola places the artist within humanity, naturally engaged in the processes of life. The 'biological' model of art criticism recognizes the inadequacy of the verbal with regard to the visual, and now relates the art object to the artist as the body's sign. It focuses on the performance of the artist from within his own nature, rather than on some concept to which he is external and for which he is but a means.

In his *Mon Salon* of 1868, Zola for the first time used the term 'naturalist' to describe Manet. Having himself sat to Manet, Zola had directly experienced the degree to which Manet's art was utterly dependent on physical nature: 'He forgot about me, he no longer knew that I was there, he was copying me as he would have copied any human beast whatsoever, with an attentiveness, an artistic conscientiousness I have never seen elsewhere. . . . Often, when he was treating some secondary detail, I wanted to drop the pose and I advised him to invent. "No", he answered. "I can do nothing without nature. I cannot invent." . . . Therein lies all his talent. Above all, he is a naturalist.'[85] Yet within a text that merely summarizes the defences of the previous year, these observations introduce the seeds of contradiction. For in comparing Manet's creative process to copying, Zola began to have expectations that Manet would increasingly fail to fulfil. As Manet came into closer contact with the Impressionists, his style became even looser, more marked with the signs of subjectivity than before. So in his 'Salon de 1879', a disappointed Zola took up a reproach he had himself refuted many years ago:

> [Manet's] hand does not equal his eye. He has not been able to develop a technique for himself; he has remained the

> enthusiastic student, who sees distinctly what is happening in nature but is never sure of rendering his impressions completely and definitively. That is why, when he starts out, one never knows whether he will get to the end. . . . When he succeeds, his painting is extraordinary. . . ; but sometimes he gets sidetracked – and then his paintings are unequal and imperfect. In short, in the past fifteen years no painter has been more subjective.[86]

Subjective came to mean erratic and uneven, qualities now incompatible with 'naturalism'. 'Originality' could no longer paper over Manet's 'weaknesses', because Zola's theory had become prescriptive and assumed the artist's ability to adhere more strictly to some 'objective' nature, as if he was expected to outgrow his biology. Manet came to look like Claude Lantier, the tragic protagonist of Zola's novel *L'Oeuvre* (1886), in which the artist's hand is never adequate to express his perception. While thus finally recognizing the impossibility of figuration, Zola made it seem the fatal flaw of visual art rather than its underlying and constructive theme.

The change in Zola's opinion relates not solely to changes in Manet's style, changes that Zola, by the way, barely discussed even if he noticed them. It testifies to Zola's own evolution, hence to the subjectivity of his own criteria. Manet corresponded to an early or transitional phase in Zola's development. Still in the wake of Baudelaire, Zola's commitment to individual expression was strong enough to provide a central critical concept, even though he thoroughly redefined it. Adopting the premises of modern science, Zola grounded sincerity of expression in psychological and physiological functions. Whatever so-called humanity or originality Zola found in Manet was predetermined by those functions rather than being an expression of virtue or will. Zola's view of Manet's art was thus congruent with a time of mechanistic approaches to psychology. The limitations of that view became apparent as soon as Manet seemed to deviate from the course on which Zola thought he had found him set. It is not that Zola had misunderstood Manet, but that both he and Manet were to evolve in divergent directions. It may be that Zola's eye ultimately remained external to nature, while Manet's, as Mallarmé would suggest for Impressionism, became more fully immersed within it.

3 Being and Immersion

Less widely known than Zola as an interpreter of Manet, the Symbolist poet Stéphane Mallarmé wrote two essays on the painter, one of which is nearly as long as Zola's famous pamphlet. From 1873 he was Manet's close companion, stopping at his studio almost daily on the way home from teaching English at a nearby *lycée*. Moreover, at the very time Mallarmé was writing about Manet, the pair were collaborating on two projects. In 1875 Manet illustrated Mallarmé's translation of Edgar Allan Poe's poem 'The Raven', and in 1876 Manet's woodcuts accompanied Mallarmé's groundbreaking poem 'L'Après-midi d'un faune'. Although these appear to be slight works within Manet's overall achievement, they afford the opportunity to study a convergence between him and his friend. In spite of the availability of these works, the opportunity has not been seized, and the most common way to relate Manet and Mallarmé is still through general parallels between their work rather than this specific historical instance of interaction. Of course, Mallarmé's suggestive, often highly visual imagery has quite understandably been compared to the breadth and freedom of Manet's brushstroke, and vice versa. Like Mallarmé's poetic structures, Manet's style often calls attention to the artifice of representation and the autonomy of pictorial notation with a wilfulness that is most explicit and appropriate in his portrait of Mallarmé (illus. 44). But what has not been addressed is a basis for such comparisons in the attitudes towards Manet and visual art that are to be found in Mallarmé's critical writings; they offer a significant and original interpretation of Manet's role in the development of modern art.

Apart from a stylistic parallelism between himself and the painter, what could a man of Mallarmé's Symbolist vision find in the ostensibly naturalist elements of Manet's painting? Whereas Zola saw Manet as an external eye analysing nature in its personal way, Mallarmé saw the painter *immersed* in nature to such a degree that he became the impersonal organ of its underlying idea or philosophical conception. Mallarmé directly answered Baudelaire's call for a painter of modern life with the name of Manet, but he did so by seeing Manet's painting as an enactment of the processes of life. As such, the key to the poetics of both Manet and Mallarmé is similar, though Manet did not articulate them as such. For Mallarmé believed that the intangible (we might say the unresolvable) effect is where poetry begins. His preoccupation with the structural, linguistic, aural and even visual (as in the appearance of words on the page) aspects of language embody an understanding of how the performance of representation itself can contribute an ineffable and poetic character to the expression of thought – can indeed itself constitute the expression of thought. We may certainly imagine that Mallarmé's awareness of such possibilities was enhanced by exposure to the work of Manet. In any case, it was in his analysis of Manet that he first confronted such questions, and in 'L'Après-midi d'un faune' of the same year, it became his explicit theme.

MALLARMÉ ON LIGHT AND AIR

The Impressionists emerged in the public eye as a distinct group thanks to the series of independent exhibitions they began holding in 1874. Manet refused to join them, no doubt because he did not need to. After all, he had been able to exhibit many of his works at the Salons, despite as many refusals. He was sufficiently well-off, and had friends enough for survival. Moreover, though stubbornly personal in his painting, he was not a man to challenge the system directly, and he had suffered when he had appeared to do so. Still, most critics agreed that Manet was either the leader of the Impressionist group or at least its inspiration. Two main reasons underlay this belief. First, Manet's originality served as an example for Impressionist radicalism, which was sometimes characterized with the politically charged word 'intransigent' (after the anarchist Spanish *intransigentes*, whose refusal to compromise caused a collapse of the Spanish Government in 1873). Second, Manet's modern subjects of leisure, his loose brushwork and high-keyed tonalities bore obvious connections to the Impressionists, though by the late 1870s he was as affected by them as they were by him.

Mallarmé also took Manet to be the leader of the

Impressionists. His principal article on Manet, which was published (in somewhat stilted English) in the *Art Monthly Review* in 1876, was entitled 'The Impressionists and Edouard Manet'. (The article was written originally in French, but no French manuscript has been found. The published translation is here reprinted complete, in the Appendix, pp. 231–42.) Mallarmé accepted the contrast with Realism, which he said had 'sought to impress itself upon the mind by the lively depiction of things as they appeared to be, and vigorously excluded all meddlesome imagination'. Presumably Impressionism was more open to the latter. (He was using the word 'meddlesome' ironically, of course.) Mallarmé thus agreed with the way Duret, Baudelaire and others had discredited Realism as uncreative, and he positioned himself as a successor to Manet's earlier reviewers. For instance, Mallarmé admired Baudelaire for having the foresight and instinct to appreciate Manet's works before 'the sufficient exposition of the principles they inculcated', that is, before the true nature of Manet's art was understood (and perhaps because Baudelaire had such a limited experience of Manet's work). He might have said that Baudelaire admired Manet as a man of temperament, without realizing that specific temperament's broader implications, which Mallarmé would explore. Mallarmé's comments on Zola are more intriguing: '[Zola] recognized the light that had arisen [i.e. Manet], albeit that he was yet too young to then define that which we today call Naturalism, to follow the quest, not merely of that reality which impresses itself in its abstract form on all, but of that absolute and important sentiment which Nature herself impresses on those who have voluntarily abandoned conventionalism.' Of course, Mallarmé was looking at Manet about ten years after Zola had. Zola's association with Naturalism was well known, but Mallarmé implied that the novelist's conceptions had been incomplete, and possibly superficial. For Zola's mechanistic explanation of the artistic process, although it accounted for individuality of artistic perception, failed to probe toward the 'absolute and important sentiment' that Mallarmé found emerging in the 1870s. This 'sentiment' was the result of nature's impressions on the artist as a representative of us all. Mallarmé claimed that 'a peculiar quality outside mere Realism', and which he found in the more profound art of Impressionism, revealed 'one of those

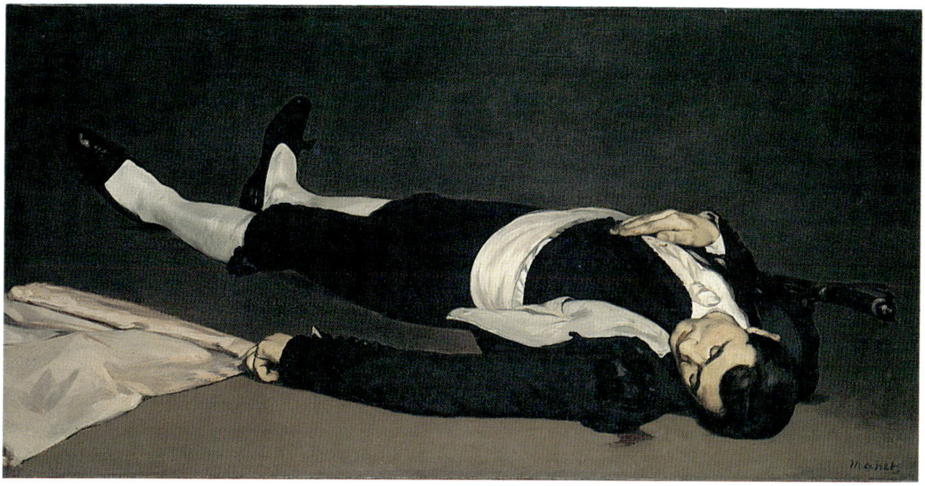

46 *The Dead Toreador*, 1864–5, oil on canvas. National Gallery of Art, Washington, DC

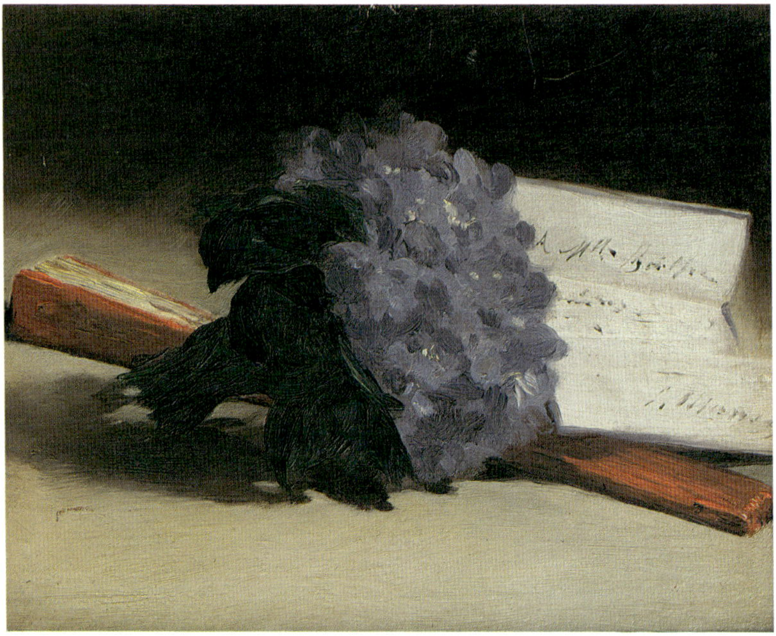

47 *A Bunch of Violets with a Fan*, 1872, oil on canvas. Private collection

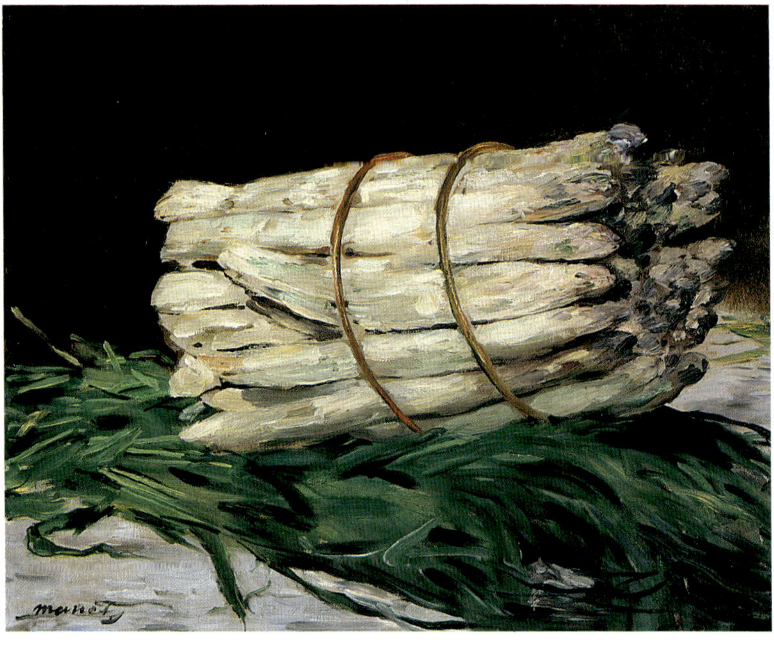

48 *The Bunch of Asparagus*, 1880, oil on canvas. Wallraf-Richartz-Museum, Cologne

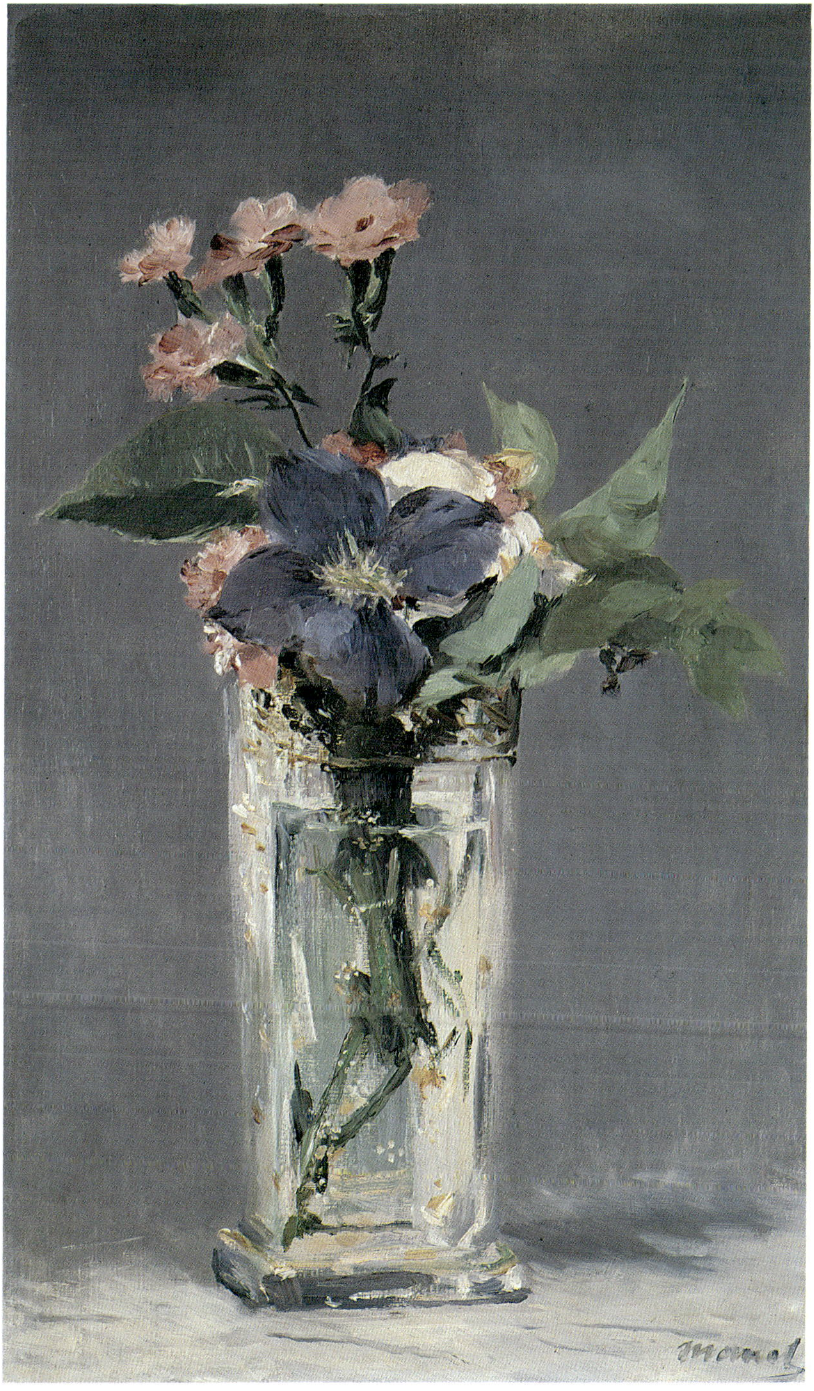

49 *Pinks and Clematis in a Crystal Vase,* 1882, oil on canvas. Musée d'Orsay, Paris

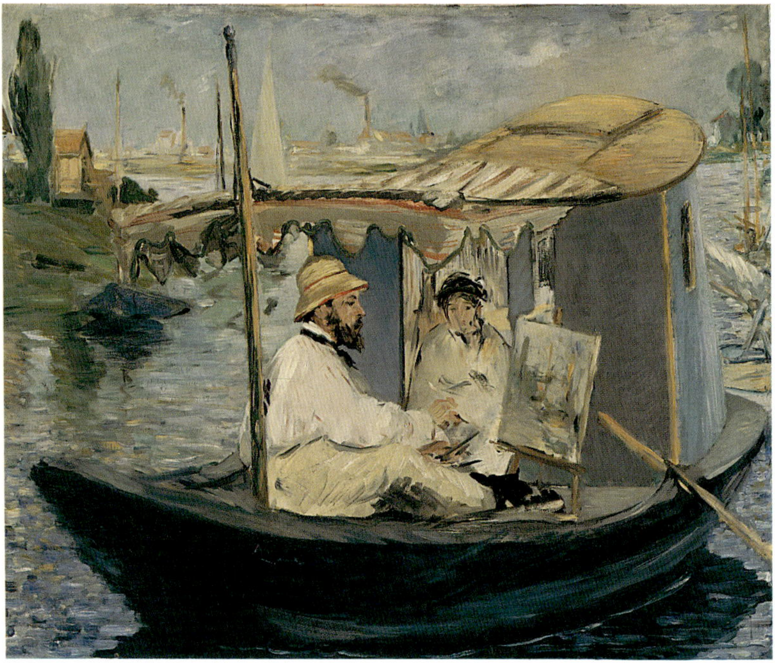

50 *Claude Monet in the Boat Studio*, 1874, oil on canvas. Bayerische Staatsgemäldesammlungen, Munich

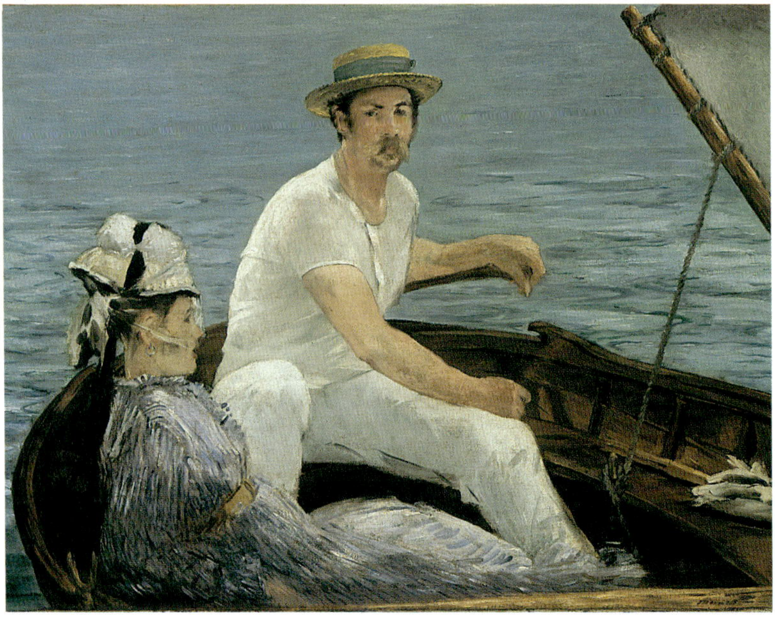

51 *Boating*, 1874, oil on canvas. Metropolitan Museum of Art, New York

unexpected crises which appear in art'. That crisis had to do with the artist relinquishing his role as domineering agent, in favour of nature itself.[87]

A short article of 1874 and some concise notes translated for the 'Fine-Art Gossip' of the British magazine *Athenæum* in 1875 and 1876 preceded Mallarmé's essay of 1876, and can help to clarify its point of view. The article of 1874 attacked the Salon of that year for rejecting two of Manet's three submissions. It argued that a jury aiming to protect the public from new and challenging work would find its tactic backfiring. Since art ultimately derives from the public (a notion anticipating the 1876 concept of art as humanity's response to nature's impressions), only the public, to which everything should therefore be available, can decide which artists have talent. One of the rejected paintings was *The Swallows* (1873; Bührle Collection, Zurich). Mallarmé admitted that by academic standards the painting 'had not been taken far enough'; in other words, it could seem 'vague' and unfinished. Yet he supported Manet's style as appropriate for representing the outdoors, where figures are but accessories lost in a general contemplation induced by the natural environment. The painter's eye had been caught by the harmony between grey frocks and a September afternoon. One more touch would have spoiled the picture's ability to embody those experiences, for it would be like over-painting them. Paintings could be over-finished as well as under-done. Before judging finish, one must consider the number of impressions a given work contains.[88]

The second, slightly later 'Gossip' is revealing, for its brevity required the simplest formulas. In the first one (1875), Mallarmé referred to Manet's painting as marked by modernity, which he associated with *plein-airism*.[89] By March 1876 his description was no longer so much of the painting itself, as it had been previously (and as it had been in Zola), as it was of effects of nature. Only in the open air could artists explore the interaction of light and ambient space, which Manet expressed through 'mobile daubs of paint dissolving into air'. On *The Washing* (illus. 52), which, having been rejected by the Salon, was exhibited privately, Mallarmé noted that 'the young woman's body is entirely bathed and seemingly absorbed by light, which leaves her with nothing but her *appearance* [*aspect*], both solid and vaporous, as is demanded

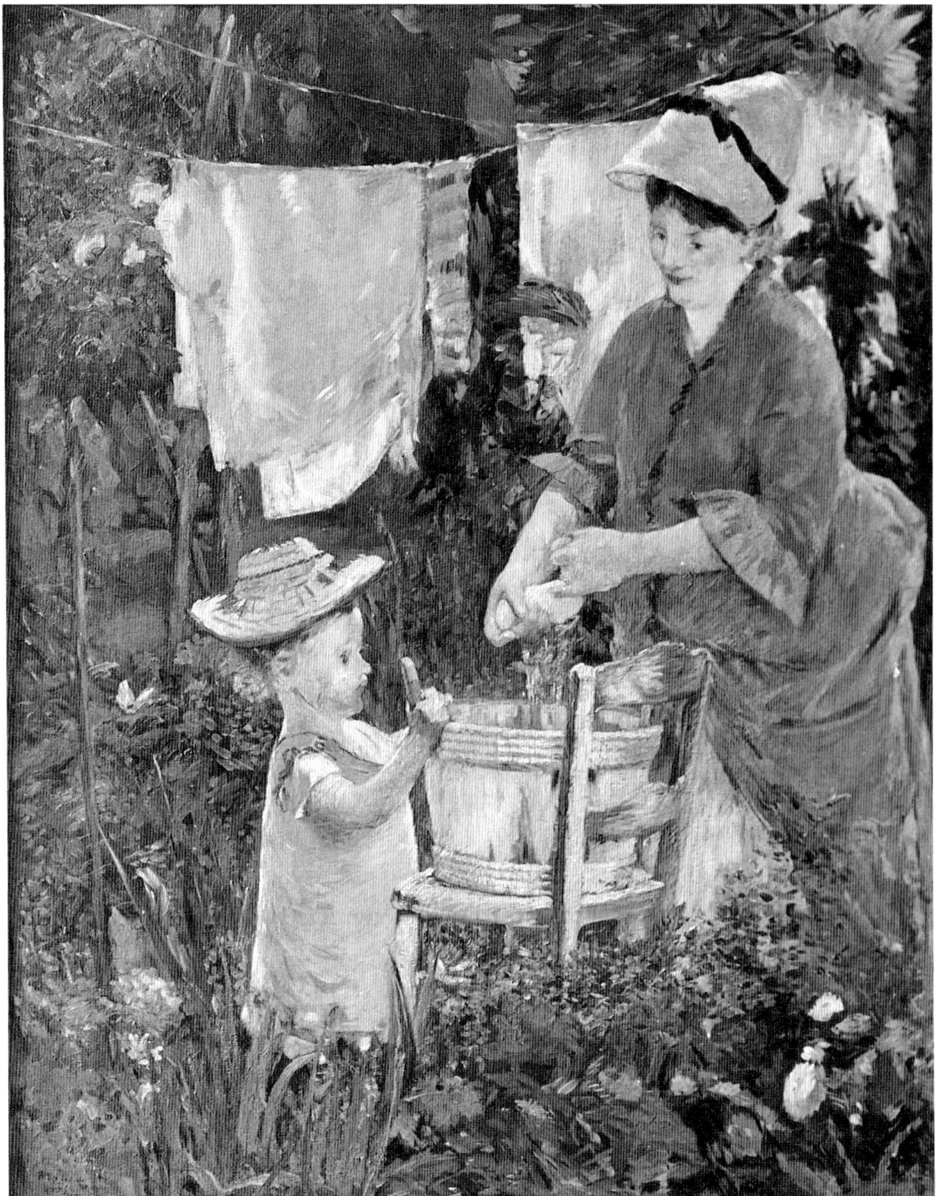

52 *The Washing*, 1875, oil on canvas. Barnes Collection, Merion, PA

by the *plein-airism* everyone is aiming for in France today'.[90] The French word *aspect* refers to visuality – that is the optical, as distinct from the architectonic, properties of form – as if to separate the eye from the body. Such a move, Mallarmé suggested, was a turning-point in the history of art.

These remarks, which preceded by about six months the long article for the *Art Monthly Review*, give a foretaste of Mallarmé's more extended attempts to relate consciousness and representation. In the *Art Monthly Review*, the poet's description of Manet's method of painting goes to the heart of that relationship:

> Each time [Manet] begins a picture, says he, he plunges headlong into it, and feels like a man who knows that his surest plan to learn to swim safely, is, dangerous as it may seem, to throw himself into the water. One of his habitual aphorisms then is that no one should paint a landscape and a figure by the same process, with the same knowledge, or in the same fashion. . . . Each work should be a new creation of the mind. The hand, it is true, will conserve some of its acquired secrets of manipulation, but the eye should forget all else it has seen, and learn anew from the lesson before it. It should abstract itself from memory, seeing only that which it looks upon, and that as for the first time; and the hand should become an impersonal abstraction guided only by the will. . . . As for the artist himself, his personal feeling, his peculiar tastes, are for the time absorbed, ignored, or set aside . . .[91]

Although there is an echo of Zola's claim that one must forget everything when looking at Manet, two interconnected and astoundingly forward-looking ideas dominate this description. First is the image of immersion; second is a definition of creativity as self-propelled process, devoid of convention. Immersion is a form of 'self-isolation' or 'self-sought insulation', Mallarmé claimed, and it could only be acquired through effort and determination. During Manet's early 'manner', Velázquez and the Flemish had led the painter toward 'living reality'. In those years, prior to the 1870s, Manet's freshness consisted of 'a co-ordination of widely scattered elements' – elements of a fresh vision spurred by diverse influences. New imagery, such as introduced by Baudelaire – and here Mallarmé refers predictably to *Olympia*, with its bouquet and black cat – could suddenly awaken the sympathies of a truth-seeker. Drawing striking themes from the world around him enabled Manet to purge artistic vision of its conventionalism and to suggest the artistic possibilities in everyday forms. Taking a cue from the democratization of culture perceived by Baudelaire, Mallarmé claimed the thrust of this first stage of Manet's painting was 'to educate the public eye . . . [in order] to see the true beauties of the people, healthy and solid as they are, [and] the graces which exist in the bourgeoisie', the latter corresponding mainly to his later work. Freed from preconception, the eyes of both painter and public would respond naturally to beauty in life itself.[92]

Mallarmé's image of the painter plunging into water in order to learn to swim suggests the integration of his consciousness with the flux of nature. His pictorial process therefore responds to natural demands that are embodied by the process itself as it procedes. In this sense it is self-propelled rather than subordinated to a set goal. Mallarmé's statement that 'the hand should become an impersonal abstraction guided only by the will' suggests Schopenhauerian terminology, in which the will to survive, like a force of nature, as for the swimmer in water, determines action. In this regard Jean Clay usefully distinguishes between technique in Manet, which is a specific means to attain a predetermined end, and procedure, which is a series of moves developed according to needs evolving out of a reactive or responsive process.[93] Mallarmé's word 'absorption' also suggests a natural process in which idiosyncratic aspects of the artist's character extraneous to natural perception itself are discarded from the psychological and physical essence. This is the way he used the word 'absorbed' in his discussion of *The Washing* in the 'Fine-Art Gossip' of 1876. The being becomes one with nature; the painter becomes a de-personalized vehicle through which nature renders its effects to the canvas. One thinks of the impressions left by light on photo-sensitive surfaces, such as a photographic emulsion or the retina of the human eye. However, Mallarmé went further. Embedded at the centre of the world rather than external to it, Manet's eye produces effects that go beyond impressions of form and colour – to repeat lines cited earlier, beyond 'that reality which impresses itself in its abstract form' (i.e., the purely external forms of Realism), toward 'that absolute and important sentiment which Nature herself impresses on those who have voluntarily abandoned conventionalism'. The abandonment of conventionalism meant the artist's merger of the self with nature, hence the abandonment of his intellectual and emotional particularity for those that are common to all at the time.

For Mallarmé, *The Washing* epitomized the parallel between the reduction of form to visuality and the artist's depersonalization. Claiming that Manet's aim was 'to impress upon his work a natural and a general law', he identified that law with the dominance of light and air 'over all else'. In seeking the necessity for representing nature as such, he concluded that light and air provided the only ambiance in which forms are truly alive. Manet's art characterizes the existence of objects as a dynamic process rather than a stasis:

> [*The Washing* is] deluged with air. Everywhere the luminous and transparent atmosphere struggles with the figures, the dresses, and the foliage, and seems to take to itself some of their substance and solidity; whilst their contours, consumed by the hidden sun and wasted by space, tremble, melt, and evaporate into the surrounding atmosphere, which plunders reality from the figures, yet seems to do so in order to preserve their truthful aspect. Air reigns supreme and real, as if it held an enchanted life conferred by the witchery of art; a life neither personal not sentient, but itself subjected to the phenomena thus called up by science and shown to our astonished eyes, with its perpetual metamorphosis and its invisible action rendered visible.[94]

Air and light, Mallarmé argued with considerable eloquence, are the medium for perception, which, though they cannot be rendered by a colour, preside over nature by their effects. The word 'enchanted' and 'witchery' imply phenomena beyond rational comprehension, yet they are precisely what science reveals to us. Thus, it is possible to see the ostensibly incomplete touches and immanent forms of Manet's painting as congruent with science, thanks to their ability to produce a natural effect. The representations of light and air are what now fill pictorial space. Mallarmé's focus on environment and ambiance in Manet, translate for him the sense of being surrounded by and circulating within nature that corresponds to lived experience.

Thinking ahead for a moment to more modern painting, one can see how Mallarmé's notions of 'immersion' and free process are linked and interdependent. They might even be considered early versions of the concepts of 'all-over composition' and 'action painting', which were adduced in the 1950s to interpret the painting of Jackson Pollock, an artist whose work has at times been compared to Impressionism. 'All-over' composition referred to the evidence of touch and the dispersion of focus that results in totally occupying and overwhelming the field of vision. Such an approach thwarts the distancing/dominating activity implied by the definition of space and the limits on form inherent in the overlay of perspective and the contours of traditional draughtsmanship, conventions with which the Impressionists sometimes dispensed at the risk of losing focus. In the concept of 'action painting', artistic process/labour is given free reign, without the demand that each trace actually represent specific form but rather that it bring forth the experience of materiality. The art work becomes an arena within which the artist acts out his creative activity. The traces of that activity put us directly in touch both with his unconscious and with his physical craft. Mallarmé's implications are similar, in that the handwork of Impressionism translates a naive and direct mode of seeing, like a force of nature, which, unburdened by conventions, can qualify as 'scientific' because it produces sensations that seem equivalent to nature; yet it also alludes to the artist as labourer, as a member of the forces of democracy.[95]

On these grounds Mallarmé held that Impressionism was the truly democratic art; hence Manet was the true painter of modern life:

> [The painter] draws from his own inner consciousness all his effects of simplification, the whole revealed by effects of light incontestably novel. This is the supreme originality of a painter by whom originality is doubly forsworn, who seeks to lose his personality in nature herself, or in the gaze of a multitude until then ignorant of her [nature's] charms.[96]

To forswear originality is to merge with both nature and the multitude, to give nature to itself. Such an approach makes the painter the expression of his age; he penetrates to the 'absolute and true sentiment' by becoming the organ of the people.

Advocating since the 1860s some of the ideas of the German philosopher Hegel, Mallarmé was here relating the 'absolute' to historical time and progress. Hegel had held that all phenomena of a given time and place are connected to a unifying, underlying concept. For Mallarmé, the historical significance of Impressionism could thus lie in its links to democracy:

> The transition from the old imaginative artist and dreamer to the energetic modern worker is found in Impressionism.
>
> The participation of a hitherto ignored people in the political life of France is a social fact that will honour the whole of the close of the nineteenth century. A parallel is found in artistic matters, the way being prepared by an evolution which the public with rare prescience dubbed, from its first appearance, Intransigeant, which in political language means radical and democratic. . . . Today the multitude demands to see with his own eyes. . . .
>
> At that critical hour for the human race when nature desires to work for herself, she requires certain lovers of hers – new and impersonal men placed directly in communion with the sentiment of their time – to loose the restraint of education, to let hand and eye do what they will, and thus through them, reveal herself.[97]

Impressionism was thus the artistic expression of the spirit of the age, nature's true self-expression. 'Intransigent' indicated less a specific political agenda attributable to Impressionist artists than the more general individualistic radicalism, with political and social consequences, of natural seeing, that is, seeing through eyes freed from élitist convention and merged with nature. Freeing oneself from convention to become an independent individual allowed one to return to a state of nature. For subject-matter the specific result was the decline of figure painting; for technique it was the rise of the sketch. Its general implication was a challenge to all sorts of standing traditions. Its result was an art of self-reflection and self-immersion.

Mallarmé's repetition of the term 'impersonal' alluded to the notion of art as the expression of a supra-personal 'Idea', a word Mallarmé used in this very context probably with reference more now to Hegel than to Schopenhauer. Through the Idea, effects as diverse as democratic politics and aesthetics were interrelated and subsumed. Mallarmé's concept of immersion also incorporated another fundamental Hegelian notion, namely that humanity combines both temporal matter and transcendent spirit. The artist's plunge into materiality reconnects him with the aspect of his nature that enables him to express the Idea, since the Idea is imminent in the material world, not external to it. Thus, he can make the Idea visible to itself, which in Hegel is the ultimate drive of all creation. Indeed, in the closing paragraph of his essay, Mallarmé directly introduced the concept of 'Idea' with a Hegelian turn of phrase. Adopting the voice of the artist, he confessed that 'I content myself with reflecting on the clear and durable mirror of painting, that which perpetually lives yet dies every moment, which only exists by the will of Idea, yet constitutes in my domain the only authentic and certain merit of nature – the Aspect.'[98]

'Aspect' is a word whose first meaning, according to Littré's *Dictionnaire* (1863), was 'the state of being before the eye'. In simple terms it means appearance, but it corresponds more precisely to what we might call visuality. Littré distinguishes between 'aspect' and 'view': ' "Aspect" is purely objective, and "view" is purely subjective. That is, in "view", what dominates is the idea of the subject seeing; whereas in "aspect", it is the idea of the object being seen'[99] – what one might crudely call its 'seen-ness' or 'see-ability', hence the more sonorous 'visuality'. Thus, aspect can also mean the side or facet from which an object presents itself to the viewer. It is an optical attribute of the object rather than of the subject's perception. Art does not literally or directly represent the Idea. (To believe so would be the mistake of all previous idealist theory.) Rather, art – or at least the art of Manet, since it stresses aspect rather than view – represents only that which it can properly represent: the visual properties inherent to forms. It takes the position of the object seen rather than of the viewer viewing. Yet the state of being seen is of course dependent on there being a perceiving subject. When that subject has freed itself from convention, as Mallarmé believed Manet and his followers had done, then the state of being seen reflected by 'the clear and durable mirror' (one thinks of the *Bar at the Folies-Bergère*, painted several years later) can only be one that embodies the Idea. Hence, it is as if the perceiving subject is imminent and active within form rather than, as in

Baudelaire and Zola, external to it. Once again, we encounter Mallarmé's concept of immersion. After one discussion of Hegel during the 1860s, Mallarmé had written to his friend Cazalis that 'my thought has thought itself, . . . I am now impersonal . . . an aptitude the spiritual universe has to see itself and develop through what once was me. . . . The universe discovers its identity in this me'.[100] While representing his authentic personal vision, the artist has merged his identity with that of the world – which Mallarmé equated with the multitude – now discovering itself through the artist's self-expression. In the essay on Manet, that self-expression was authenticated by its concentration on 'aspect' rather than 'view'.

As Mallarmé continues (in the voice of the artist), modernity will no longer tolerate an art of dreams:

> It is through her [the Idea] that when rudely thrown at the close of an epoch of dreams in the front of reality, I have taken from it [reality] only that which properly belongs to my art [i.e., the visual], an original and exact perception which distinguishes for itself the things it perceives with the steadfast gaze of a vision restored to its simplest perfection.

We generally associate dreaming before nature with Symbolist painting, more specifically, with Paul Gauguin, as sometimes directly inspired by Mallarmé's own writings. Yet in this admittedly complicated sentence, Mallarmé implies that Realism was a fantasy reaching toward its end. But an art devoid of dreams certainly does not have to lead to Realism. Earlier in the same paragraph, Mallarmé defined art as being 'true as nature, fair as remembrance, and imperishably my own'. And he added: 'the better to satisfy my creative artistic instinct, that which I preserve through the power of Impressionism is not the material portion which already exists, superior to any mere representation of it, but the delight of having recreated nature touch by touch'. That is, Impressionism preserves in its traces on the canvas the joyful and often playful, but in any case personal and evocative, process of recreating nature. Of course, that recreation can only take the aspect as its object. But it was one that corresponded, as Mallarmé asserted at the end of the paragraph, to the 'exact perception' of a 'steadfast gaze' restored to simplicity, and, as he had said before that, loosening 'the restraint of education' in order to 'let hand and eye do what they will'. The viewer's experience of art was of a record of the free and sincere artist-individual's 'touch by touch' process of recreation. That very freedom and sincerity made hand and eye the impersonal instruments, as it were, of nature, of the 'will of Idea'. They were not enslaved by the objects of reality (as positivist art might be) but gave the lead to an individual subjectivity rooted in human nature (thus shared by and accessible to all – hence democratic) and to the process of representation that were its means of expression.[101]

In his effort to convey the link between art and motivating forces in nature, Mallarmé repeatedly referred to Manet's expression of vitality. The phrase 'living reality' was a way of distinguishing Manet's representations from 'lifeless' Realism – a Realism perhaps identical with the positivism despised by Baudelaire. The phrase 'that which perpetually lives and dies at every moment' stressed the artist's attempt to seize organic processes rather than inanimate properties. The metaphors Mallarmé used to translate this notion into visual terms were the visually ambiguous concepts of light and air. He seems to have been the first to understand the Impressionist preoccupation with light as more than merely an interest in the way light falls on objects and alters their colouration or contours. Like the contemporary scientist Amédée Guillemin,[102] Mallarmé saw light as life itself. The medium of all perception, it sustains life. Familiar from Mallarmé's poetry, the image of light here reacquired its traditional association with being and knowledge (enlightenment), while carrying overtones of Hegel's association with the Absolute. 'That which perpetually lives yet dies every moment' evokes Mallarme's description of *The Washing*, in which forms 'struggle' – another key word – as if for their existence, or his comment on a painting by Sisley: 'on his canvas the live air moves and the leaves yet thrill and tremble'.[103] One thinks of Walt Whitman, or of Wordsworth's 'Whose dwelling is the light of setting suns, / And the round ocean and the living air . . .' (from 'Lines written a few miles above Tintern Abbey', in *Lyrical Ballads*).

Although as an instructor of English, and one who had even lived in England and written extensively on the English language, Mallarmé may well have read Romantic poetry, it is more to the point to show how the imagery he summoned to explain Manet's painting suggested a resolution of its opposed readings. Manet was no Romantic, merely expressing his personality through the images of nature. Nor was he the Realist (positivist), impassively depicting a nature still-born and inert. Of course, the element of self-expression was so obvious that it was a recurring theme in writings on Manet prior to Mallarmé. At the same time, Manet's audacious departure from accepted norms of technique and decorum was equated with the search for greater naturalism, in the sense of nature expressing itself through the artist. Armed with Hegelian terminology, Mallarmé reconciled the ostensible contradictions of these interpretations by phrasing Manet's self-expression as self-discovery, a self-recognition in which the new (less educated, hence more 'natural') audience of the current historical phase could recognize its own human visual process. In Hegelian terms, Manet's self-discovery was the self-recognition of the Idea – philosophical language that absorbed politics into metaphysics and made the artist's position all-inclusive. In his early correspondence, Mallarmé once wrote that 'the artist creates himself before the paper'. Mallarmé's biographer Guy Michaud remarked on Mallarmé's obsession with mirrors and his desire, expressed to Cazalis, 'to paint not the thing, but its effect'.[104] But to express oneself truly, one must be able to see oneself from outside. This act of separation was called 'crisis', another Hegelian concept used in Mallarmé's analysis of Manet and featured in his later essay on poetry, *Crise de vers*. The duality of Manet's art is like that act of separation: we find the eye both inside and outside his painting; it is *his* vision, yet it is the impersonal gaze of the multitude. And though Mallarmé's essay was aimed at resolving this duality, in the same year, in 'L'Après-midi d'un faune', it came to appear unresolvable.

THE RAVEN

The paradox between immersion and externality Mallarmé saw underlying Manet's art was indeed a central theme of their collaboration. Mallarmé was one of several writers with whom Manet had worked, but prior to Mallarmé actual collaboration was extremely limited. Manet's relationship to Baudelaire was one of association and occasional community of thought. Collaboration is too strong a word to describe the poem Baudelaire sent to accompany the *Lola de Valence*. It might apply to Manet's portrait of *Edgar Poe*, an etching that was probably done in anticipation of Baudelaire's project for an edition of criticism on Poe. In the case of Zola, a plan to illustrate an 1867 re-edition of Zola's *Contes à Ninon* never bore fruit. Of course, Manet alluded to Zola's writings on art in his portrait of Zola, and in *Nana* he used a character from Zola's *L'Assommoir*. But these were not collaborations either. Manet did do the famous poster lithograph for Champfleury's book on cats (illus. 13), a smaller version of which was published in the book itself, but in this case illustration is a better word than collaboration, for despite the heightened impact obtained by using Manet's bold image to represent the text, the artist's contribution to Champfleury's ideas does not seem crucial. For Mallarmé, however, the opposite is true: the unpretentious drawings accompanying 'Le Corbeau' (Mallarme's translation of Poe's 'The Raven') and 'L'Après-midi d'un faune' have a Mallarméan character that sheds light on poet and painter at crucial points in the careers of each. For the poet, of course, 'L'Après-midi d'un faune' was the first major example of his mature and personal structure and style. For the painter, the mid-1870s saw the consolidation of his departure from a wilful dialogue with past styles and historically charged themes and his movement toward the greater informality we associate with Impressionism.

For both Manet and Mallarmé, 'The Raven' may seem a backward-looking choice, for it connects them both to the legacy of Baudelaire, Poe's first great admirer in France. Yet the convergence in Baudelaire and Poe makes sense if one accepts eroticism as a metaphor for experience and creativity. Moreover, Mallarmé's translation of the poem into freely cadenced prose and Manet's broadly brushed wash illustrations (lithographically transferred) are far from nostalgic or old-fashioned. Beginning with the 'portrait bust' of the raven on the edition's cover, we know we are in strange territory. Its lumpy, anthropomorphic features suggest anything but an ornithological study. Manet endows it with the intelligence and wisdom of a judge, presiding not only through its position on the cover, but through personality as well – an *alter ego* for the poet. The edition was a large folio size, with the English text and the French on opposite pages. The four illustrations were printed on inserted sheets. Though the poem is primarily an internal monologue, the illustrations record distinct stages in a sequence of actions that might be described as follows:

1. *Once upon a midnight dreary . . .* (illus. 53): The poem opens with the weary poet lost in meditation over his books when he hears a strange tapping, 'As of someone gently rapping – rapping at my chamber door'.

2. *Open here I flung the shutter . . .* (illus. 54): After going to the door, only to hear the echoed naming of his desire ('Lenore') in the empty hallway, he opens the window shutters to let the raven enter 'with many a flirt and flutter'.

3. *Perched upon a bust of Pallas . . .* (illus. 55): The bizarre bird alights on the bust of Athena over the door, while the poet pulls up a 'cushioned seat' and stares up toward the bird, which croaks 'Nevermore'.

4. *That shadow that lies floating on the floor . . .* (illus. 56): Finally, nothing but a malevolent shadow remains, from which the poet's forlorn soul 'Shall be lifted – nevermore!'

The stages of action correspond to the poet's state of mind, increasingly aroused and desperate as the raven – like the inner self – relentlessly reminds him of the irrecoverable loss of Lenore. In the first two plates, Manet's deep tones emphasize shadow and gloom. In the second plate, the poet's open hand is a subtle expression of surprise, highlighted as it is by the deepest surrounding darkness. In the third plate, diagonal brushstrokes suggest a stifling atmosphere ('Then, methought, the air grew denser, perfumed from an unseen censer . . .'), and the enfeebled poet seems pressed into the chair, almost erotically, his head barely rising above the cushion. In the fourth plate, shadow has itself taken on life, becoming the most prominent form. At its bottom it resembles that cast by the bird perched upon the bust, but then in much freer strokes it becomes a dense vapour rising and trailing into oblivion. The emptiness of the lightly sketched chair is emphasized by the chair's juxtaposition to much heavier shadows: the poet himself has disappeared, spent and merged with his other self, as it were, in the ambient ether. In the three illustrations showing the poet's features, we recognize those of Mallarmé rather than of Poe, and the rooftops seen through the window of the second plate are those of Paris. But scrupulously respecting the text, especially in the

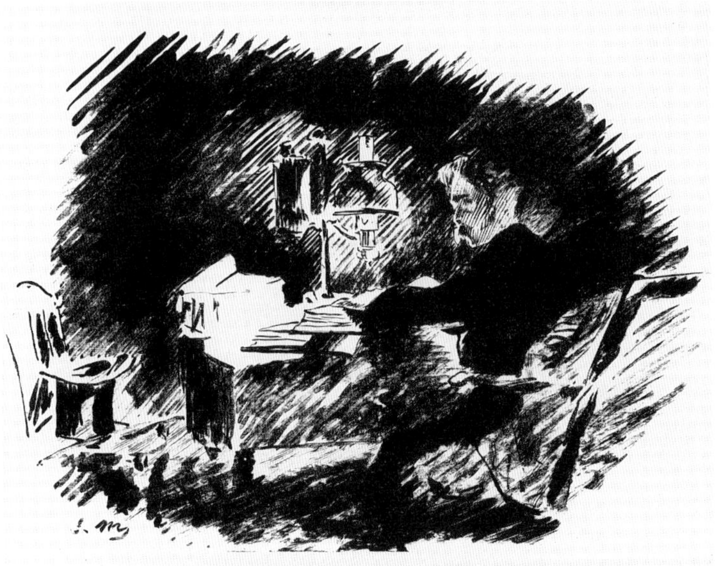

53 *'Once upon a midnight dreary . . .'*, illustration for *Le Corbeau*, 1875, brush and ink transfer relief-plate, unique state.

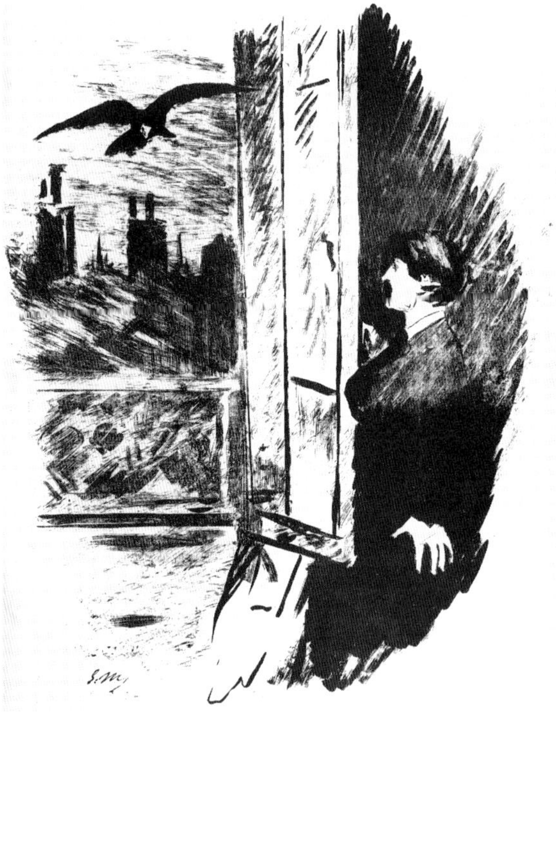

54 *'Open here I flung the shutter . . .'*, illustration for *Le Corbeau*, 1875, brush and ink transfer relief-plate, second state.

55 *'Perched upon a bust of Pallas . . .'*, illustration for *Le Corbeau*, 1875, brush and ink transfer relief-plate, second state.

56 *'That Shadow that lies floating on the floor . . .'*, illustration for *Le Corbeau*, 1875, brush and ink transfer relief-plate, unique state.

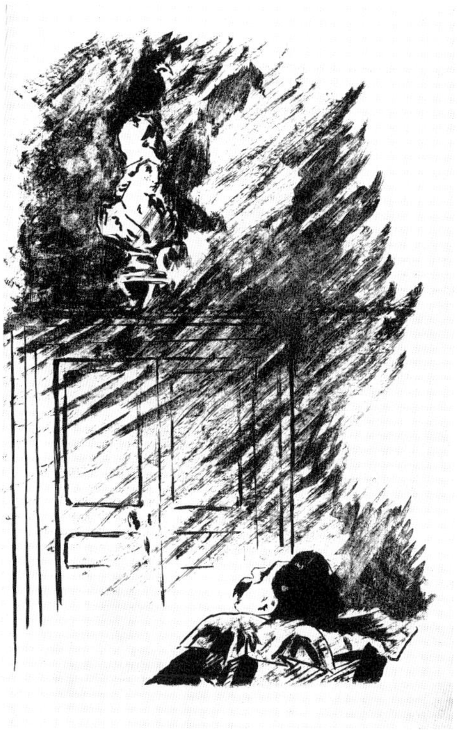

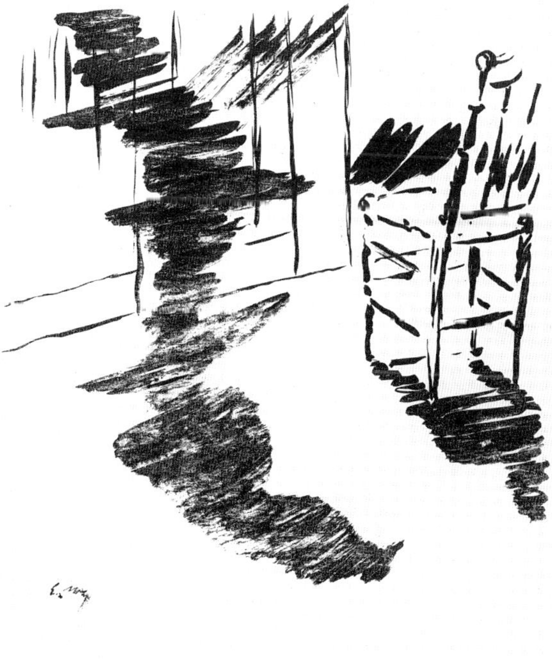

last two plates, Manet has used techniques like those Mallarmé so well observed in his painting to translate the poem's psychological expression into effects of the natural world. Though the context is much opposed to that of *The Washing* – that is, we experience the close confines of the poet's room rather than *plein air* – the basis of both is none the less in light and air. The black and white of the lithograph evokes the positive and negative of solid and void revealed by light and shadow. And Manet's relatively free draughtsmanship readily suggests the quasi-fragmented technique – Mallarmé called them 'mobile daubs' – of Impressionism and its connotation of the world revealed to vision through light.

The last two plates also relate to the concept of vision through which Mallarmé's critical essays interpreted Manet's work. The raven can of course be regarded as a poetic device – the voice of the poet's mind. In 'Perched upon a bust of Pallas . . .', bird and poet stare at one another from the extremities of the image. In the final plate, the poet seems to have been physically absorbed by the raven's gaze: he disappears by merging with the bird's indecipherable spectre. This exchange of glances parallels many of those in Manet's various paintings. But unlike in those examples, here, as the object of another's gaze, the viewer (poet) is appropriated by it, conforms to it, and loses his consciousness and identity in it. Although the forlorn poet is a far different character from the painter of Mallarmé's essay, his merger with the world is like a mystical and erotic version of Manet's self-immersion. In both, loss of self and immersion are performed through vision.

The logic of the connection between two apparently so unrelated exercises as the Mallarmé–Manet Poe and the essay on Manet may lie partly in the joint relationship to Baudelaire, who avidly devoured Poe's literary theories. It is enough to quote Baudelaire paraphrasing the American's *The Poetic Principle* to measure the latter's appeal: 'All certainty is found in dreams'; 'the value of a poem lies in the excitement, in the *carrying off* [*enlèvement*] (one might say absorption) of the soul'.[105] Of course Baudelaire revelled in erotic or hallucinatory states of consciousness. If we think of concurrent definitions of reality as a 'true hallucination', that is, if we think of reality as the product – the representation – of consciousness, then Manet's ostensibly naturalist painting is not inconsistent with the poetics of Poe, Baudelaire or Mallarmé. In 'The Raven', the poet's feelings drive toward an inevitable conclusion, in which consciousness fails at possession. We shall see that 'L'Après-midi d'un faune' plays much more overtly upon that same conception – the irresolvable conflict between the physicality of experience and the uncertainty of consciousness in the world. For it flaunts a network of levels of perception in which representation is a multivalent sign of consciousness rather than an infallible guide to reality, and the verbal exercises of consciousness are inadequate to the visuality of its experience.

THE FAUN

Mallarme's 'L'Après-midi d'un faune' was finally published (with Manet's woodcut illustrations) in 1876, the year following the translation of Poe. (It is here reprinted complete, with a following translation, in the Appendix, pp. 225–30.) We leave behind the morbid and shadowy world of Poe for the sparkling vision of rococo pleasures in an open airiness suggestive of *plein-air* Impressionism. A reading of the poem, sometimes clarified by its manuscript version of 1875, may suggest parallels to the understanding of the artist Mallarmé expressed in the *Art Monthly Review*. That is not to say the poem speaks directly of Manet, or even refers to his illustrations. But since its account of inspiration takes vision as its model, its relevance to the painter's art is unquestionable. The very first line: 'Ces nymphes, je les veux perpétuer' (These nymphs, I want to perpetuate them), coming just before the description of a vision, invokes the artistic enterprise. In the French, the positioning of the word *les* (them) before *veux* (want), conflates the desire the nymphs themselves arouse with the artistic desire to preserve their memory. In the world of vision, reality and memory are both confused and merged; perpetuation creates as effective a world as original experience. And, as the poem proves, original experience has no more reality than art. It is hard to believe that in the version of the poem Mallarmé tried to publish a year earlier, the word 'émerveiller' (to amaze) was used instead of 'perpétuer'. The last-minute change completely altered the introductory discourse from a mere narrative of desire, in which the poet wishes to act upon figures within the scope of his vision (thus still granting them a degree of reality), to an allegory of the artist, in which vision itself is a mysterious object of desire. With this single stroke, Mallarmé moved closer to the position of his essay on Manet and gave the poem a far more universal reach.

The parallel between the allegory in 'L'Après-midi d'un faune' and the concept of the artist's enterprise in the essay on Manet affords some insight regarding the importance of the visual for Mallarmé and the possibility of the poetic in Manet. The first several lines set the stage for the poem's shifting and questioning points of view:

> *Ces nymphes, je les veux perpétuer.*
> *Si clair,*
> *Leur incarnat léger, qu'il voltige dans l'air*
> *Assoupi de sommeils touffus.*
>
> *Aimai-je un rêve?*
> *Mon doute, amas de nuit ancienne, s'achève*
> *En maint rameau subtil, qui, demeuré les vrais*
> *Bois mêmes, prouve, hélas! que bien seul je m'offrais*
> *Pour triomphe la faute idéale de roses –*
> *Réfléchissons . . .*

> These nymphs, I want to perpetuate them,
> So clear,
> Their lightness incarnadine, that it lilts in the air
> Drowsy with tufted slumbers.
>
> Did I love a dream?
> My doubt, heap of ancient night, culminates
> In many a subtle branch, which, remained the true
> Woods themselves proves, alas! that quite alone I offered myself
> The ideal fault of roses as triumph.
> Let us reflect . . .[106]

The faun wants to prolong the presence of the nymphs, who seem to have faded into air. The word 'incarnadine' alludes both to their colour and their flesh, so light and bright, yet material. As if awakening, he wonders if all was a dream. The break in the line after 'perpétuer' is echoed by the break before the mention of the dream. We are quickly shifted to different viewpoints and different levels of reality. The first sentence announces what can be read as artistic purpose as well as erotic wish. The next lines describe the vision; and then we are made to think it might have been a dream. Looking through the grasses, the faun suspects he merely triumphed over roses – flowers that allude again to the nymphs' colour, but which additionally characterize them as not just physical but as aesthetic presences. The ironic conclusion to this group of lines is the ambiguous and multivalent 'Let us reflect', which alludes both to the reflecting role of art (as mirror of both mind and nature) and to the need to explore further the philosophical consequences of the faun's vision.

These consequences are adduced within different viewpoints from the continuation of the poem. Shifting to the second person singular, as if in a dialogue with himself, the faun considers whether his vision might be an illusion created by desire, or whether it is the 'visible and serene artificial breath / Of inspiration'. Removing himself then further from the vision, he commands, in the more formal second person plural, 'CONTEZ' (that is, 'tell', or, more literally, 'recount'). There follows, set off by italics, a poem within the poem, a highly imaged account of the vision, which reintroduces the first person singular. The vision's colours – greens and whites – suggest a landscape by Fragonard, where the confusion between swans and nymphs is like that between nature and art, referent and sign.

The italicized vision finishes with the image of immersion, but appended are some lines directly alluding to art: 'Inerte, tout brûle dans l'heure fauve / Sans marquer par quel art ensemble détala / Trop d'hymen souhaité de qui cherche le *la*:' (Inert, everything burns in the tawny hour / Without marking by what art together ran off / Too much hymen desired by the one who seeks the *la*'). The two references to art are, first, the deception or ruse that made the vision disappear and, second, the musical note *la*, which suggests the entreaties, sexual (hymen) or otherwise, of the artist, player of pipes. That is: what art makes visions appear in the first place, only to disappear when the artist tries too hard to capture them for permanence? (In the 1875 version, the line reads 'Tant d'hymen par mon art effarouché. Hola!' – So much hymen frightened away by my art. Hola!). Indeed, the faun compares the nymph's kiss to the 'bite' of 'arcanum'. Evoking the azure – Mallarmé's constant symbol of the Absolute (as in a poem, 'L'Azur', of 1864) – under which the twin reed of art is played, the faun turns again to the dream for an image of 'false confusions' between 'beauty of surroundings', that is, nature, and 'credulous' art. The inextricable entanglement of art and nature is a mystery; both evaporate as one tries to approach them more closely.

Next, Mallarmé introduces two very traditional images: painting will stand for art as a whole; grapes will stand for inspiration:

Moi, de ma rumeur fier, je vais parler longtemps
Des déesses; et par d'idolâtres peintures,
A leur ombre enlever encore des ceintures:
Ainsi, quand des raisins j'ai sucé la clarté,
Pour bannir un regret par ma feinte écarté,
Rieur, j'élève au ciel d'été la grappe vide
Et, soufflant dans ses peaux lumineuses, avide
D'ivresse, jusqu'au soir je regarde au travers.

I, emboldened by my murmur, will speak at length
Of goddesses; and with idolatrous paintings,
I will lift bodices from their shadow:
Thus, when from the grapes I have sucked the brightness,
To banish a regret by my ruse discarded,
Laughing, I raise the empty cluster to the sky
And, blowing into its luminous skins, avid
For drunkenness, till evening I gaze through them.

Art ('murmur' – i.e. sounds – and 'idolatrous paintings') is the means to lift restraints (bodices) from the desired nymphs, though the faun now alludes to them as otherworldly – either goddesses or phantoms. Regretting their disappearance, he uses the ruse of the grape to conjure up their memory; until the evening, he gazes toward them through the luminosity of inspiration.

The next group of lines begins 'O nymphes, regonflons des SOUVENIRS divers' (O nymphs, let us reflate these varied MEMORIES), and is followed by two more italicized accounts. 'MEMORIES' recalls the capitalized 'CONTEZ', which precedes the first artistically cast (italicized) account of the vision. The new word ('MEMORIES') implies a further remove, as does 'reflate'. In the first line of the reflated vision, the eye is the instrument of desire, as it pierces through the reeds toward its immortal prey. Prodded by the effects of the grape, this now desperate vision is more violent and erotic than before. But the excitement and exaltation reach a climax before the third italicized account. There, more soberly detached and reflecting on his adventure, the faun begins with 'My crime', thus recognizing the violence done to nature through an artistic act that has progressively become more explicitly dominating (as if sexual – recall: 'reflate', or earlier, the phallic 'Droit et seul' – Upright and alone). The crime consists of having separated an interlaced couple of sleeping nymphs, an allusion to the labia, but also perhaps to the inseparability of the different visions – of art and nature, or of the various aspects that constitute nature's whole. That is, the faun's theorizing is doomed to end in failure; it tries vainly to make distinctions when undecidability is in fact the crucial point. Here the poet ironically casts doubt on his own excessively selfconscious enterprise.

Still, the poet's horns will always be susceptible to the maidens of desire. As the poem nears its close, Mallarmé uses the obvious images of ripening fruit, bees and the lava of Mount Etna visited by Venus to evoke its overflowing. And in the final verses, the faun, its tired and heavy body lying thirsty on the sand, still opens its mouth toward the wine-making sunlight of its visions. The final verse, 'Couple, adieu; je vais voir l'ombre que tu devins' (Couple, farewell; I am going to see the shade you became), suggests a farewell to direct experience, which is by its nature transitory ('couple' suggests sexual coupling), and a devotion to the world of art, through which, though transformed, it is perpetuated. (Could Jules Laforgue have been thinking of 'L'Après-midi d'un faune' when he wrote that 'art is but the perpetuation of desire'?)

Oddly enough, this ending echoes the spectre at the close of 'The Raven', where the poet loses himself in the raven's gaze, to which he is fatally attracted despite its remindful 'Nevermore'. All that remains is the raven's shadow, that is, its representation, like the poem itself. Manet's illustration of this scene added a Mallarméan complexity to Poe. 'L'Après-midi d'un faune' goes beyond Poe's relative simplicity to evoke something like the experience Mallarmé found in Manet. The faun, poet or artist, is absorbed by his own visions, but as an expression of the tension between self and world. The faun's position, inside or outside his visions, as expressed by varying voices, is confused, multiple and universal, like the position of the artist in perception and the position of perception in representation.

It is true that in many ways Mallarmé's vision coincides with Manet's. The poet's vivid imagery, as in 'Les Fleurs' (1863) or 'L'Azur' (1864), and his allusiveness rather than narrative clarity must certainly have made his sympathy for Manet's visual suggestiveness inevitable. His use of typography and the positioning of words and phrases on the page could be called 'painterly'. Of course, Mallarmé's remarks on *The Swallows* and *The Washing* confirm the parallel, but the philosophical cast of the longer essay goes well beyond it. Both it and 'L'Après-midi d'un faune' deal with the contradictions exemplified in art and poetry; hence, they embody different levels of a similar discourse. The essay appears schematic next to the poem because it attempts resolution rather than an exploration and enumeration of those contradictions. But a principal theme of both is the idea of vision as the paradigm of a complex, multivalent perception; and their shared conception of the artistic process lies in the artist's attempt to capture and perpetuate experience by exploring his ambiguous vision from the inside, which is to say both inside the world and inside the mind. 'L'Après-midi d'un faune' reuses the traditional guise of bucolic poetry and casts its treatment of sensuous experience in sexual terms. Underlying those poetic strategies, however, is the same question about the relationship of reality, perception and art that is to be found in the critical essay on Manet.

In Mallarmé's account, Manet possesses none of the ironic and critical selfconsciousness of the poet/faun. The painter is cast as more or less naïvely producing effects the faun finds both confusing and intoxicating. Ironically, then, Mallarmé at first seems to preserve a hierarchy between painter and poet, for although the painter's confrontation with nature most directly embodies the creative process, the poet stands above it with his philosophical questions and resolutions. Yet if certain changes made for the 1876 version of 'L'Après-midi d'un faune' have a consistent theme, they are to disguise in poetic suggestiveness some of the more didactic aspects of the earlier effort. The beauties of melodious sonority, or of the shape of words on a page are more striking as semi-opaque rather than transparent signs. The poem becomes more of an artistic object in its revision. Thus, rather than moving beyond

Manet – as the poet's position in 'L'Après-midi d'un faune' could imply – Mallarmé has in fact moved closer to the selfconscious artifices of representation found in Manet. He moves toward the 'performative', as I have suggested the term might apply to Manet's painting. We experience the faun's poetic responses by ourselves becoming involved in a process of deciphering similar to that of the faun's search for meaning, a search that ultimately confirms the uncertainty of words in capturing the visual and the inequivalency of the verbal and the seen. A dual reading of Mallarmé's poetry as both symbolic and concrete is thus not so distant from our experiences of Manet's art as simultaneously mimetic and semiotic. So if his discussion of Manet has affected the poetic evolution of Mallarmé's poem, it may be because Mallarmé was able to articulate what he admired Manet for doing so instinctively. Hence, there may be an obverse to the hierarchy between painter and poet that at first seemed to emerge in Mallarmé's two publications of 1876. That is, the poet/faun's need to step outside his vision results in a loss of that spontaneity – that sincerity – which marks the true representative of the Idea. The grape becomes the ally necessary to its recovery. Mallarmé's selfconsciousness is a betrayal of the directness of nature's self-expression – what he admires so fully in Manet. By the very nature of visual art, Manet is immersed in the centre of his world, while the poet, given the nature of his art, must remain outside. The painter produces contradictions that, as in the experience of the faun, are the essence of his poetry. Their effect on the viewer/reader is of aporia, undecidability and uncertainty, effects that produce a subject whose footing in the positive world of Realism is suddenly unsure.

At first glance, Manet's illustrations for this poem seem among his slightest works. Mere vignettes, two evoke the bucolic themes of the satyr (illus. 57) and nymphs (illus. 58), while two seem like fragments – a bunch of dark grapes (illus. 59) and a tuft of wild flowers (illus. 60). All four, of course, allude to the content of the poem, and quite sensitively so. Manet separates the satyr from the nymphs, for the faun's vision of their presence is of questionable status – Are they a vision? Are they memories? Were they ever real? The grapes make the important allusion to poetic intoxication, whereas the wild flowers seem more like a signature, an appendage, and – like so many still-lifes in Manet's paintings – a bouquet.

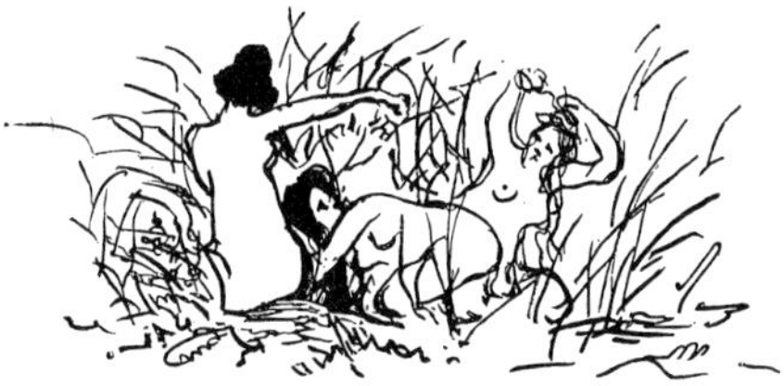

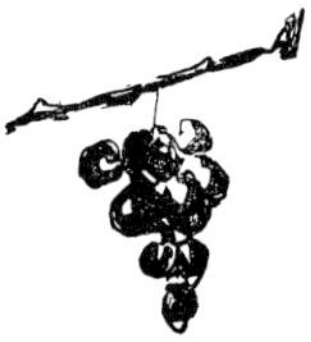

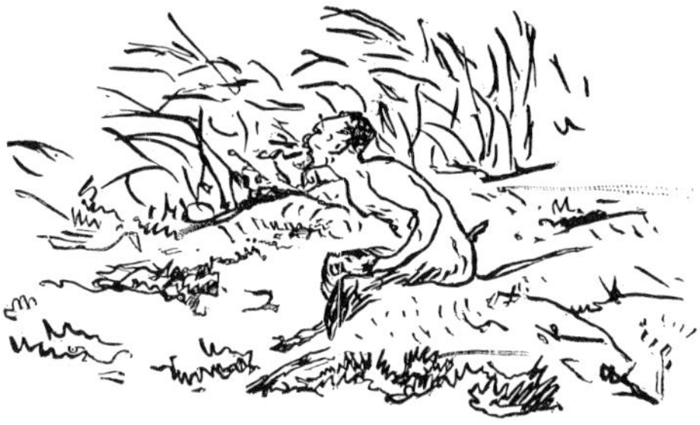

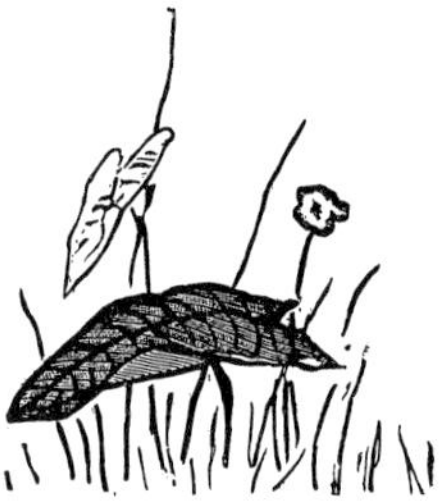

Four woodcut illustrations for Mallarmé's *L'Après-midi d'un faune*, 1876. Clockwise from bottom left:

57 *Satyr*
58 *Nymphs*
59 *Grapes*
60 *Wild Flowers*

(The wild flowers precede the title-page and have the words 'ex libris' printed below them.) The simple style of Manet's woodcut technique based on outline lends appropriate insubstantiality to his forms; they suggest calligraphy, and parallel Mallarmé's preoccupation with the look of his poem as markings on the page. That this style was inspired by the Japanese print designer Hokusai is not surprising, but that the image of the wild flowers is a direct appropriation from one of Hokusai's woodcuts might be, until we recall Manet's other borrowings.[107] Yet here, the second-hand status may remind us of the process of mediation through which we acquire all knowledge and which underlies all representation. In any case, Manet's illustrations certainly capture the lightness of Mallarmé's verse, and suggest the tentative reality of the faun's imagined or remembered world. In the visual realm, like Impressionism itself, they are poetic approximations paralleling Mallarmé's use of words to suggest and circumscribe, since they can never substitute for or define. Only the grapes are mostly filled in. They and the flowers, though much smaller than the other two illustrations, may allude to the ultimate realities – subjective inspiration and the visionary beauties that result.

4 A Poetics of Bouquets

Among the most often repeated criticisms of Realism was its failure in the poetic mission of art. In an article on the 'Salon de 1852', Ernest Chesnau wrote: 'In our times . . . nature is studied with more sincerity; however, Realism . . . has been more contemptuous than it should be of any poetic interpretation of reality.' And in *L'Artiste* of October 1855, Charles Perrier said: 'The Realists' argument is that nature is enough. To believe them, the fine flower of poetry which artists strive to impress upon art, and which is called the Ideal, is nothing but a vain subtlety. . . . To make art and poetry incompatible is a contradiction in terms.'[108] 'Poetry' referred to the quality that raised art above nature and to which artists aspired in order to endow their productions with lasting spiritual value. It designated the 'humanistic content' of art taken by traditional theory as moral justification for the existence of art and for its practice. Chesnau and Perrier claimed that eliminating the distinction between art and nature eliminated the 'poetic' too. For them, there was no poetry in what they believed was the mere material process of seeing because there was no creativity or subjectivity in a mechanical reproduction. Of course, for them, the 'poetic' would have been revealed through idealization, that is, through signs that the artist had appropriated nature for purposes beyond itself and hence beyond the visual. This kind of poetry was still linked to what I have called the 'externalist' paradigm of reading, in which the artist/viewer remains distant and omniscient.

Here I shall suggest that what might be called a 'poetics of bouquets' derives poetry from a world inhabited by the eye rather than distanced by it. Its aesthetic relates to the leisure and spectacle characteristic of modern society, in which the eye revels in nature as a source of security and pleasure rather than fleeing it for a refuge in the ideal. The desire to transcend reality traditionally signified by poetry is replaced by affirmation of contact with it. However, the tension between reality and the ideal that underlay traditional art still exists, though now in a different form. For with the disappearance of the ideal, the non-real becomes an empty chasm; immersion in the world thus seems conditioned by the possibility of its loss. The need for reaffirmation through the manipulative exercise of still-life takes on a certain poignance. While few images so completely express the beauties of the present as bouquets, they may also be shadows masking an underlying sense of absence. Bouquets are often substitutes for words. Alluding to the unverbalizable and unknowable, theirs is a poetry of ambiguity and silence.

In the age of photography and naturalism, the flower and its plural, the bouquet, emerged as captivating images of the relationship between art and nature through which visual poetry could be expressed. Romantic painters of the early decades of the nineteenth century referred to art as the flowering of imagination. Charles Baudelaire used flower imagery repeatedly. Following the death of Delacroix in 1863, he described the painter as 'a volcanic crater artistically hidden behind bouquets of flowers'.[109] Baudelaire did not say which he found truer, the elegance and artifice of the mask or what lay behind it. In the same essay, Baudelaire described his hero's palette as 'a bouquet of skilfully arranged flowers'.[110] The flowers of the palette, awaiting the artist's intervention, were the raw material for artistic bouquets. In his project for a preface to the second edition of *Les Fleurs du mal* (first published in 1857), Baudelaire explained his own poetic intentions as the infusion of nature with beauty. His title made what was hardly an unusual allusion: flowers stood for poetry, for the beauty of the ideal. Extracting beauty through poetic form from nature, which he saw as inherently corrupt, exactly paralleled proposals he would make in *The Painter of Modern Life*. Flowers could thus become signs of human virtue exemplified by artistic activity. They were elements of self-imagery, for, as in the description of Delacroix, they embodied the face the poet presented to the world. *Les Fleurs du mal* is a bouquet: an arrangement of beautiful forms and of poetic self-presences. As personal recreations of nature, then, bouquets are paradigms for artistic representation. In Mallarméan terms, they allude to the merger of self and world that produces art. They epitomize the conversion of objects to signs, which is to say representations that embody the subject, a process defined by the materiality of language, particularly in visual art.

Of course, the term *bouquet* also suggests the role of flower imagery in poetic language. For bouquet is an odour or flavour, by extension a sensual emanation of objects, hence both an aspect of them and yet one dependent on a perceiving subject. The associations that result, reawaken (re-present) the mind to memories of experience. Common as commemorative offerings, bouquets are both inducements to memory that may signify pain and loss and yet are promises of pleasure. They can stand both for remembering reality and for the desire to transcend it, as in Mallarmé's sonnet of 1877, 'Sur les bois oubliés':

Sur les bois oubliés quand passe l'hiver sombre
Tu te plains, ô captif solitaire du seuil,
Que ce sépulcre à deux qui fera notre orgueil
Hélas! du manque seul des lourds bouquets s'encombre . . .

In forgotten woods when the dark winter passes
You complain, oh solitary captive of the threshold,
That this sepulchre for two that will make us proud
Alas! is encumbered only by the lack of weighty
bouquets . . .

The bereaved subject's memories seem vain efforts to cross the threshold beyond which he would be reunited with his beloved, whose voice addresses him. The lover's tomb is 'encumbered' by the absence of bouquets (it is winter), which provide our thoughts with a means to satisfy the yearning to escape ordinary life, to control destiny. As in art, the bouquet alludes to an existence that is both of 'external' nature and of our personal ('internal') experience and needs.

When the bride tosses her flowers she bestows the promise of happiness on whomever catches it. The bouquet symbolizes harmony and order, in short, an ideal. But it also entails sacrifice. For the flower is cut from nature; the bride gives up innocence and freedom. In the act of celebration is contained an act of mourning. In visual art, bouquets were often the basis for what was more or less called 'material painting' – painting that affirmed both the materiality of the medium and of the world. Yet that very affirmation harboured all the uncertainty of flower imagery itself, that is, their allusion to the absence of world and the fragility of self (*vanitas*). The poetics of bouquets is thus a poetics of opposites expressed together, of poignance and of paradox. Knowledge is faced with undecidability and gives way to aesthetic desire.

FLOWERS OF THE PALETTE

Flower arranging is an aesthetic practice with obvious connotations for the processes of visual art, since the bouquet that results is an exemplary still-life. And still-life, as an essentially material art through which the artist none the less expresses creative vision, was commonly said to epitomize painting as a whole. Baudelaire's allusion to such ideas in his remarks on Delacroix had many echoes, contemporary and otherwise. For example, according to the mid-nineteenth-century writer on art Charles Blanc, Sir Joshua Reynolds referred to the painting of Rubens as a 'bouquet of colours'.[111] In his discussion of flower painting, Blanc noted differences between Dutch and French conceptions. The French, he held, 'paint flowers in order to regale the artist's eye with unexpected juxtapositions of all colours under the sun. The Dutch address their work to amateurs of the garden.'[112] That is, while the Dutch merely created the illusion of nature, the French used flowers as painting incarnate: their flower pieces were pretexts for creating art.

In allegorical representations of the attributes of the arts, still-lifes were often emblems for the art of painting.[113] Bouquets are often present in such works, though they themselves rarely refer directly to visual art. The tradition of allegorical still-life painting really begins with allegories of the senses, in which bouquets are common attributes of the sense of smell. However, such identifications are not always clear, nor are such compositions necessarily limited to five different objects standing for the five distinct senses. In Pierre Subleyras's *Attributes of the Arts* in Toulouse, for example, the attributes of the arts are almost interchangeable with attributes of the senses, the bouquet standing for the 'art' of agriculture. And in Jean-Baptiste Oudry's *A Table in an Artist's Studio* in Schwerin, a bouquet is juxtaposed to a palette, a bust, a candle, a holder for a rare stone or medal, and the attributes of music. It seems unlikely in the latter case that the bouquet stands either for the sense of smell or for the art of agriculture. Rather, it evokes something more intimate to visual art itself, perhaps its subject-matter or its production. Some flower paintings, particularly those in which the bouquet is accompanied by birds or insects, combine all the senses. Recalling representations of agriculture, they imply an allegory of nature, though it would have to be a nature cultivated by the creative mind, as in the art of gardening. In this sense, flower painting parallels artistic representations of beautiful nature – *la belle nature*. The point is not that allegories of gardening refer necessarily to art, but that they provide historical models for bouquets as expressions of nature creatively perceived.

Few observers failed to notice the unprecedented resurgence of flower painting in particular and of still-life in general during the second half of the nineteenth century. It is always hard to establish causality in the event of basic changes, but certainly the still-life revival did accompany a century-long revaluation of the ranking of genres or categories of painting. Castagnary claimed the still-life revival was specific to France, which had outdistanced all other nations in that category.[114] His particular pleasure in the increasing number of still-lifes stemmed no doubt from their presumed connection to naturalism. Widely practiced in the seventeenth and eighteenth centuries, especially in Holland, still-life had been eclipsed in France because of official and academic preferences for heroic or historical themes and their appropriate classical forms. The nineteenth-century revival was obviously part of the decline of that so-called 'grand tradition'. Noting just such a connection, one observer complained in the *Revue des Deux-Mondes* (1851): 'Grand painting is becoming weaker every day. It is not a good sign when, in order to find talent, we must make ourselves small and take refuge in still-lifes.'[115] Influential writers increasingly recognized that humble subject-matter, even the everyday objects of still-life, could be vehicles for great art. The basic belief in the poetic enterprise of art had not changed; rather, its association with the classical tradition shifted toward a poetic perception of the natural and the everyday. Concomitantly, the processes of still-life – its arrangements of forms and colours – gradually emerged as an expression of that perception.

The still-life revival was coupled with renewed interest in past schools other than the Italian school of the grand tradition. Of course, Théophile Thoré was deeply versed in the history of Dutch art, about which he wrote under the pseudonym 'W. Bürger'. He is renowned as the rediscoverer of Vermeer. Collecting Dutch and Spanish art had been popular since well before the Romantic period, and the indebtedness of painters even as original as Courbet to their style is well known. Thus, Manet's interests came well within already established currents. His knowledge of Dutch and Spanish art was quite expectedly confirmed by travel, but he also used books, especially Blanc's well-known *Histoire des peintres de toutes les écoles*. Published in the 1860s, these volumes constitute one of the master works of nineteenth-century art history. In them Blanc treated schools traditionally viewed as secondary with enlightened justice and praise. The books were also an important source for the rationale behind the still-life revival. Writing about Willem Kalf, Blanc asserted:

> If one wanted a definition of painting, one could just as well find it in a *Kitchen* by Kalf as in a heroic subject. Art is just as present at the bottom of that copper kettle gilded by light, or on the edge of that silver goblet, as in the midst of those serious compositions for which history and philosophy have given the subject. How strange and at first paradoxical! The better artist is the one who can make a prize painting from an overturned cauldron and a bunch of leeks, rather than the painter nourished at the breast of academies . . .[116]

Going beyond Blanc, Thoré explained this paradox by the ultimate artificiality of representation. Because the art of painting is a fiction, 'a wholly arbitrary optical play . . . grounded on convention', he wrote, one could risk fantastic forms, vulgar subjects, caricatures, even deformities. 'The Spanish, the Flemish and the Dutch represented bohemians, the lame, the drunk, the poor and all sorts of eccentrics.' Painting can represent all levels of life and even the most lowly objects. 'A painting of fish, of insects, or of molluscs can be a masterpiece.'[117]

So still-life embodied the most fundamental principles of art; its compositions displayed the basically material language of painting; its qualities were those on which history would ultimately judge all painters. Castagnary noted that in still-life 'beauty consists in the rendering [of objects], and it results from the execution'.[118] Process-related values are the key to what had traditionally been equated with poetry. Of course, the rise of still-life is only second in the nineteenth century to the rise of landscape. But landscape is often a metaphor for the external reality of nature (though infused with our perception of it), whereas still-life, artificial by definition, is more directly a metaphor for art. I would not go so far as to suggest that in an age of naturalism the still-life and flower piece were deliberately used as allegories, as they so often were in Symbolism and Post-Impressionism, a generation later. The point is, rather, that they offered the unmediated experience of a material art. Indeed, many artists were conscious of the degree to which flowers allowed them to concentrate on fundamentals of aesthetic content and composition. As Renoir told Georges Rivière:

> Painting flowers is a form of mental relaxation. I do not need the concentration that I need when I am faced with a model. When I am painting flowers I can experiment boldly with tones and values without worrying about destroying the whole painting. I would not dare to do that with a figure because I would be afraid of spoiling everything. The experience I gain from these experiments can then be applied to my paintings.[119]

In front of the model, representation was subjugated by the requirement of verisimilitude. Flower painting permitted a more purely aesthetic creativity. Fantin-Latour stated the case more succinctly, though with slightly different criteria, when referring to his own flower paintings in a letter of November 1862: 'If one can faithfully paint the most prosaic object in the world . . . one can paint the universe.'[120] Still-lifes, and flower paintings in particular, then, are emblematic of the shift in emphasis from a narrative to a visual poetics.

In 1860 the Galerie Martinet, where Manet was to have an important exhibition in 1863, showed works from the collections of some progressive connoisseurs. Their taste focused on the eighteenth century, where, according to the review by Thoré, the most remarkable discovery was some twenty-five examples of painting by Chardin. The exhibition is generally credited with giving a crucial impetus to the French still-life revival. Thoré's admiration of Chardin's ability to express the 'fullness and interiority' of form was so great that he even questioned the implications of the French term for still-life – *nature morte*. He preferred the emphasis on *life* of the English or German (*Stilleben*) expressions, for though Chardin represented nature as immobile, in his work it was anything but dead.[121] Two years later, Charles Blanc's volume with a chapter on Chardin appeared. Although Blanc found it natural for Chardin to move beyond still-life to the study of living forms (in about 1738, Chardin switched to genre painting, then later switched back to still-life), he so praised him for breathing life into inanimate objects that distinctions between genres seemed unimportant: 'Material objects . . . have their own existence, a way of being and of uniting with light that reveals their diverse properties, their substance, in an instant. . . . Just as air supports living organisms, light gives life to material objects.'[122] In order to deal with Chardin's greatness, Blanc's explanation almost seems applicable to Impressionism and foreshadows Mallarmé's concept of immersion in light and air. While he saw Chardin's mastery of the painterly touch corresponding to the return of materialism in eighteenth-century philosophy, he clearly justified renewed interest in Chardin by the striking parallel with his own time.

A similar view obtains in the exquisite essay on Chardin by the Goncourt brothers, first published in 1864.[123] They saw still-life as the special strength of Chardin's genius: 'He raised this secondary genre to the highest and most marvellous condition of art. Never had the enchantments of material painting, which touches upon the most commonplace objects to transfigure them by the magic of rendering, been brought further.' Playing upon differences between close-up and normal viewing in a way we found in Zola a few years later, (and first used by the eighteenth-century critic Diderot for Chardin, as well) their exclamations of wonder at Chardin's 'unique handling [and] inexplicable representations of nature' are tributes to what they termed his technical *cuisine* and its miraculous powers of imitation. Thus, their expression 'material painting' alludes to an art rooted in physical process rather than in distancing description. A passage describing their examination of some flowers exemplified their approach to still-life:

> See these rare bouquets, which are like the flowers of his palette, and through which the painter outshines all previous copiers of flora: see these two carnations: they are no

> more than smears of white and blue, a sort of scattering of silvery enamels in relief; look at them attentively from a little farther away, and the flowers rise up from the canvas; the leafy design of the carnation, the heart of the flower and its tender shadow, its ragged forms, everything comes together and unfolds.

In other passages, again contrasting close and distant viewing, the brothers marvel over the way flecks of contrasting unblended colours and little twists of the brush create sensations of actual presence:

> Look at his work for some time, then move back a few steps; the glass solidifies, it is real glass, it contains real water. . . . Brushwork, everywhere broken up, glimmers awakening in shadows, full lights posed like fingertips on the glass's edge, that is all you see in approaching the canvas. Here, in a corner, there is apparently nothing more than the dried mark of a brushstroke, then suddenly a walnut opens . . . and appears in every detail of colour and form.

These experiences suggest Impressionist vision, one whose point of departure is the undifferentiated physical data of seeing. They recall Zola on Manet. Chardin eschews narrative in favour of what might be called the 'story of perceptual experience'.[124] Note how many sentences begin with the imperative verb-form 'see' or 'look', as if an extra effort to do so would reveal the essence of the art. The eye becomes immersed in reality, not just because of the reality itself, which is so often taken for granted, but because of the eye's consciousness of the artist's process of representation. Recapitulating that process, the Goncourts' descriptions imply the fundamental role of 'material painting', exemplified by still-life, as its poetic embodiment. There, the artifice of representation is itself a poetic practice, and its result is the celebration of matter.

THE FIGURE IN THE STILL-LIFE

In 1871 Renoir painted *Still-life with Bouquet* (illus. 61) as an *hommage* to Manet. Hanging on a wall is Manet's etching after the painting then attributed to Velázquez called *The Little Cavaliers*, a print Manet considered significant enough to exhibit no less than three times during the 1860s. On a table in

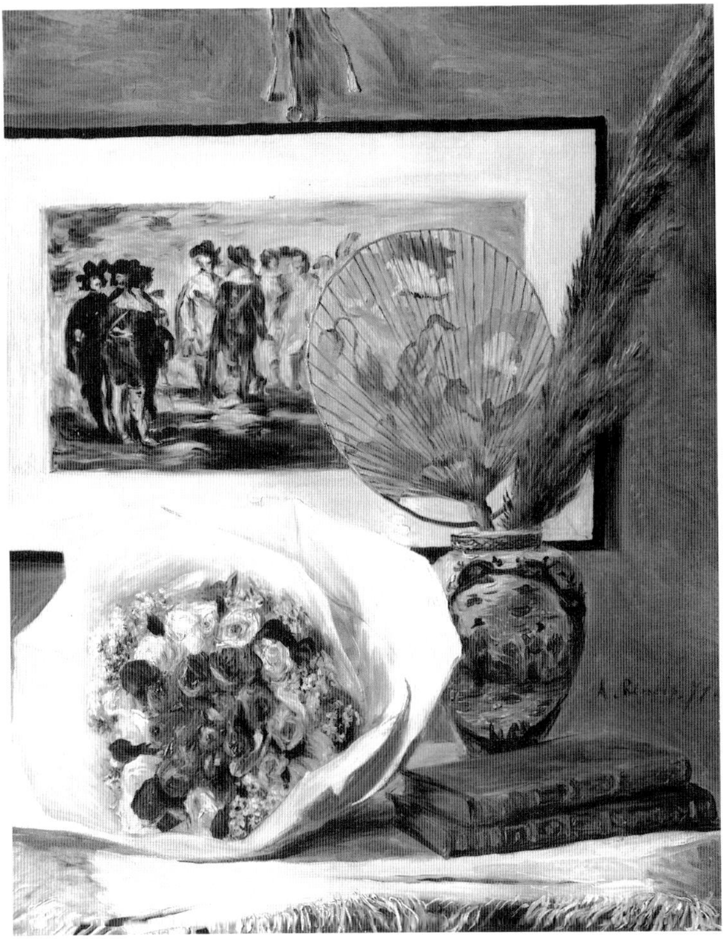

61 Pierre-Auguste Renoir, *Still-life with Bouquet*, 1871, oil on canvas. Museum of Fine Arts, Houston

front of the print lies a bouquet in a wrapper clearly reminiscent of the *Olympia*; and in an arrangement alluding to the portrait of Emile Zola, Renoir placed a Japanese vase containing a feather and a fan alongside a pair of books. Besides their allusion to paintings by Manet, these three groups have in common the process underlying their creation, a process based on selection and juxtaposition, which is the guiding principle of still-life. The *Little Cavaliers* is an assemblage of figures, like several in Manet's major early works. The bouquet, of course, is a gathering of selected flowers, and the composition with vase and books is a traditional still-life. The comparison between figure painting, flower painting and still-life is unmistakable. Thus, Renoir not only used objects individually to refer to different figures (in paintings by

Manet), but by putting those references together as a still-life made up of still-lifes (a kind of master or meta-still-life), he referred beyond individual paintings to Manet as an artist. He established that connection not simply through various elements that refer to Manet by recalling his works, but by calling attention to the process lying behind those works. For by the time Renoir had made his fascinating picture, still-life had in certain circles become synonymous with the name Manet.

Indeed, one of Zola's best remembered and most influential remarks about Manet's painting is that Manet treated figure painting the way academic painters treated still-life. That is, he regarded painting simply as an arrangement of colours and forms:

> Dear master, . . . for you a painting is but a pretext for analysis. You needed a nude woman, and you chose Olympia, the first comer; you needed some bright and luminous touches, so you put in a bouquet; you needed some black touches, so you put in a negress and a cat. . . . Obviously, given the mechanism of his talent . . . [Manet] does very powerful renderings of groups of inanimate objects, which we call still-life.[125]

Théophile Thoré, one of the first to give more than a few lines to Manet in articles of the early 1860s, came to a remarkably similar conclusion after a few years of hesitation. Disconcerted by Manet's affinity for Spain and his predilection for dubious themes, Thoré nevertheless had always appreciated Manet's bold colour and handling. In 1868, perhaps taking his cue from Zola, he attained an integrated view in which still-life again was a paradigm:

> I will take the risk of saying that Monsieur Manet sees very well. That is the first quality to be a painter. . . . When one has put onto the canvas the 'spot of colour' that a figure or an object has made on its natural surroundings, he is through. Don't ask for more, at least for the moment. . . . His present vice is a sort of pantheism, which gives no more value to a head than to a slipper; which sometimes gives more importance to a bouquet of flowers than to a woman, for example in his famous painting of the black cat [the *Olympia*]; and which represents everything uniformly, . . . as in the portrait of Emile Zola.[126]

Castagnary more or less agreed about the Zola portrait: 'Everything that is still-life is treated with a master's hand.'[127] Reflecting such views, though with more reservations than Thoré, Paul Mantz wrote of *The Balcony* in his 'Salon de 1869' that it would be futile to look for

> the accentuation of a type or the expression of a sentiment or idea. . . . Let us admit that it is about colour combinations and let us look at it as we would the wild arabesques of Persian pottery, the harmony of a bouquet, or the decorative imprint of wallpaper. Yet M. Manet has not quite succeeded. . . . His painting is no more interesting than a still-life.[128]

By the end of the 1860s, then, one approach to Manet's aims and to the essential character of his art held that he composed by areas of colour, with little regard to the significance of figures or objects themselves. His pictures were arrangements of colour patterns, like still-lifes or bouquets. Whatever dissatisfaction followed from the perceived limitations of his painting, such statements laid the ground for the later claim (first made by the Post-Impressionist Maurice Denis) that any painting was ultimately an arrangement of lines and colours on a flat surface – an abstraction, in other words. They provide a context for seeing still-life, epitomized at this point by bouquets, as essential to Manet's artistic profile.

Still-life was indeed an important part of Manet's work from its very beginnings. Not only were independent still-lifes a successful genre within his production, still-lifes were prominent, usually in the foreground, in a majority of his figure pieces. Given the view of Manet's art shared by many of his contemporaries, it may not be too much to see those still-lifes as standing for his artistic presence or persona. Of course for the figure paintings, we must avoid excessive distinctions between deliberate compositions of inanimate objects that constitute a traditional still-life within the larger picture, and those that may form part of a setting or may be the attributes of the figure. Even the latter can be pretexts for objects whose primary justification is the pleasure their representation provides. Hence, an approach to the problem of still-life in Manet's art might temporarily turn Zola's statement on its head. That is not to say Zola was wrong but, on the contrary, that the full implications of his intuition are best understood by asking to what degree Manet's still-life expresses the concerns of figure painting, concerns that go beyond arrangements of colours and forms. How does Manet's still-life, perhaps as much or even more than figure painting, embody the 'humanistic content', the 'poetry', still sought in the most ambitious art? How does still-life express the artist's presence in seeing and in being seen – the relationship of self to other so emphatically traced in figure paintings by exchanges of gaze? How does the still-life, and the bouquet in particular, embody the merger of self and world Mallarmé saw effected in Manet's art?

If, as Mallarmé suggested, Manet's painting expresses (we might say, performs) the artist's immersion in the world's materiality, then what better painted sign for self than the material art of still-life? Certainly, still-lifes are both more discrete and yet more pertinent than self-portraits. The only time Manet literally included himself in a picture with others, the *Concert in the Tuileries*, he made his position marginal. Earlier, we saw how he playfully used signatures and other devices as signs of his artistic control and decision-making. With still-lifes, he could be both more subtle and more forward. Indeed, his placement of still-lifes in the foreground of many major compositions borders on the systematic. Of course, and especially in the first works, they are often props and attributes that relate to the primary subject. Their use in the portrait of *M. and Mme Auguste Manet* (illus. 16) is entirely traditional, and even the bottle lying on the ground in *The Absinthe Drinker* (illus. 2) reads as the figure's sign. However in *The Guitar Player* (illus. 3), Manet used a jug and two garlic bulbs as echoes of the picture's primary forms. Naturally, they allude to the Spaniard's Mediterranean culture, but the way they anchor the composition's right-hand side is worthy of Chardin. The single garlic clove points along a diagonal that ends at the top of the guitar to suggest the calculated structure Manet refused to change even when told the instrument was being held contrary to the way it was strung. In another early painting, *Boy with Cherries* (1859–60; Museu Calouste Gulbenkian, Lisbon), the stone ledge and cherries in their wrapper are integral parts of the composition. Even so, three cherries make a play of colour against the grey and emphasize the diagonal formed by the brilliant reds. In a freeze-motion effect, they seem to have fallen from the package (unless they are held back by a finger?). Though obviously related to symbols of the precariousness of life, the device also focuses attention on subtle and equally fragile effects of artistic choice. They vaguely reiterate the composition, while complementing the signature, which looks etched into the stone and is thus, too, a part of still-life, at the opposite corner.

Subordinate to compositions in which they are placed, still-lifes are more available than are figures as vehicles for play, whether of wit or of the brush. In the portrait of Nadar's mistress called *Reclining Woman in Spanish Costume* (illus. 8), Manet alluded to such ideas through a kitten playing with two oranges. Again at the corner position, and echoing the main figure, the little group is here placed just above the signature. Of course, the oranges are vitalizing spots of colour. And cats were often used by artists and poets for various symbolic overtones. (The cat was a favourite pet of Baudelaire.) Perhaps the look from its glistening eyes suggests more than playfulness and innocence. But whether or not the kitten and its oranges allude to the relationship between man and woman, lover and mistress, they may also suggest the rituals and freedoms of art. Indeed, combined with the cat's play, Manet's representation of still-life can be taken as a code for his presence – not unlike a signature, with which it is here associated. Declaring the artifice of his means through objects drawn from reality, the artist's commentary reposes on the notion of still-life as paradigm for art that we already saw to be widely accepted – the artist-cat playing with and upon nature. Three figures of the artist's presence – animate, inanimate, and signature – are here combined.

In the same year (1862), Manet put a cat in an etching from a series where one of his most overtly symbolic still-lifes had an important role.[129] In the first cover design for the collection of etchings called *Eaux-fortes par Edouard Manet* (illus. 62), the animal stands near an open portfolio of prints with the title as its label. Looking outward, it seems to present the collection of prints to the viewer. From this relatively simple design Manet moved to a more complex composition, in which a Polichinelle looks out from between theatre curtains labelled with the title *Eaux-fortes*. Tacked to the curtain is the image of a balloon over the outskirts of Paris (illus. 63). The latter evokes, though

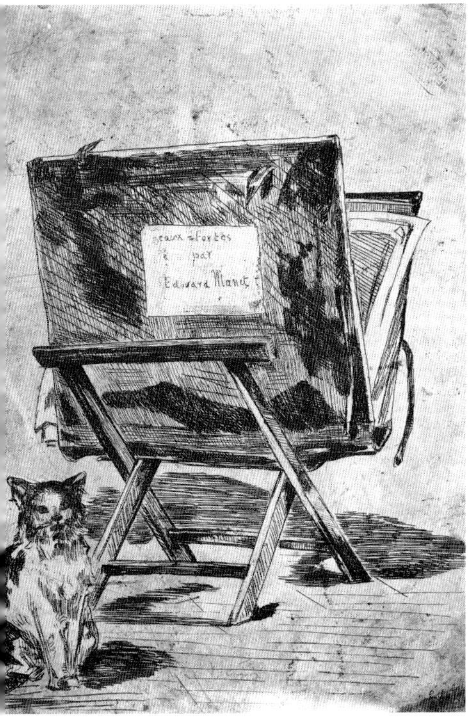

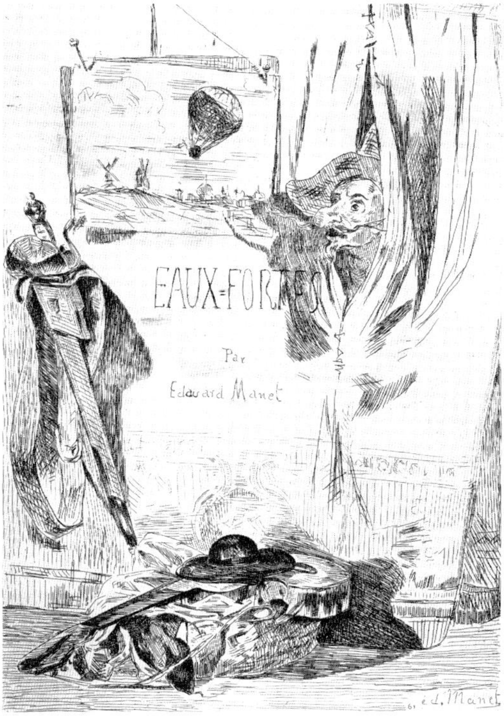

62 First cover design for *Les Eaux-fortes par Edouard Manet*, 1862, etching. New York Public Library

63 Second cover design for *Les Eaux-fortes par Edouard Manet*, 1862, etching. New York Public Library

without at all reproducing, Manet's lithograph of *The Balloon*, which, like Polichinelle's theatre, belongs to the kind of outdoor festivities one might have enjoyed at the Invalides Esplanade or in the gardens of the Tuileries. This version of the cover design contains two significant still-lifes. The first is the sword used by Manet's son in the *Boy with a Sword* (illus. 64), a painting of 1861. Manet had intended at first to include an etching of this composition in the collection, but left it out. Here he used a single element, the sword, as a metonym; that is, he used a part to refer to the whole, not to the boy but to the composition. It happens that this particular prop was the component of the painting most utterly dependent on arbitrary choice; it gave the painting a unique identity, like a signature. Not so much Léon's personal attribute, then, the sword is, rather, the sign of his transformation into art. The second still-life in the etching is the basket of objects at the bottom of the composition. Each item in the basket alludes to other paintings by Manet. Most easily identifiable are the guitar and sombrero, which refer to his most successful work to date, *The Guitar Player*; with them appears to be the cape

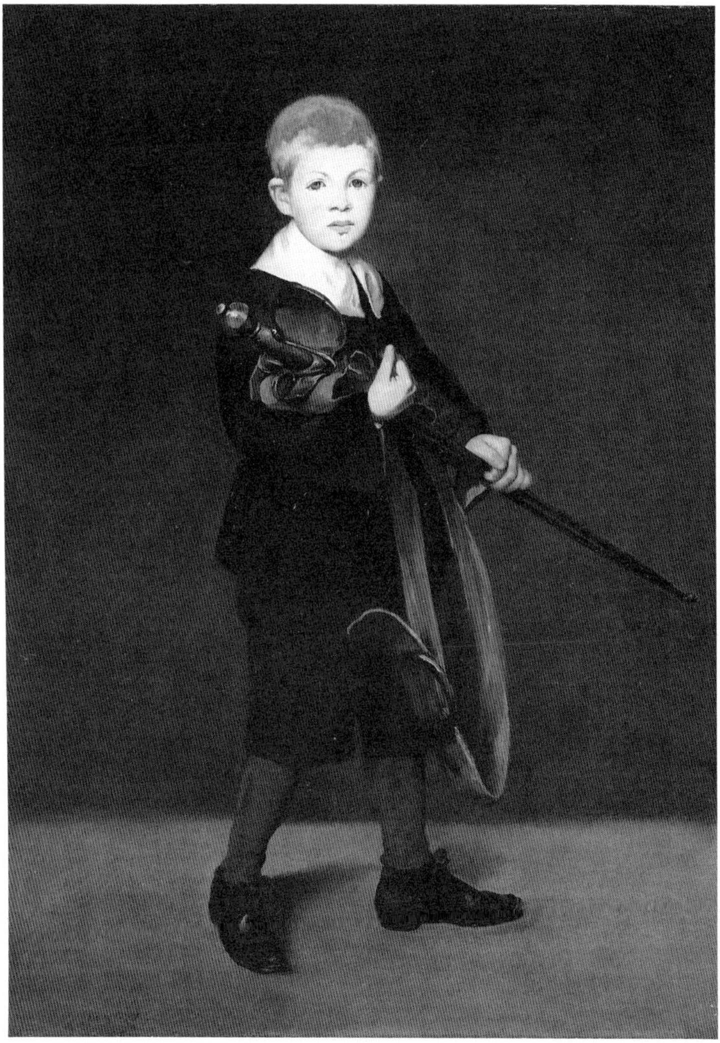

64 *Boy with a Sword*, 1861, oil on canvas. Metropolitan Museum of Art, New York

from the *Victorine as an Espada* (illus. 22). (This composition of objects in the basket was important enough for Manet to have made a painting of it, called *Guitar and Sombrero*, in the Musée Calvet, Avignon; since the painting is in reverse, it probably preceded the print.) Culminating a process of distillation like that used for choosing the motifs of which it is constituted, this still-life itself became the sole motif for Manet's final version of the cover for the etchings collection (illus. 65).

Manet's repertory of attributes – the cat, Polichinelle's theatre, the balloon, the still-lifes – clearly alludes to his artistic poses of the early 1860s. All derive from forms of public entertainment and leisure. Gradually, however, Manet moved away from this early allegoricism toward a use of still-life that embodies rather than literalizes. In the cover plate for the etchings Manet had used still-life to bring together various significant objects. In the early versions the still-life was juxtaposed to other elements within the composition. In the final version the relation of the guitar/sombrero still-life to the whole was like that of a single object within the guitar/sombrero still-life to its own overall arrangement. That is, the still-life within the larger composition was sufficient to stand for the composition as a whole. What is less obvious, but can now be argued, is that still-lifes within other larger compositions may stand metonymically for them, for they sufficiently

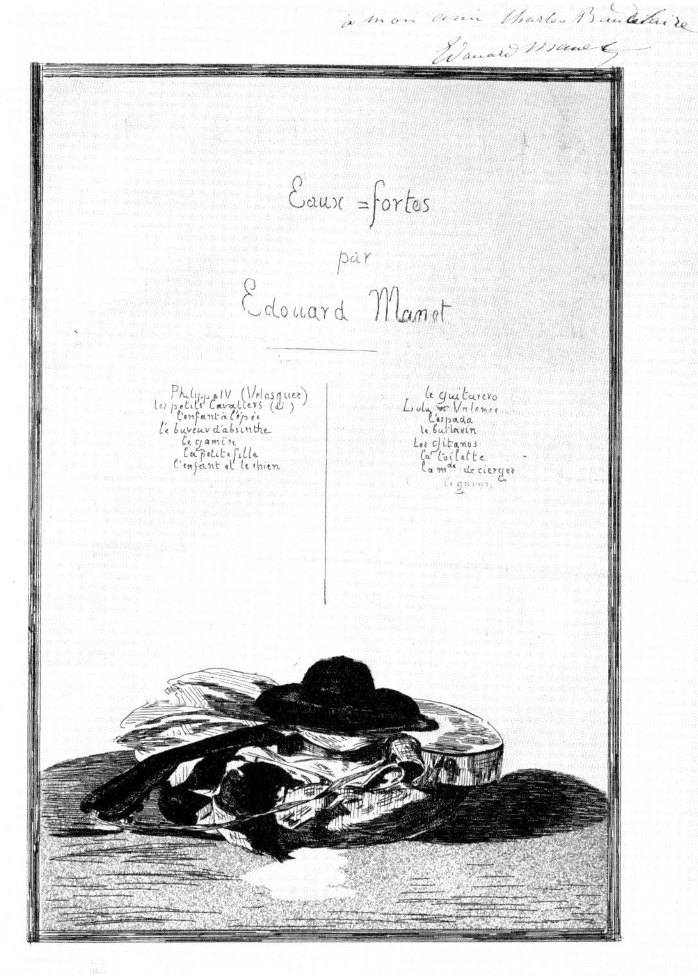

65 Proof for the frontispiece of *Les Eaux-fortes par Edouard Manet*, 1862–3, etching with aquatint and drypoint. Nationalmuseum, Stockholm

embody the values and identity of the composition as a whole. So it is not simply that Manet's figure painting, as Zola maintained, embodies the values of still-life – arrangements of inanimate forms – but rather that Manet's still-lifes also embody the ultimate values of figure painting – the poetic animation and interpretation of forms. In his foregrounds, then, they are like both Manet's signatures and his cats, *alter egos* of artistic presence. Gazing on them, we view the essential Manet, whose persona is now embodied by signs for artwork that define it as consciousness and process.

Nowhere is the role of still-life more visible than in Manet's two largest and most controversial compositions of the years that immediately followed the *Déjeuner sur l'herbe* and the *Olympia*, the former with its magnificent display of Victorine's dress, straw hat and basket of fruit and brioches, the latter with its prominent bouquet. In the *Déjeuner*, certain objects – hat, dress and basket – suggest links to the *Guitar and Sombrero*. Although we are now in a contemporary outdoor setting rather than experiencing exotic entertainment, the composition still evokes the modern association between visual spectacle and leisure. It is a world where didactic reading has given way to aesthetic experience *qua* consumption. The artist's presence as 'spectacle master' (like Polichinelle or the cat) has been subsumed into the expressive handling of form. The model, who by returning our gaze becomes another kind of artist's *alter ego*, draws us into her world, which is a world of visuality – of being seen (of 'aspect') – as well as a world of seeing. Victorine's temporarily discarded clothing emphasizes the distinction between her ordinary person and her artistic function, that of a model in the artist's employ. In the *Espada* her look seems to ask if the way she poses with the cape and sword is just right. In certain pictures, exotic costumes or props (like the sword in the *Boy with a Sword*) projected Manet's figures into the realm of art as picturesque subjects. In the *Déjeuner*, the model's nudity itself, with the still-life reminding us of its dependence on the artist's command, accomplishes a similar effect.

In Manet's *Olympia*, figure and still-life – nude model and bouquet – are side by side. Bertall's caricature of the painting (illus. 66), which so exaggerates the size of the bouquet, suggests the importance of the latter for Manet's contemporaries: the caption ironically refers to the painting as 'the bouquet

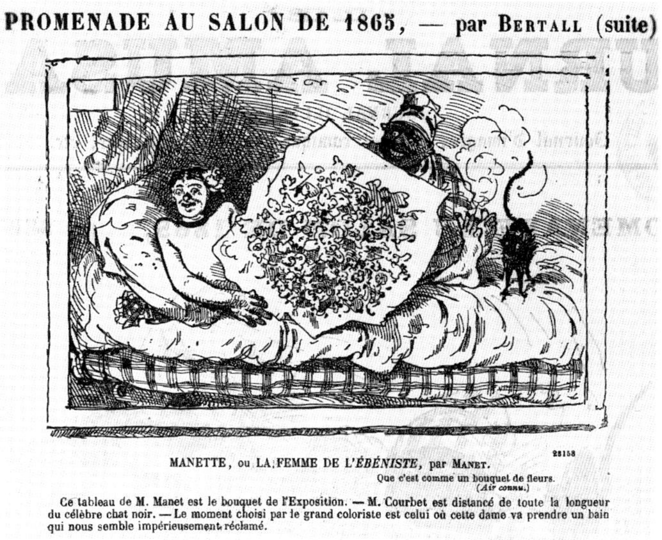

66 Bertall's caricature of *Olympia* from *Le Journal amusant*, 27 May 1865, Paris

of the exhibition'. The juxtaposition of figure and still-life offered several critics the opportunity to discriminate between their admiration for Manet's abilities as a still-life painter and their disgust for his figure of the prostitute. Linked to the ritual of courting, the bouquet is a traditional part of the iconography of the seductive nude. It is a traditional painterly element as well. But if Manet really made the statement attributed to him by Antonin Proust ('I render, as simply as can be, the things I see. Take *Olympia* – could anything be plainer?'), it must have been meant as irony.[130] For it was inevitable that the nude would cause a stir, and the cat is now a knowing accomplice. Indeed, the cat's startling prominence is captured by Thoré's reference to the *Olympia* as 'the famous painting of the black cat'. Viewed as the cousin of Manet's other cats, this one again alludes to the artist as playful presenter and master of ceremonies, watching us and noting our response to the spectacle. Recalling how criticism of the *Olympia* was so divided between its polarities of figure and still-life, it may not be too much to see the painting as implicitly proposing an equivalency between the two. In this regard, Olympia's bedsheets are especially worth noting. For in ways paralleling his use of table-linen in still-life (as we shall see), and anticipated by the theme of the picnic spread upon a blanket (though in the *Déjeuner* it is actually Victorine's dress), the bed-linen is the vehicle for strikingly broad and arbitrary

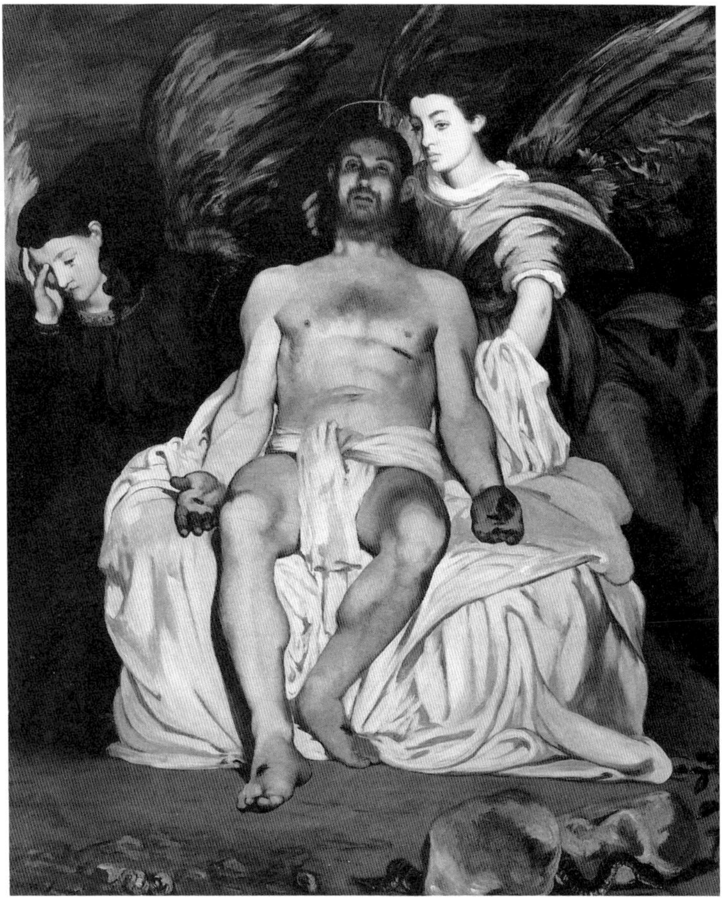

67 *Dead Christ with Angels*, 1864, oil on canvas. Metropolitan Museum of Art, New York

painterly effects. A painting done just after the *Olympia* (though exhibited before it), namely the *Dead Christ with Angels* (illus. 67), complements it as a male nude frontally presented, like a 'still-life' displayed on a background of complexly patterned cloth. Here, too, a traditional theme has been subverted by transforming a hallowed body into the substance of an aesthetic display. The pun on the cadaver of Christ as a *nature morte*, both dead and yet living as art, is almost too ostentatious. Shifting the wound made by the centurion to the *left* side of Christ's chest recalls the arbitrary choices made in the *Guitar Player* (the instrument strung and held in reverse) and elsewhere. The only realist explanation is that we are looking at a mirror reflection of Christ – a pun on the art-as-mirror-of-reality concept. Otherwise, the wound can only allude to the artist's assertion of his independence from nature, to his unwillingness to have his representation subjugated by the referent, and thus it alludes to the manipulative process underlying the making of art. In that sense, all look back to the cape of Victorine's espada, and thus to the basket on the cover for the *Eaux-fortes*.

We have noted the essential role of Baudelaire for both cat and flower imagery. In the later 1860s Champfleury's book on cats, with its poster and illustration by Manet (illus. 13), figured prominently in that context as well. The book contained illustrations by Edmond Morin of Baudelaire with a cat on his shoulder next to a potted plant, and of Champfleury himself with a furry head and cat-like ears. Though not published until 1870, when it accompanied a new edition of Champfleury's book, Manet's etching of *A Cat and Flowers* (illus. 68) makes an essential reduction of these motifs, to which the addition of an iron railing refers to the grid we found in *The Balcony* (illus. 30), on which he was working at the time, and then in the later *Gare Saint-Lazare* (illus. 32). Like the still-life of guitar and sombrero, the reference to the artist and his flowering, yet ordering imagination is unmistakable. In the *Olympia*, prostitute, bouquet and cat all are Manet's

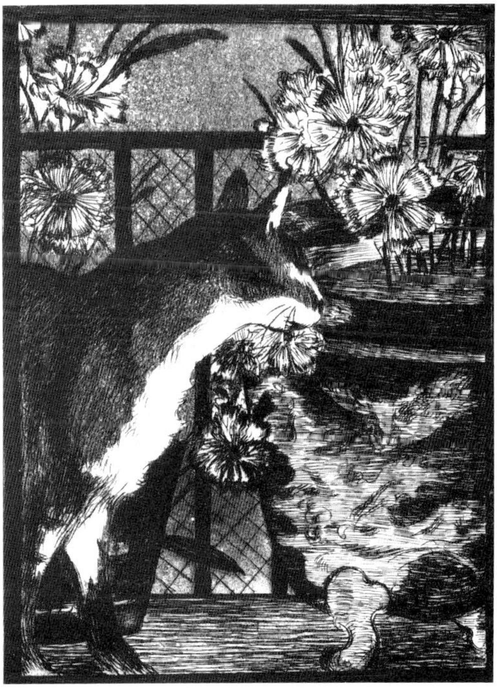

68 *Cat and Flowers*, 1869, etching and aquatint. New York Public Library

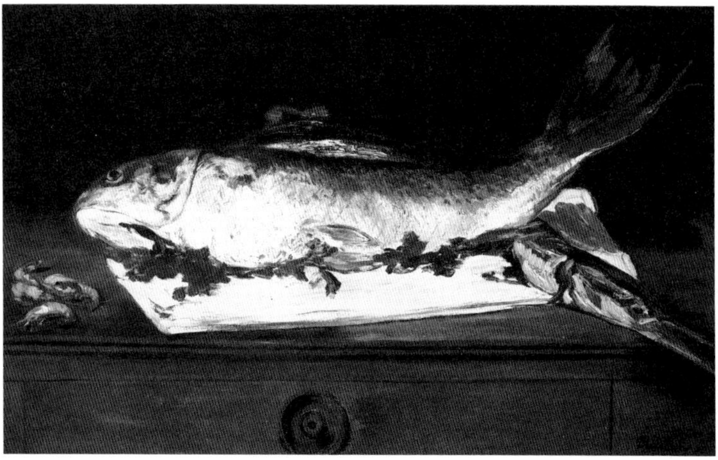

69 *Salmon, Pike and Shrimp*, 1864, oil on canvas. Norton Simon Art Foundation, Pasadena

artistic *alter egos*, for all are signs of artistic vision and creative presence. The cat makes its final appearance posing near the helmet of the *Luncheon in the Studio* (illus. 29), confirming the retrospective character of its introspective atmosphere.

By this time Manet was doing large, formal still-lifes that were earning him such critical success that he could be considered an important still-life painter in addition to his more notorious role as a figure painter. Surely they contributed to the growing concept of his painting as stemming primarily from the principles of still-life? Several, such as the *Salmon, Pike and Shrimp* (illus. 69), the *Still-life with Fish* (illus. 24), the *Fruit on a Table* (illus. 70), the *Melon with Peaches* (National Gallery of Art, Washington, DC) and the *Salmon*

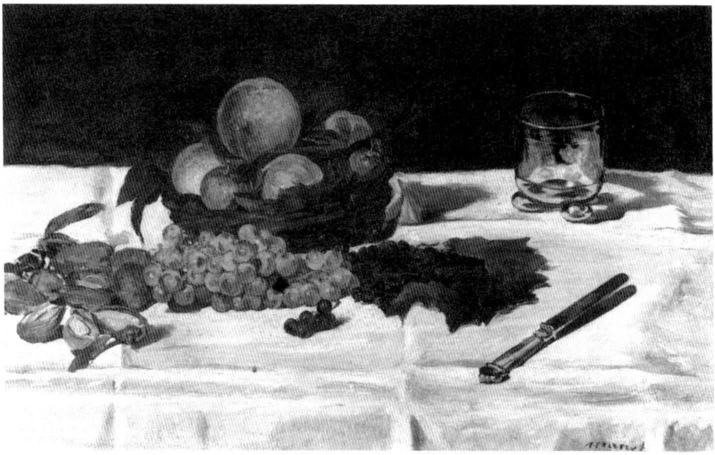

70 *Fruit on a Table*, 1864, oil on canvas. Musée d'Orsay, Paris

(Shelburne Museum, Vermont) were exhibited publicly, either at Martinet's in 1865 or at Manet's Avenue de l'Alma exhibition in 1867. All are reminiscent of the studied arrangements of Chardin, except that in most of them, the table-linen (and in the *Salmon, Pike and Shrimp*, the wrapper) heightens the contrast of colours and the tension between spatial and planar readings of their structure. *Fruit on a Table* is divided into sections by the creases in the cloth, the front edge of the table suggested underneath it without corresponding to a fold. In *Still-life with Fish*, spatial reading and the edge of the table are confused by the painting of the cloth in the area of the knife and lemon, objects whose allusion to Dutch painting is therefore probably ironic, since, for most painters of Manet's

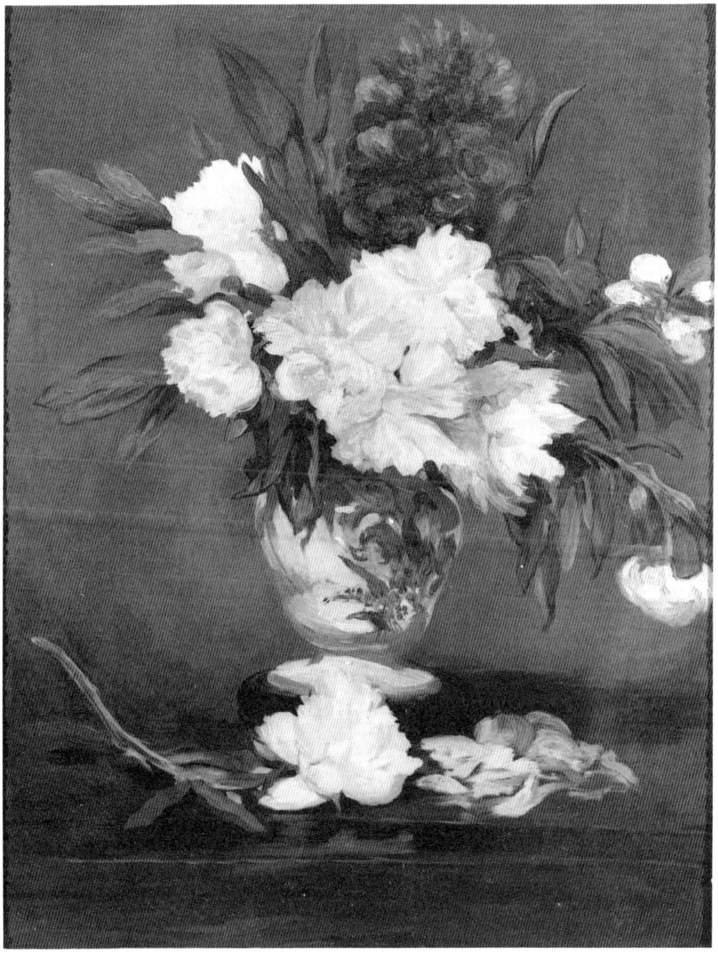

71 *Peonies in a Vase*, 1864, oil on canvas. Musée d'Orsay, Paris

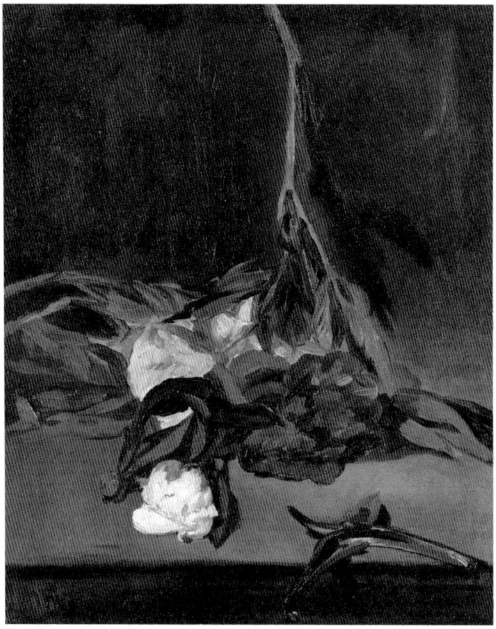

72 *Peony Stems and Pruning Shears*, 1864, oil on canvas. Musée d'Orsay, Paris

generation, spatial clarity (as opposed to Manet's ambiguity) would have been considered an essential quality of Dutch painting. In the *Salmon, Pike and Shrimp*, and especially in *Melon with Peaches*, Manet began to play freely with the tablecloth, creating the kind of arbitrary patterns that are also evident in his sea pieces of 1864 and were later taken up in Paul Cézanne's still-lifes.

Another composition of 1864, the *Peonies in a Vase* (illus. 71), was especially admired by Manet's contemporaries. For Ernest Chesneau it revealed Manet's 'incontestable pictorial qualities'.[131] It was accompanied or followed by some smaller and less formal pictures. In one of the latter (illus. 72), pruning shears are prominently featured in the foreground; one stem seems as yet unprepared for the final arrangement. In an even smaller work with two white peonies, now in the Musée d'Orsay, the handle of the shears is visible to the left. The theme of the series taken as a whole is floral arrangement – again, as already suggested, a fitting paradigm for the concept of still-life and, by extension, art itself.

In many of Manet's ambitious paintings of the second half of the 1860s, the concerns of figure painting and still-life are more completely merged. The most carefully studied works are single figures with costumes that almost seem to be

Manet's primary interest. Removed from social context and physical setting, these figures look very much like portraits, even when they are not identifiable as such. They also function as social types, a characteristic of which is to operate as aesthetic rather than sociologically insightful allusions to their worlds. Indeed, it could be argued that, from *The Street Singer* (Museum of Fine Arts, Boston) of *c.* 1862 and the *Young Man (Eugène Manet) in the Costume of a Majo* (Metropolitan Museum of Art, New York) of 1863 to the portrait of *Philibert Rouvière as a Tragic Actor* (illus. 21) and the *Fifer Boy* (illus. 43) of 1866, Manet's figures are bearers of still-life. (I said earlier the idea was more literally true for the *Dead Toreador*; illus. 46.) That is, the patterns and colours to which their costumes give rise seem the veritable subject-matter of such canvases. They embody the values of still-life to the same degree as drapery studies by the Old Masters, except that Manet's are independent works. Moreover, the figures' poses and their relationship to the indeterminate space of their setting create the sensation of a foreground in the centre of the canvas, where most of the pictorial activity takes place. As in the *Olympia*, these paintings produce an aesthetic of display, rather than narrative. Spread over the surface, indeed, pressing toward the eye, Manet's pigments create a world physically manipulated – like that of still-life objects, except here more intimately infused with the painter's eye as expressed through gesture and touch.

Of course Manet continued to use still-life as prop, attribute and commentary, especially in portraits of friends, such as those of Astruc, Zola and Duret, the last-mentioned suggesting a Spanish model for the pose and the play on the signature, and a Dutch model for the still-life. Indeed, Duret himself gave an account of the still-life in his portrait that suggests just how pictorially motivated Manet's process was. He tells how, to the virtually completed portrait, Manet added first an upholstered stool, then a green book, which he tossed to the floor beneath it. The artist successively placed additional objects and then painted them: the lacquer tray, the carafe, the glass, the knife, and finally the lemon for a touch of yellow. Duret himself said that this process revealed how Manet viewed his entire picture according to the paradigm of still-life.[132] We might add that joining the still-life to his nearly completed portrait composition reintegrated the picture, into

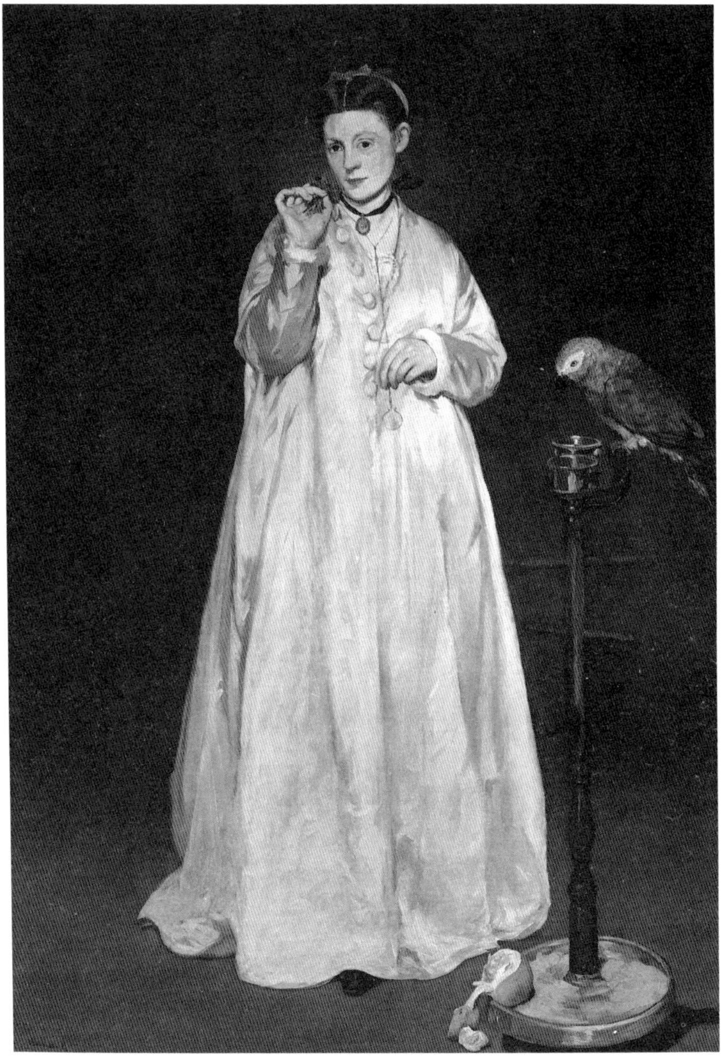

73 *Woman with a Parrot*, 1866, oil on canvas. Metropolitan Museum of Art, New York

what we might call a still-life-like essence. The exquisite *Woman with a Parrot* (illus. 73) of 1866, perhaps even better combines Manet's painting as still-life concept, and actually represented still-life, for its painted objects are even more prominent than in the Duret portrait. But such a combination is also explored in the more complex arrangements of *The Luncheon* (illus. 29), where figures and still-life elements are thoroughly interspersed. Castagnary concurred in this view when he wrote of this painting that 'Monsieur Manet is more of a fantasist than an observer. . . . He takes his subjects from

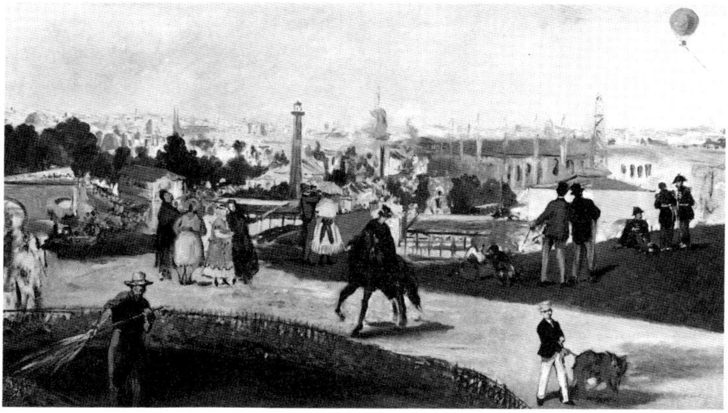

74 *The Universal Fairgrounds in 1867*, 1867, oil on canvas. Nasjonalgalleriet, Oslo

poetry or from his imagination rather than real life. Thus, there is much in his compositions that is arbitrary.'[133] This definition of poetry continues the tradition of opposing art to nature. But rather than a literary gloss, poetry is found in the arbitrary and fantastic arrangement of compositional elements. In some pictures, the arrangements seem contrapuntal, as in the *Universal Fairgrounds in 1867* (illus. 74) and the *Beach at Boulogne-sur-mer* (Museum of Fine Arts, Richmond, VA). The beginnings of such strategies can be found in Manet's 'pastiches', like *The Old Musician* (illus. 4) and *The Little Cavaliers* (illus. 5). In *The Balcony* (illus. 30), the figures themselves, though each is carrying a prop, form an ensemble as artificial as the potted plant and as removed from 'nature' as the lap-dog with its ball. The foreground's proximity itself, not just its contents, signals artifice too, for to observe the scene directly the viewer would have to stand in mid-air. Manet is less interested in illusion than in spectacle and visuality.

What has so often been called Manet's flattening of pictorial space can be given various interpretations. If we continue to view his paintings in spatial terms, as his contemporaries surely did, it is apparent that Manet has reduced space to a shallow envelope. This reduction or compression is not so far from the tradition of French history painting since the late eighteenth century, which, as in the work of Jacques-Louis David, staged its figures in a frieze-like array in the foreground of its compositions. However, Manet's paintings have also been compared by Richard Wollheim to nocturnal dreams, in which events seem to occur in real space, but where there is no sense of additional spatial context around the figures themselves of the dream.[134] I believe Manet's handling of spatiality, or disregard for it, is linked to his preoccupation with what I described earlier as a 'centred' foreground. Such a location of the foreground is different from its placement at the bottom of compositions that follow the traditional perspectival system. It is the consequence of Manet's concept of the canvas as the table-like support for still-life. What once was an illusionistic space is now the space of imagination or creative thinking, similar perhaps in its physical translation to the space of dreaming, but rendering a quite conscious state and altogether differently motivated. Foreshadowing the Cubists, Manet neglects the edges of his composition, for, if space is created, it is not by reference to the external element of the frame but rather, to the operation of the process of visual representation within its site. Again, one thinks of how Jackson Pollock's 'all-over' composition, as I suggested earlier, thwarts the distancing/dominating paradigm and brings forth the experience of materiality. Manet had not so much reduced a previously spatial conception of art (though that is the historical effect), as he has produced an art where contact between the creative self and the realm of its creativity – a virtually physical contact – is maintained by treating the canvas as the supporting slab for materials represented by paint. The signs of Manet's presence remain virtually in his possession by never leaving the physical present for the illusory and timeless realm of art. Thus, the eye seems at the centre of the representation brought so physically close. The appeal of Japanese prints and the importance of the tablecloth are simply versions of the painting *cum* still-life, animated and poeticized by the traces it bears of the artist's vision, that is, by the artist's presence embedded in it. The signs of reality, which in the case of painting are physical and opaque, and display that condition in Manet's case by hovering at the borderline between figuration and defiguration, appear quite literally manipulated through the intermediary of the brush. Representation is merged with physicality by locating its site within the painting rather than outside or over and above it – at its surface rather than beyond its frame. That surface, though effaced by the show of innovative handling, is none the less sufficiently expressed to replace the frame as *parergon*, as the absent yet defining condition underlying the artwork's constitution of its subject. Through its sense of participation in the process of representation, the subject now discovers its congruence and integrity with the world inside the frame – not simply its materiality, but its potential otherness and susceptibility to manipulation as well. The bouquet, with its natural elements artistically displayed, will be the subject-matter within the broader category of still-life that most effectively embodies these effects.

BOUQUETS ON THE CONSCIOUSNESS OF BEING

As Manet moved toward an Impressionist style, the world he created appeared more and more obviously inhabited and selected by his eye. Every visible inflection of brushstroke and every fragmented spot of unblended colour are retinal stimuli reminding the viewer of the activity of seeing, and transforming its natural experience into a spectacle for aesthetic contemplation. When Mallarmé referred to the artist's immersion in the world, he was responding to sensations produced by the proximity and sensuality of Manet's painted surface, which he saw as the poetic yet manual index of the artist's abiding presence in representation. Moreover, the ordinary viewer becomes a participant in the process by completing through imagination what the painter merely summarizes. Mallarmé's concept of the world's self-revelation through art located Manet's historical significance in the philosophical and democratic ramifications of this practice. Inhabiting the world as its creature rather than distancing it as its sovereign, Manet took his surroundings as capital for his economy of delectation. The paradigm of art as bouquet/still-life suggests not only how Manet invested that world with his ordering consciousness, but how he merged his art with the concerns and attitudes of everyday, domestic (natural) life.

We all use flowers, plants and other objects, most notably artworks, to create an environment for ourselves according to personal ideals – to attain a more liveable world. Hanging pictures on walls often follows the same basic principle as arranging objects on a table or flowers in a vase. The aim is a harmonious setting and a sense of comfort, which in turn are signs of taste and culture. Within pictorial compositions, bouquets and still-lifes may indicate the kind of environment being represented. They can also, and at the same time, be used to complement other elements in order to achieve an overall arrangement pleasing to the viewer. In *La Gare Saint-Lazare* (illus. 32), the composition as a whole unfolds along the diagonal from the flowers on Victorine's hat to the grapes in the lower right-hand corner. Those inanimate elements provide a framework evoking leisure and pleasure for the figures and their activity. In the *Masked Ball at the Opéra* (illus. 34), a bouquet occupies the composition's central point along with an orange. Alluding to artifice, they underscore the occasion as festive and contrived. In *Argenteuil* (Musée des Beaux-Arts, Tournai), virtually the brightest spot of colour is the bouquet in the woman's lap. In spite of their outdoor activity, her companion has presented her with something chosen and arranged, groomed just as she is – a gesture that also reminds us of the limitations on adventure imposed by a rented rowing-boat. *In the Conservatory* (illus. 33) shows a prosperous couple whose surroundings reveal the artificial cultivation of natural floral beauty. In the portrait of *Eva Gonzales* (National Gallery, London), made in 1869–70, Manet represented his friend at the easel engaged in painting a floral arrangement. One can hardly avoid the link it makes between female leisure and that particular branch of the art of painting. But it also appropriates Gonzales and her painting into his, Manet's, arrangement and therefore becomes a doubly self-reflexive expression of the creative process. In the portrait of *Berthe Morisot* (1872; private collection, Paris), the subject holds a bunch of violets, a motif whose associations are certainly personal, but, given Manet's other uses of such juxtapositions between figures and still-life, may continue to allude to artistic process. In Manet's *Autumn (Portrait of Méry Laurent)* (1881; Musée des Beaux-Arts, Nancy), the flowered background evokes wallpaper patterns, again a sign of cultivated comfort. Whether functioning as mere ornament or as obvious symbol, whether offered for praise or for consolation, the bouquet's touch of colour is always a sign of artistry. It represents the human and the humane, the ordering mind and the thoughtful gesture. As an embodiment of artistic practice, it expresses the cultured and the cultivated – a refinement of nature attained through and bearing witness to human intelligence and sensitivity.

Indeed, the world of Manet's later, 'Impressionist', paintings, is a world of domesticity and leisure, in which art is the ornament, the purpose and the expression. A painted map of

Manet's world includes places of public socialization familiar to the upper bourgeoisie: *Races at Longchamps* (Art Institute of Chicago), the *Universal Fairgrounds* (illus. 74), the *Opéra* (illus. 34), and cafés. Looking back on Manet's work of the early to mid-1860s, we can see the beginnings of this pattern in the *Concert in the Tuileries* and the *Déjeuner sur l'herbe*, even though in those paintings Manet's preoccupations were more overtly programmatic. Then, his environment was the world of museums and of contemporary poetry and literature, however abrasively reflected in the *Lola de Valence*, the *Olympia* and the *Dead Christ with Angels* (said to be inspired by the naturalist history of Christ, written by Ernest Renan). Later, it included vacation spots like the Normandy beaches and harbours, or farther afield, as in *Venice: The Grand Canal* (Shelburne Museum, Vermont). These are places chosen for personal pleasure that had become sufficient justification for their representation in art.

Manet's few street scenes were taken from close to home, practically from the window of his new studio. Although virtually archetypal for his Impressionist friends, Manet had not even tried street views until attracted by activities of unusual interest, as in *La Rue Mosnier with Pavers* (1878; Fitzwilliam Museum, Cambridge) or the Third Republic celebration of 13 June in the *Rue Mosnier with Flags* (illus. 75). In the

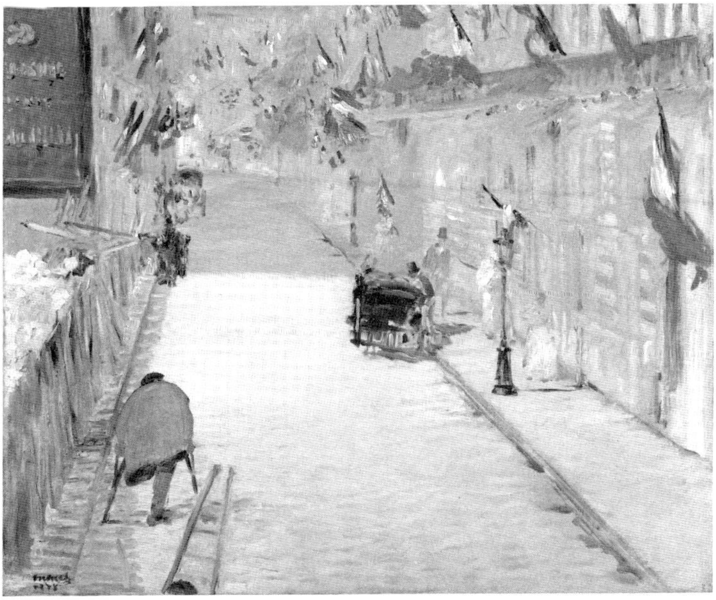

75 *Rue Mosnier with Flags*, 1878, oil on canvas. J. Paul Getty Museum, Malibu

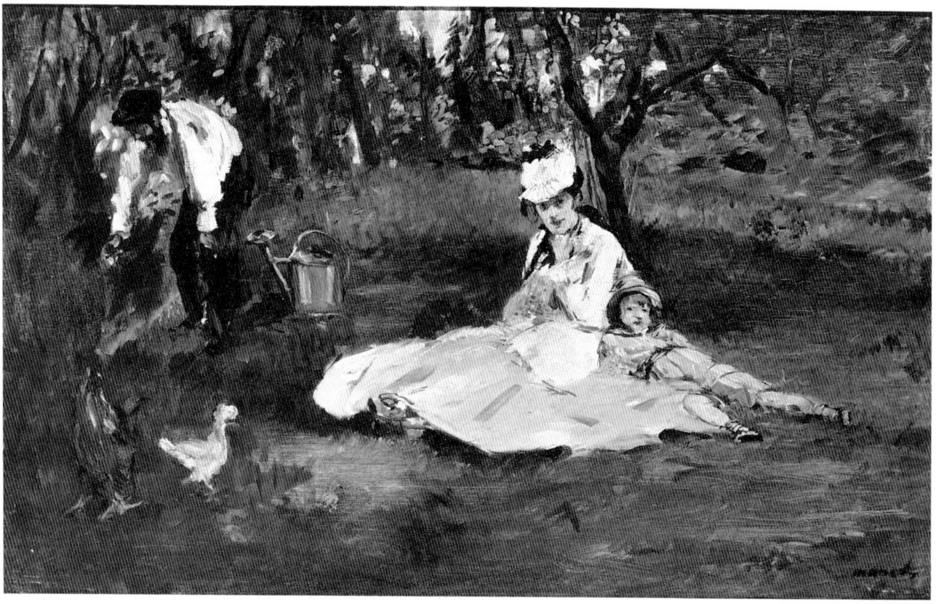
manet

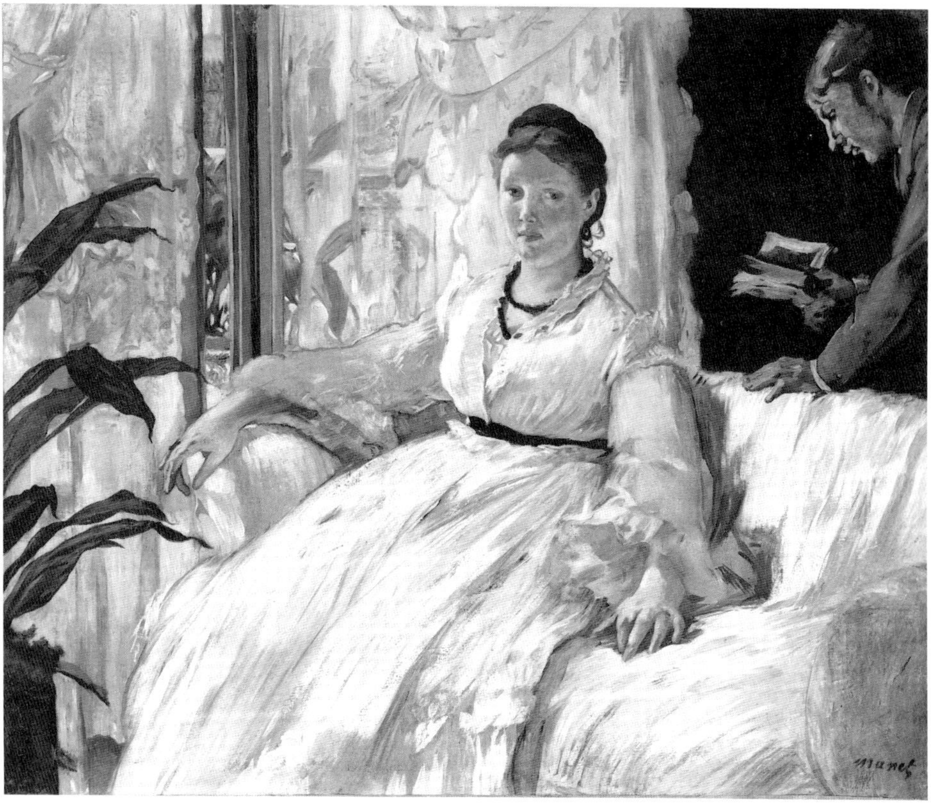
manet

76 *The Monet Family in the Garden*, 1874, oil on canvas. Metropolitan Museum of Art, New York

77 *Reading*, c. 1865–73, oil on canvas. Musée d'Orsay, Paris

former it is not the street itself, but its improvement into a paved thoroughfare – an aesthetic as well as a practical improvement – that incited his composition. In the latter it was the display of flags for a public holiday, in which the fête's political meaning, however Manet may have appreciated it privately, seems subordinated to the aesthetic spectacle it produced, and muted by the irony of the one-legged man in the foreground. Increasingly, Manet's world became that of private gardens (illus. 76), houses and interiors – a world chosen and arranged, a lived still-life, sometimes bouquet, for bourgeois pleasure. Music was an important presence, too, important enough for Manet to have depicted his wife at the piano (1867–8; Musée d'Orsay, Paris): she was a talented pianist who seems to have enjoyed performing for friends. Only on rare occasions did politics break in upon that domestic harmony, with the political works we have already discussed.

How could Mallarmé see the world expressing itself through a painting like *The Washing*? The answer is that Manet's image of femininity in suburban sunlight evoked the life Mallarmé had chosen for himself – a life that made his refined and contemplative poetry possible. It is a world to which artists like Monet and Renoir gladly withdrew after earlier 'bohemian' years of struggle (though it can hardly be called poverty). Perhaps we should not be surprised that one of Manet's most stylistically precocious pictures took as its subject his wife and son, lit only by a window in their living room (illus. 77). Within their relatively stable environments of marriage and child-rearing, in which social obligations and domestic concerns were satisfied, the painter and the poet quietly pursued personal artistic aims. Their 'revolution' – in the literal sense of 'turning' or 'returning' – was a turning away from public art, back on the self as the source not just of art but of faith in culture. It had its beginnings in Romanticism – hence Manet's links to Delacroix and his taste for Spain, Mallarmé's espousal of German Idealism, and the role of Baudelaire for both. But their radical assertion of personal freedom had its conservative side too, for their concentration of creative energy upon the language of the self, which is so often seen as laying the foundation for modernism and hailed as an expression of democratic individualism, also isolated the artist from history and public causes, and was firmly indebted to the bourgeois status quo.

What Mallarmé seems to have understood is that Manet and the Impressionists unapologetically centred their vision within the social conditions that made their careers as artists possible. Withdrawn from the traditional moral theme, the language of poetry and art had no more function other than to function. It sought objects for its own expression that are pretexts for that expression rather than metaphors of morality, unless morality is reduced to the impulse to seek harmony in an outside world perceived as generally unstable and inhospitable. For that reason their paintings take the subject-matter that is natural to their functioning, that is, the environment from which the possibility of art derives. In a series of fascinating essays Norman Bryson has suggested how still-life as a genre represents a generally overlooked domestic (in his terminology, 'feminized') space, which exists in opposition to the world of history and action – the masculine, or high art – and is subjected to its values.[135] For Manet, domestic space became the space of the natural; art became the affirmation of the familiar; for it was precisely because of the security inherent in the familiar that his art could be produced. As Manet's career progressed, history and action were increasingly subsumed within the scope of the ordinary. They consisted in the day-to-day process of living that Manet's painting both embodied (recorded) and performed. That is not to say Manet rejected the values of high art, but rather that he neutralized the powerfully ideological opposition between high and low genres (ideological in this case because it indicates status and worth) by vesting the values of the former in the most basic enactment of perception and representation. Pleasure itself, with no particular moral claim, could be accepted as the purpose of living and the subject of art. And pleasure could be found in the everyday enjoyment of life, towards which Manet's attitudes were quite conventional.

Indeed, during the last decade of his career Manet's roving gaze more and more frequently settled on non-controversial targets. Other than still-life, what more socially convenient and acceptable form of painting than portraiture was there, especially portraiture of women, when experimentation rather than formality was the aim? For it was still possible in the nineteenth century to regard women as aesthetic objects –

78 *George Moore*, 1879, pastel on canvas. Metropolitan Museum of Art, New York

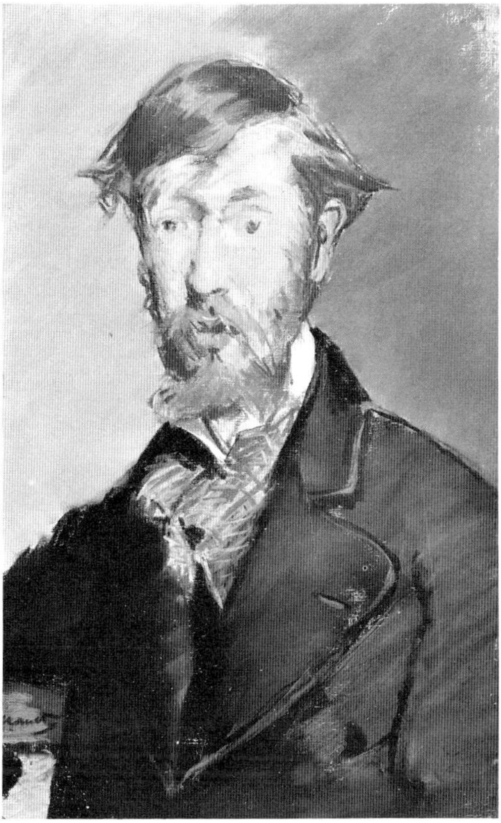

not necessarily vehicles for the erotic fondling of the brush, despite examples in Manet's painting such as *The Blonde with Bare Breasts* (Musée d'Orsay) – but as a traditional inspiration for artistic exploration. Indeed, during these years Manet's portraits of women were far less formal, less finished and more technically experimental than were those of men. It was as if the male does not pose casually, whereas the woman of leisure has the time.

Even most of Manet's male portraits are of artists, writers or men of culture, such as the painter Marcellin Desboutin, the actor Jean-Baptiste Faure or the Irish writer George Moore (illus. 78) – men with whom Manet shared flexible day-to-day schedules and the ideology of culture as the profession of the man of leisure. Posing for one another, socializing in cafés, attending the Opéra and listening to concerts were collective affirmations of the seriousness of leisure. Art that represented them and their places promoted social bonding that reinforced the sense of value in their own creative activities. Entertainment, however literary and cultivated, became the subject-matter of modern painting, replacing moralizing history painting, though counting on the traditions of the latter to proclaim the new worth of modern life. That is, the artistic representation of any theme could imply its dignity and stature. Painting gave Manet's private social practices a public justification and professional content.

Concurrently Manet located his artistic practice at the centre not of a professional world separate from the 'natural' world of social relations, but of that natural world itself. Manet's persona as artist and his social practice were mutually reinforcing. So, toward the end of his career, the still-life, usually fruits or flowers, became instruments in Manet's social relations. The objects themselves performed social acts. He used them as marks of homage or admiration – as offerings, like the bouquets they sometimes pictured. (Mallarmé frequently did the same with little poems.) They suggest a man of breeding and gentility, who can afford the generosity of time and effort to bestow a bouquet of visual poetry on a friend. The first of these gifts was the *Bunch of Violets with a Fan* (illus. 47), the exquisite little composition of 1872, signed and dedicated to Berthe Morisot. The combination of bouquet and fan alludes of course to Manet's earlier portraits of her. In those portraits, *The Balcony* and *Berthe Morisot with a Bunch of Violets*, they were more than props; they were important elements of an arrangement in which figures and objects were part of a larger compositional 'still-life'. And in contrast to the picturesque use Manet made of props, such as in the *Boy with a Sword*, these objects are clues to Morisot's taste and social status. In a sense, the picture of 1872 is his friend remembered by her attributes; it is the sign of his friend metonymically transformed into still-life – into art. Again, the objects embody the figure, the part refers to the whole.

In 1880 Manet sold his *Bunch of Asparagus* to Charles Ephrussi, who overpaid its price of 800 francs by two hundred more. In response, Manet sent the small *Asparagus* (illus. 79) with a note that played on the illusionistic function of art: 'Your bunch was one too short.' (The painting of an asparagus was a substitute for the asparagus itself.) Here, the slight, informal still-life became a gift conveying not just affection, but a sense of pride and fairness that prevented Manet from

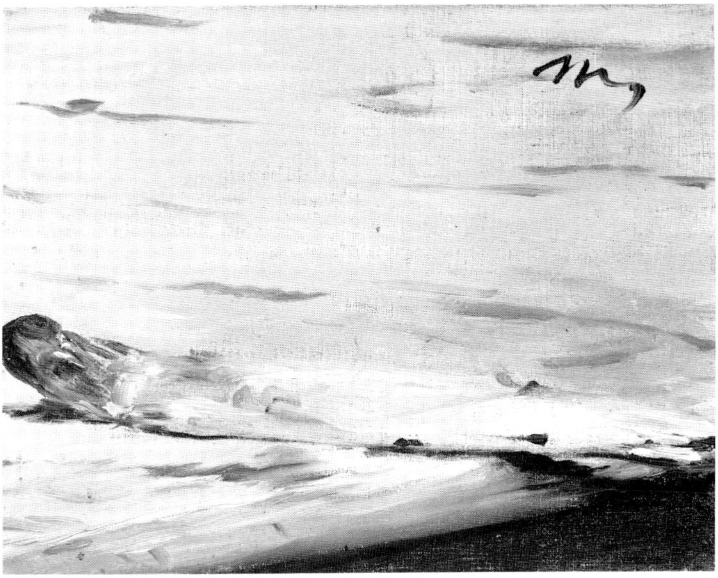

79 *Asparagus*, 1880, oil on canvas. Musée d'Orsay, Paris

accepting deliberate overpayment without some gesture in return. It deftly reaffirmed his status as artist, distinct from the artisan who merely fabricates commercial products, and that of an equal in the society of his patron. Along with the letter, it was a good-humoured gesture of control over his work that maintained its fiction as a vehicle of social rather than overtly economic transaction.

Two years later Manet dedicated a small picture of *Three Apples* to Méry Laurent. Like Morisot, Laurent was a close friend Manet frequently used as a model. Perhaps paintings such as this one and the *Bunch of Violets* can be related to the *Asparagus* as forms of compensation, in this case for the models' efforts. Following Manet's play on the illusionistic function of painting, painted apples or flowers are gallant little gifts, such as would have been the objects themselves, except they are here transformed into new objects of the sort these women had made it possible for Manet to create with themselves as his subject-matter (i.e. objects). Having in a sense possessed Morisot and Laurent through his painting, Manet returned to them something of that which they had given him. Such an offering may be an apology of sorts for the time and boredom of posing. But even while showing affection for women who, unlike Victorine, were not paid professionals, what Manet rendered to them was again an affirmation of the

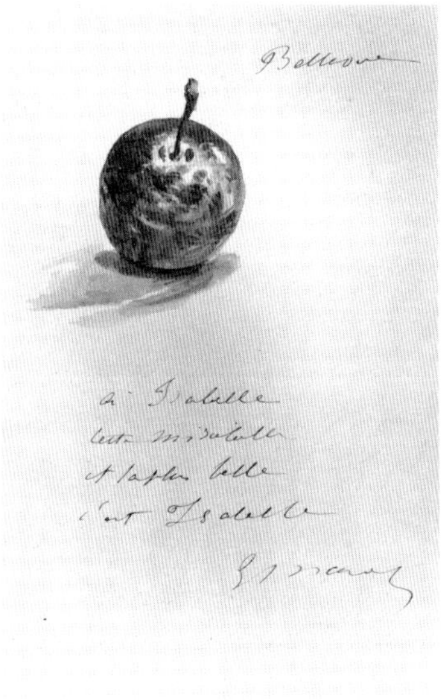

80 *Mirabelle*, 1880, watercolour with note. Musée du Louvre (Cabinet des Dessins), Paris

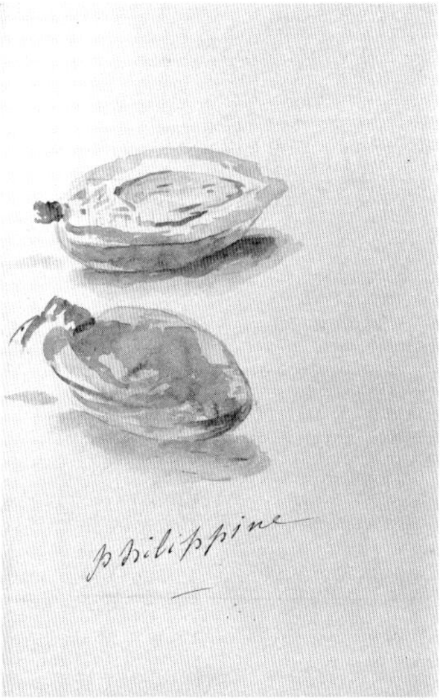

81 *Philippine*, 1880, watercolour. Musée du Louvre (Cabinet des Dessins), Paris

artist's transformative vision. As with the *Asparagus*, the still-life satisfied Manet's sense of fairness in a situation where not only could he not take something without offering a token in return, but where the final word in a visual statement reaffirmed that statement as an expression of his own artistic self.

In a series of letters sent to friends, Manet extended such gestures to the paper on which his notes were written. Using a watercolour of a fruit as a sort of letterhead or watermark, he alluded to a kind of equivalency between his own identity and the painting of a still-life. A series of such letters addressed to Isabelle Lemonnier clearly suggests the role of artistic self-image in a game of seduction. One, with a mirabelle plum (illus. 80), contains the following verses:

à Isabelle
cette mirabelle
et la plus belle
c'est Isabelle

In another, with a peach, he writes: 'Dear Mademoiselle, It is not my fault if the peaches are ugly at Bellecour, but the prettiest girl can only give what she has – Write to me of the events on the beach. . . .' Manet was ill during the summer of these and other notes in which he gently pleaded with Isabelle to keep him abreast of the social events he was missing. He hoped to entice her at least to answer, that he might continue to partake of (to possess a part of) the social scene. Another *billet*, with an almond and the word 'Philippine' (illus. 81), fits exactly into such a scheme. According to a French custom, the first to find a double fruit and call out 'Philippine!' could claim a present from the other. What gift could Manet have more desired than a reply from Isabelle – than a written representation, that is, of herself?

Like the offerings to other women, especially to Morisot, Manet's bright and clever works belong to a project of dissimulation. Here, of course, bouquets allude to favours done or hoped for; as I mentioned earlier, they speak of the unspeakable. Nowhere is their silent testimony more eloquent than in the increasingly frequent flower pieces Manet did at the end of his career. With his health deteriorating, he was confined to bed early in April 1883; he died on the last day of that month. In his final year or so, continuing right through those final weeks, he painted a number of small canvases (illus. 82) based on flowers that were often sent or brought to him by friends. Tokens of their feelings, these bouquets became the motivation for Manet's art now functioning on its most basic level. The artist's response to their gesture of caring was the act of painting – which used the flowers as its excuse, but which had always reinforced his social bonds. Here it

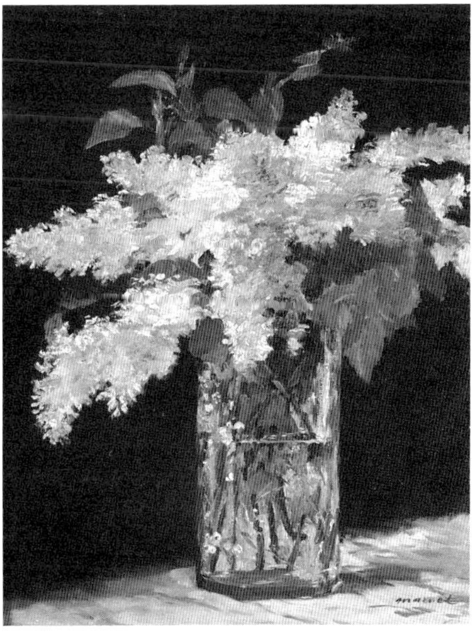

82 *White Lilacs*, 1883, oil on canvas. Nationalgalerie, Berlin

approaches an act of love returned. To paint these blossoms surely extended the pleasure Manet took in contemplating them and savouring their associations. Through such stand-ins, he could hold his friends close. What better offering to an artist than the object of beauty that epitomizes and gives rise to his art? What better way to cherish that offering than to immortalize it? Slight as they appear at first glance, then, these paintings summarize the links between Manet's art and his immediate world, the *sine qua non* of his art. Aesthetic performance was both the motivation and the product of that life, and these late bouquets go to the very heart of that symbiosis. Thus it is certainly appropriate to find front and centre in Manet's last major painting, the *Bar at the Folies-Bergère* (illus. 45), a flower arrangement much like those of his final years. It stands there like the signature of his debonair consciousness. Similarly, the delicate petals at the barmaid's bosom are like the signature of his poetics of bouquets.

None of these paintings bears the slightest visible hint of sadness or regret (illus. 49). Other than our own knowledge that blooms are destined to wilt, there is no overt link to the theme of vanity or the transitory. Their cheerfulness may imply Manet's disdain for conventional and laboured emotion; perhaps they testify to the importance of outward appearances – of persona and of spectacle – in his world. They are certainly far from a 'realistic' recognition of his failing strength; they are more a refuge from it. Their vibrancy celebrates the joy of colour and delicate form, the vitality and refinement of a life in art. On the verge of death, the artist creates what appears to be its opposite. Yet despite the brilliance of these works, the interdependence of opposites such as celebration/mourning, artifice/reality and figuration/defiguration that is ever present in bouquets is nowhere better embodied than through these late ones. For in their particular case, their affirmation of the material realm is also quite literally a dissimulation of its potential loss. They are like enactments – performances, rather than allegories – on the eternal theme of *vanitas*. Their very presence, in the context of the medical facts and social relations of Manet's final year, embodies the bittersweet poignance of mortality. When one plucks the flower, however exquisite the arrangement it engenders, there is no pretence that its beauty will last.

Most of us lead relatively separate social and professional

lives. In the nineteenth century the vast majority of artists outside the avant-garde still acted as if art were a career rather than a calling, although in opposition to official figures like Ingres there existed the highly personal alternative exemplified by Delacroix. Manet seems to have achieved a harmonious integration of the two extremes. Hardly the lofty academic or the romantic rebel, he made art a natural and a social activity rather than a marginal or commercial one. Manet's social origins and attitudes help explain this phenomenon. That a man of the upper bourgeoisie would make art his profession testifies of course to an important evolution. The Romantic notion of artistic genius and superiority was attracting practitioners whose ambitions had nothing to do with careerism and could be a vehicle (as was especially the case for Degas) for a certain social superiority based on 'vision', taste and intellect. Although Manet's persistent originality placed him outside the professional mainstream, his obvious identification with the Parisian world of the new intellectual and leisure class has in the end made him seem more mainstream than the so-called professionals of his day – the Gérômes and the Bouguereaus. Not only does Manet's art represent the world of his class – its places and its social practices – it is so infused by its pleasure-oriented values that its apparent radicalism of artistic language comfortably became its emblem. Manet's painting cultivates ordinary objects to the pleasure-seeking ends of the casual, yet discerning eye. Eschewing the expression of effort embodied by formal and finished work, it implies the warmth and affection of the *amateur*, a man of leisure, and the informality of the rapid sketcher and *flâneur*, rather than the laboriousness and moral ambition of the professional. The later, Impressionist paintings were not conceived as museum paintings; they evoke not the public dialogue of the Salon but the privacy of domestic surroundings. Even in his more formal and programmatic works, Manet's attitude is to appropriate the world to his personal aesthetic rather than to adjust his art to the profession. Thus, Manet's way of seeing, increasingly rooted in his private life, *is* his world; and for his art to express the world through his way of seeing is to express the position of his eye within it – diffident, of course, but embedded (immersed) at its very centre.

5 The Death of Realism

'Illusions', Baudelaire quoted Manet as having said, 'are as innumerable, perhaps, as the relations of men to each other and of men and things. And when the illusion disappears, when, that is, we see persons or things as they really are, detached from ourselves, we have a strange, complex feeling, half regret for the vanished phantom, half agreeable surprise at the appearance of this novel, of this real thing.' While Manet indicates that every being or thing appears to us through our own projection, that is, informed with our own preconceptions, he accepts the possibility, though rare, that reality can make itself directly known. The occasion for Baudelaire's account was the story, in the prose poem 'The Rope' (1864), of the suicide of Manet's young model, who hanged himself in the studio while Manet was out. Manet had posed the lad with all sorts of props – angel's wings, a vagrant's violin, a crown of thorns and the torch of Eros. But after the boy's death, it was the rope with which he had hung himself that became his attribute, or at least this is suggested by the clamour his neighbours made to be given a piece of it. The boy's mother eventually got the treasure, apparently – as Manet suddenly realized – in order to sell it. So much (this was the point of the poem) for the illusion of motherly love! (Here, again, Baudelaire allows Manet to appear slightly naïve.)[136]

The contradiction in this story may be illuminating for our purposes. Its harsh view of human nature suggests that truth lies in dispelling illusions, even though doing so may leave us bereft. Yet it also claims that we live our lives within illusions, that it is human nature to do so. We invest the world with meanings derived from our own needs and subjectivity, and that process is so fundamental that we feel abandoned when those illusions are unexpectedly withdrawn. Manet's own painting, particularly the early work, operates systematically to dispel illusions, even at the risk of social unpleasantness. Yet, as Manet's art develops, it more and more selfconsciously accepts that even an ostensibly 'objective' (i.e., demythifying) form of seeing is still itself part of illusion; the subjective element to vision will always be inherent in it. If art is no more than the process of transcription without the object, that is, deprived of equivalency to reality not only by its materiality and technique but by the nature of vision itself, then its approximations and tentative recreations of experience can be viewed autonomously. The growing acceptance of such a concept of art finds its expression, for example, in comparisons between visual signs and music as well as in the paradigm of the bouquet. For it certainly makes more sense to arrange the elements of art according to undeniable desires, however subjective, than to strive in frustration toward the unattainable goal of realism. When the artist-framer discovers that reality is a chimera, his practice becomes a charade. His consolation is to become a shaper, even if he serves only himself.

BEYOND COURBET AND DELACROIX

This development in Manet's art is evoked by Manet's relationship to his predecessors and his followers. Fantin-Latour's group portraits constitute but one kind of commentary on artistic relationships and art-historical positioning. There is the evidence of art itself. The style Fernand Desnoyers described as half-way between Romanticism and Realism required a resistance to Courbet manifested by a renewal of ties to Delacroix. For Manet, there is relatively little proof of direct response to Courbet, though we did see how the latter's *Desmoiselles des bords de la Seine* could have generically inspired the *Déjeuner sur l'herbe*. Even so, the basic premise of painting modern life owed a great deal to the man from Ornans; and according to Manet's friend Antonin Proust, Manet said Courbet had got it right except that he used too much black.

Perhaps Courbet was too partisan and too ostensibly plebian for Manet to flaunt connections openly; certainly the kind of contemporary subject-matter Manet chose reflected both his very different social position and a far less political notion of the avant-garde, a concept that was not of particular concern to him. Yet despite these differences, both artists shared an underlying acceptance of the interdependence of facture and visuality, of making and seeing. Indeed, the association between art and manual activity was a prominent theme in Courbet's *Studio of the Painter*, which had been the centrepiece of the notorious Realism exhibition he opened across from the Universal Exposition of 1855. This complex painting was intended to summarize Courbet's career and theories, the latter much indebted to Courbet's friend Pierre-Joseph Proudhon. At the time, Proudhon was for many the most compelling Hegelian in France. His interpretation of Hegel as grounding humanity in materiality – recall the Hegelian source of Mallarmé's later concept of 'immersion' – led him to view labour as the defining characteristic of man. Courbet certainly drew on Proudhon's idea that the perfection of labour found in art was the supreme expression of human virtue. So in the *Studio of the Painter* Courbet showed himself in the actual process of art-making – painting a landscape – hence physically engaged with the world while placing himself at its centre. (He claimed to pass all the world through his studio.)[137]

Indeed, much of Courbet's work is involved with the materiality of both human existence and our natural surroundings, which he insisted on representing through his own perceptions – hence his constant focus on himself. Through Proudhon's Hegelianism he saw the process of representing those perceptions as a high and philosophical form of labour – and art a meta-enterprise – that embodied the essence of humanity. Manet's response to Courbet, or at least his position in relation to him on these issues, may be understood through the way the gaze merges with the hand to both define and produce the world at the centre of which (rather than panoptically external to which) the individual stands. Manet's art focuses on the visual as the plane of the activity Courbet took to be one of labouring. It may be worth recalling that Manet's reviewers, Zola in particular, said that Manet saw the world in terms of spots. The French word for spot, *tache*, is related to the word for touch (*touche*); and a related word, *tâche*, means task or work. Manet's 'labour' (to think of it in Courbet's terms) – his physical and optical engagement – is psychological and phenomenological. Of course flower arranging is a physical dialogue with nature of a different order from Courbet's artisanal labour: it is less plebian and less polemical, more private and more domestic. Indeed, sometimes the poetics of bouquets aestheticizes the overt political and social messages that often inform Courbet's version of the avant-garde. And we ourselves, often ravished by the seductions of painterliness, associate this art with leisure and harmony rather than with conflict and concern. (Incidentally, Courbet did some sumptious flower pieces in the early 1860s). Yet there can be no doubt that both artists shared a belief in the validity of their own performances as bases for art, and in the appropriateness of the artifices of handling to convey them.

Although Delacroix precedes Courbet in standard narratives of art history, it must be recalled that he was still alive and a potent force throughout Manet's early years. Odd as it may seem, Manet's response to Courbet may have been to approach the principles of materiality, individualism and modernity that Courbet so loudly trumpeted through the more diffident and aestheticized vision of the older man. For in ways that Manet could easily appreciate, Delacroix shared those principles as well. Of course, a certain artistic sympathy between Manet and Delacroix can easily be explained through Baudelaire, whose writings on Delacroix, as we saw, cast him in precisely the terms that Manet would find relevant. But there are also specific links between Delacroix and Manet that reveal the younger artist's intense curiosity and respect. During the mid-1850s, Manet made two copies of Delacroix's *Dante and Virgil*. Proust confirms the painter's admiration and tells of a visit to Delacroix's studio to ask permission to copy the work, then in the Luxembourg Museum. Conversation apparently centred on the older artist's admiration for Rubens. We know from Manet's *Landscape with Fishermen*, a painting bearing some stylistic affinities to the copies of the *Dante and Virgil*, that in at least one case Manet looked closely at Rubens too. Though Manet claimed a distaste for Delacroix's *métier* (perhaps it was still too smooth for him), he never forgot that Delacroix had supported his submissions to the Salon. And even though he soon moved in other directions, these early lessons were assimilated; they provided the first elements of Manet's original stylistic character.[138]

For example, Delacroix's use of a contrasting stroke to tighten forms that had first been created freely out of colour anticipated Manet's method of using shadow or other natural effects to suggest contour, as in the *Olympia* or *The Fifer Boy*. (It would also lead to Cézanne.) This technique was a conscious departure from tradition on Delacroix's part. In fact, in his project for a dictionary of art (of around the time he met

Manet), he wrote: '*Contour*: Must come last, contrary to custom. Only someone very practiced can get it right.'[139] Yet here was the kind of handling that made critics angry over Manet's 'dirtying' of his colours by using what looked like 'shoe polish', thus spoiling illusionism. In spite of a related technique, therefore, Manet drew attention to his unique artistic persona more confrontationally than had Delacroix, for the latter's indexing of artistic presence was mediated by the imaginative connotations of his literary and picturesque themes, whereas Manet's figures claimed reality.

There are episodes in Delacroix's career when, momentarily free of literary preoccupations, his work acquired a character prophetically close to that of his later admirers. It is no accident that one of the great still-lifes of the nineteenth century is Delacroix's *Still-life with Lobster* (illus. 83), a work that looks backward to Baroque colour and exuberance and forward to pure painting, a work that epitomizes Joshua Reynolds's term 'bouquet of colour'. And while sitting out the Revolution of 1848 on the family property at Champrosay, Delacroix painted some magnificent flower pieces that suggest a bridge between the Rococo Revival and Impressionist colourism. Several flower still-lifes were shown in sales and exhibitions held in 1864, the year following Delacroix's death. Their influence is certainly felt in Degas's famous *Woman with Chrysanthemums* of 1865 (Metropolitan Museum of Art, New York), and it is entirely fitting that such a novel expression of calculated composition-making harbours a backward glance to Delacroix. It confirms what Delacroix's later admirers perceived, namely that his heroic and literary gestures were an overlay on a system of the poetic uses of form for self-expression. It is worth noting that even Delacroix's *Sardanapalus*, as it now hangs in the Louvre and must have in the studio, confronts us at eye-level with an extraordinary still-life of oriental paraphernalia, vigorously impastoed and impetuously brushed (illus. 84). If we are to believe Baudelaire's contention that one should stand far enough back from a picture to appreciate its rhythms and harmonies rather than its narrative, then the abstract qualities of such a still-life convey the essence of *Sardanapalus* without the necessity of narrative. We saw a similar metonymic parallel between still-life and figure composition in the painting of Manet, beginning with the *Guitar Player* and the *Déjeuner sur l'herbe*.

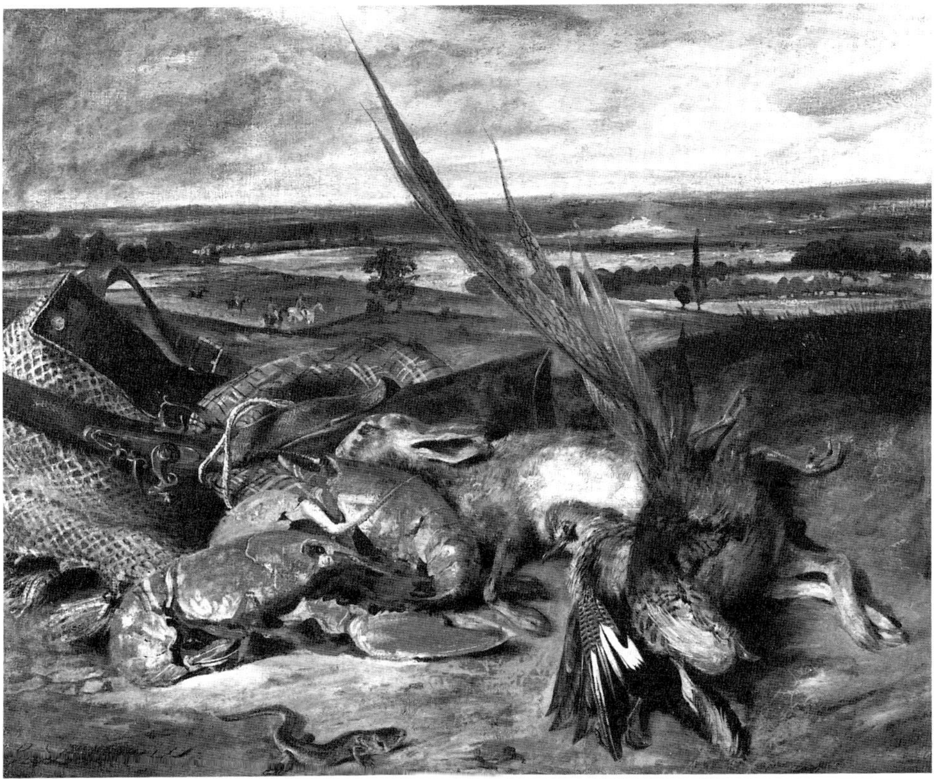

83 Eugène Delacroix, *Still-life with Lobster*, 1827, oil on canvas. Musée du Louvre, Paris

84 Detail of the foreground still-life in Delacroix's *Death of Sardanapalus*, 1827, oil on canvas. Musée du Louvre, Paris

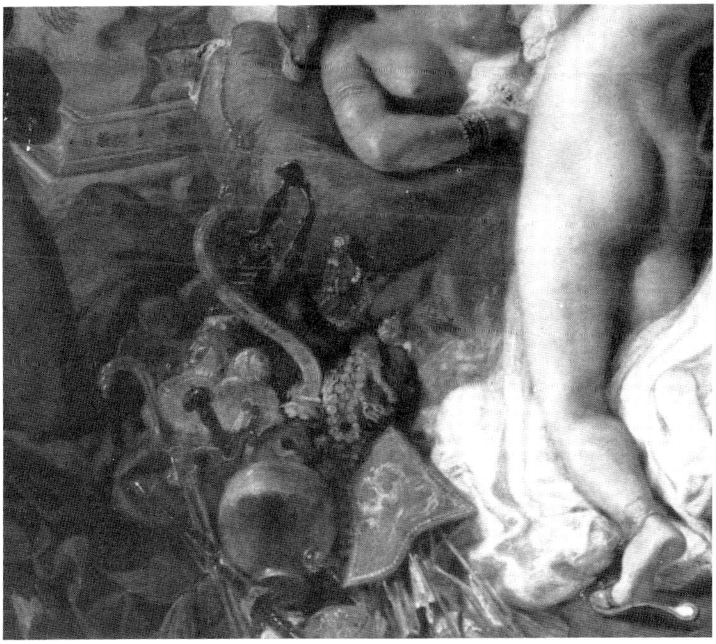

Perhaps the *Sardanapalus* was for Delacroix what the *Bar at the Folies-Bergère* became for Manet.

So Manet's position may not be so much between Romanticism and Realism, as we heard Fernand Desnoyers say, as it is beyond them. For it is neither a compromise nor a transition but rather a response to the truths of each. It is a 'Post-Realism' – an aftermath, dependent on what went before yet a critique of it, as in Post-Impressionism and Postmodernism. Recalling Courbet's absence from Fantin-Latour's group portrait, we might propose that painters like Manet were looking beyond what was called, however unjustly, the 'unpoetic' art of Realism. For Realism seemed the death of an art whose essence was still defined as subjective and imaginative by powerful voices, including Realist theorists themselves. If Realism was that, then one could certainly look at Delacroix, particularly the less literature-bound Delacroix of the art of still-life, for its antidote.

BOUQUETS AND THE HAND

In the close-knit group of younger Realists and early Impressionists, recognition of influence, dialogue or exchange generally took less literal forms than group portraiture. Just as Manet's perspective on Delacroix casts light on his own position, younger artists' engagement with Manet illuminate it from another angle. There is no need to rehearse the familiar story of the development of early Impressionism, in which Manet's presence and style played such an important role. Rather, it may be useful to focus on the interface of two themes to which I have attributed special significance: bouquets and the hand. I have argued that Manet's art operates through performative, that is, through physical activity that seizes us directly through form and structure rather than mediating content through narrative or narratives in disguise. Its poetics of bouquets embodies and affirms a fundamental shift from the paradigm of the artist as framer and describer to that of the artist as shaper and performer. In the responses of Manet's followers to his achievement, we can focus on the increasingly visible motif of the hand. For it is the hand that transforms the referent to sign and imprints the artwork with the marks of the artist's performance, as it represents forms in ways that more and more readily reveal its role in creating them. How did Manet's contemporaries and followers link the making of bouquets to their shapings by the hand?

We have already seen in Manet's portraits of his writer friends, Astruc, Zola and Mallarmé, how representations of the hand contain particular allusions not only to the writer's own character but to the artist's self-conception. In each painting Manet's playful focus on the hand reminded us of its importance as the physical translator of ideas and vision. In the *Olympia* the hand played the double role of hiding the woman's prostituted genitals while at the same time focusing attention on the very thing it hid. Thinking of her as an artist's *alter ego*, we can see the hand as the instrument for the artist's own introduction of ambiguity and duplicity. In certain other instances, as in the *Déjeuner* or the *Fifer Boy*, hands are strikingly outlined in black or grey. They are indices of the painter's seemingly brutal manual intervention; they produce the kind of effect that challenged convention, calling forth complaints of Manet's technical inexperience. Sometimes hands are used to point, as in the *Philibert Rouvière*, where they lead to signs of the painter himself. In *The Balcony*, by contrast, the hands of Fanny Claus are produced so loosely, without particular outline, that they recall handling in flowers like those in the *Peonies*. Gestural brushstrokes, dissimulating a barmaid's cleavage or drawing a dead toreador's blood, reaffirm the visual hand's controlling presence at points of supreme poignance.

Manet's fascination for the representation, positioning and signature of hands may have been shared by his friend Degas. The latter's portrait of *The Duke and Duchess of Morbilli* (illus. 85) – the painter's sister and her first-cousin husband – of about the same time as Manet's *Zacharie Astruc* (illus. 15), exhibits a preoccupation both with the placement of hands in the composition and for the pictorial handling that produces them. Of course, the picture contains many passages of deliberate, yet loose and unresolved areas; attention is easily dispersed over its surface from one autonomous element to the other. But more perhaps than any other feature of this double portrait, the hands call attention to the artist's presence, bearing as they do the highly visible marks of the painter's brush. The most prominent are the Duke's, the right hand dangling relaxedly over the back of the chair, the left hand over the table-edge in the most immediate foreground

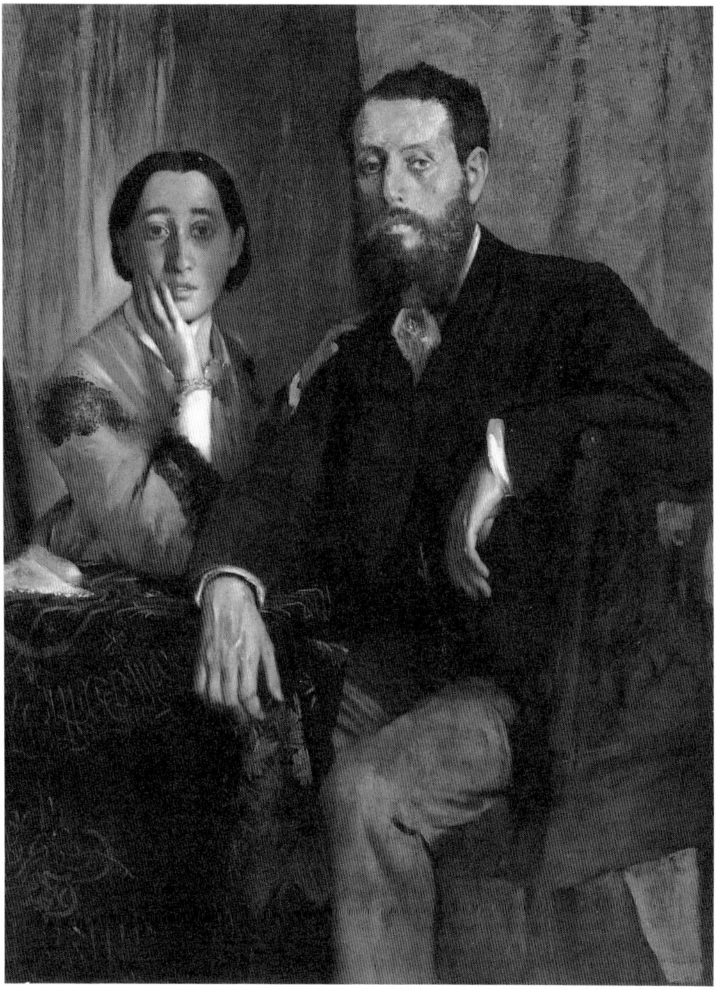

85 Edgar Degas, *The Duke and Duchess of Morbilli*, c. 1865, oil on canvas. Museum of Fine Arts, Boston

and seen against the calligraphically traced patterns of the tablecloth. Signs of the Duke's own sense of ease and composure, they suggest similar attitudes on the part of the artist who has understood the Duke and is capable of staging his appearance. The Duchess's hands, especially her right one, with its little finger moving furtively across the lips, express her nervousness about being seen. It is no surprise that Degas seized the chance to assert control at that very spot, with brushstrokes that are broad and unmodelled, while confident and definitive. The Duchess's fear of acquiescing to another's vision was well-founded, for by producing her and leaving his imprint on her, Degas seems to have wrested away her sense of privacy and self-determination. Neither her hands nor her husband's shoulders can protect her against the probing of the artist's manually wrought gaze.

A very different case is Claude Monet, who was among those Fantin-Latour showed in Manet's atelier. Monet's *Women in the Garden* (illus. 86) of 1866–7 was of course a considered response to Manet, in particular to the *Déjeuner sur l'herbe*. Having painted on the beaches, Monet was already committed to *plein-air* when he arrived in Paris from Le Havre in the early 1860s. Seeing the *Déjeuner* at the Salon des Refusés, he could easily tell that despite the park-like setting it was a studio concoction. Yet as affected by Manet as the *Women in the Garden* would be in composition and facture, Monet insisted on painting his large canvas out of doors. In order to do that with the same kind of freedom he enjoyed

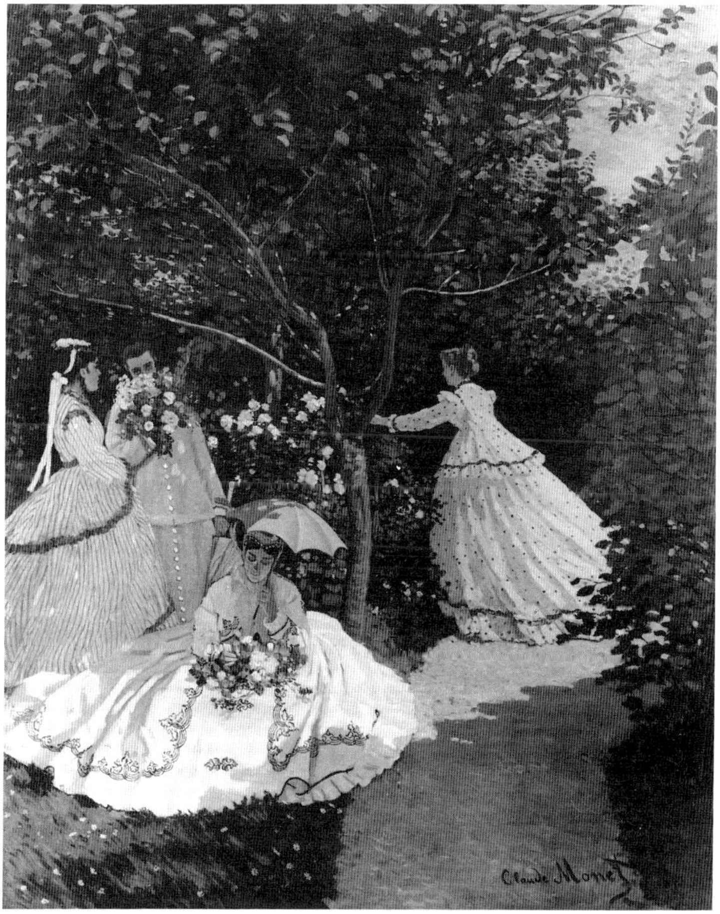

86 Claude Monet, *Women in the Garden*, 1866–7, oil on canvas. Musée d'Orsay, Paris

when painting smaller, easel works, and to allow himself easy reach to the top of the canvas, he dug a trench to set it in, and raised and lowered it with a rope and pulley. He had to reshape nature in order to paint according to nature. Several of Monet's figures, all posed by his mistress Camille, hold bouquets, which through their colours become focal points of the composition. In this, they may allude directly to *Olympia*, but they are also suitable props for a garden scene. Both they and the dug trench embody Monet's artistic conceptions. For although based on nature to the extent of posing the model in natural light and setting up outside, the painting was rigorously planned and patterned. Its combination of overlapping and linked figures with differently designed dresses based on fashion plates, and its contrasts of light and shadow, are as much an arrangement of nature as are the bouquets within the picture, and as bouquets themselves are of flowers. Indeed, the art of Monet epitomizes the poetics of bouquets – nature arranged by the pleasure-seeking eye as a garden for both aesthetic enjoyment and immersion. In the 1860s Monet had done a number of flower still-lifes. But when he settled in Giverny, in 1891, he made his entire surroundings into a flower arrangement; he spent the rest of his life as the physical shaper of an environmental bouquet. The shimmering surface of his many *Waterlilies* determines a self-contained world occupying the entire field of vision; the flowers floating on it become the marks of a lifetime of seeing. Underlying this vision is Monet's transformation of his garden, and the creation of a lily pond by damming up a little stream. His works done at Giverny thus exemplify the extent to which, though derived from nature, the bouquet embodies cultivated surroundings shaped physically to the artist's taste. It may at first seem far-fetched to take the planting and digging Monet did in his garden to be a concrete manifestation of the relationship between the hand and eye in art. But we must remember that the art of flower arrangement physically involves the activity of the hand – cutting stems and placing specimens – as do the arts of painting and gardening.

Van Gogh admired the 'firm impasto' of Manet's *Peonies*.[140] Even more to the point are his own deliberate, sometimes mortar-like or building-block brushstrokes, which often serve as the field for representations of flowers. Van Gogh's sympathies with a pre-modern civilization rooted in rural

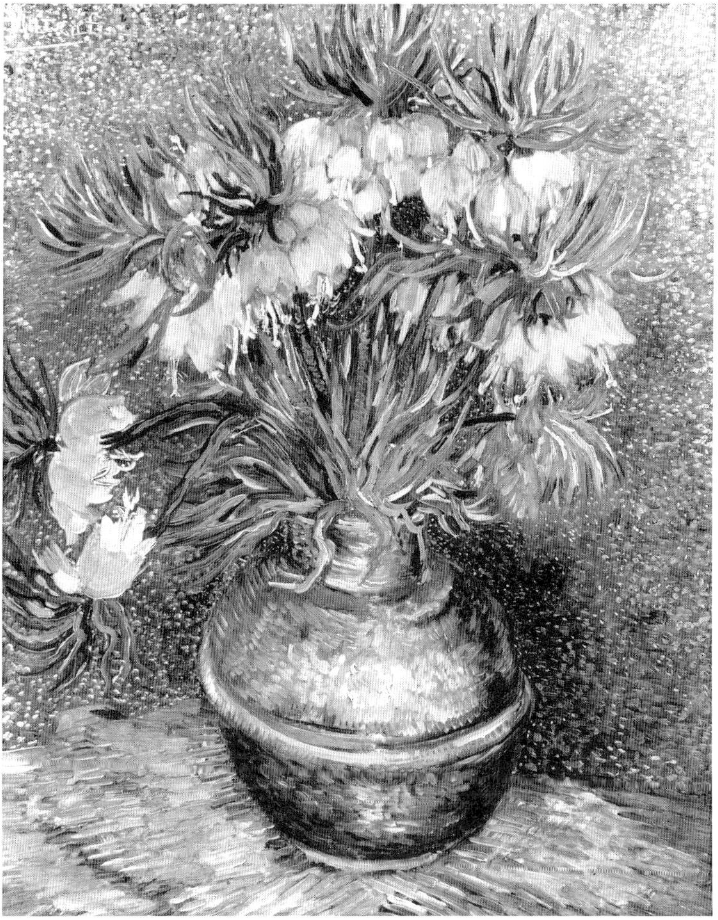

87 Vincent van Gogh, *Fritillaries in a Copper Vase*, 1887, oil on canvas. Musée d'Orsay, Paris

labour and handcraft (in this he was close to Courbet) led him to admire weavers as prototypes for the artist creating two-dimensional, designed surfaces. In emphasizing an absolute identity between the object and its means of representation – as between woven images and coloured thread, or flower petals and strokes of paint – he embedded representation in the process of its production. In *Fritillaries in a Copper Vase* (illus. 87), done in Paris in April or May 1887, the flowers' extraordinary botanical forms are conflated with brush-strokes, which assimilate them to pictorial gestures. And for all their symbolic associations, van Gogh's painted *Sunflowers* insist no less upon their crafting by the artist's hand. Touch signifies manual effort. As in Manet, although even more selfconsciously, the hand embodies artistic thought and crea-

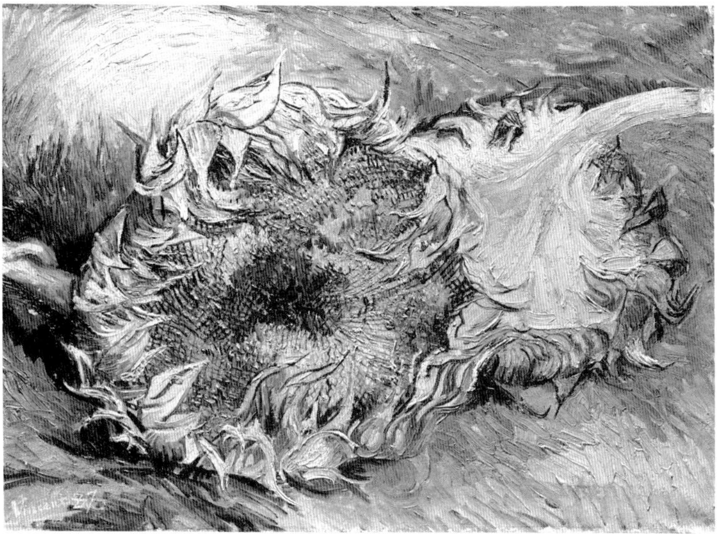

88 Vincent van Gogh, *Sunflowers*, 1887, oil on canvas. Metropolitan Museum of Art, New York

tive will. Flowers in van Gogh's *œuvre* are a particularly powerful metaphor for the artistic enterprise – indeed, the six sunflower compositions of January 1889 were to decorate his own studio, like talismans for his inspiration. Associated with the flowering of thought and so with the process of artistic perception that would give rise to the hand-produced object (a process van Gogh compared to giving birth), the twisted, turning forms of the sunflowers are especially appropriate for the artist's theme. Embodying as they do his creative process, they are symbols of the self, which is still located within the organic and physical process of representation and identified with the material of the painter's craft. The 'life' they derive from the sun, whose trajectory the sunflower follows (in French, *tournesol* means 'turn-to-the-sun'), suggests the symbiosis of light and artist's vision and the material sustenance the artist derives from nature while acting on it in his primal manner. His representation of the sunflowers as beings in motion compares physical creativity to nature's mysterious life forces. Indeed, in an earlier study (illus. 88), a sunflower looks uncannily like an eye; in a letter, van Gogh referred to his sunflowers as his children.

The knarled hands of those in van Gogh's *Potato Eaters* and *La Berceuse* (illus. 89) speak of ethos and morality as well as of social class and physical occupation. They allude to the manual labour the painter called 'honest', and which his own

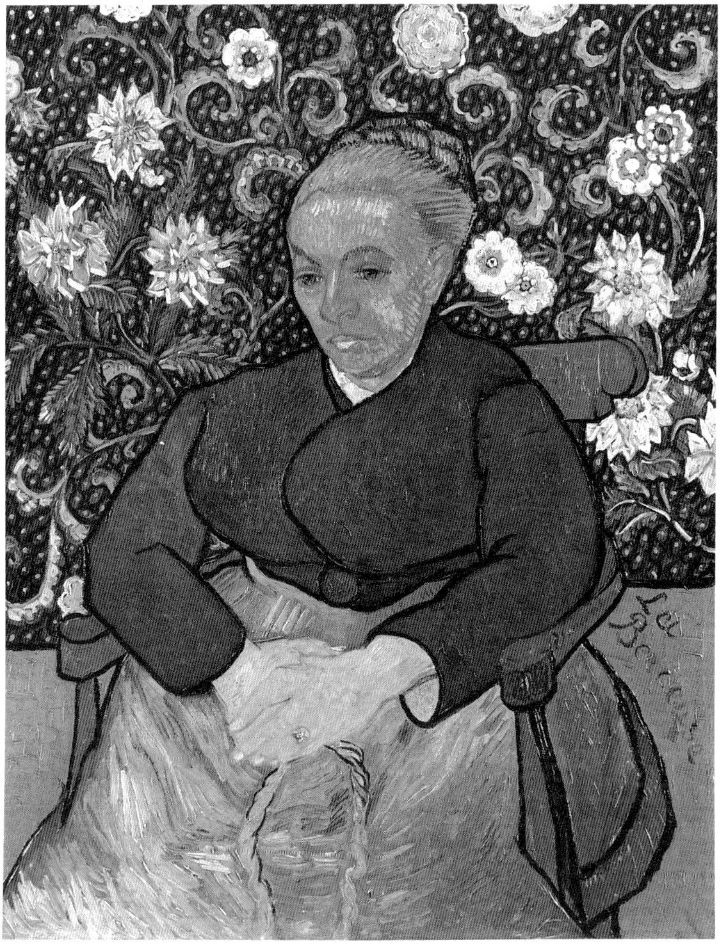

89 Vincent van Gogh, *La Berceuse (Augustine Rollin)*, 1889, oil on canvas. Rijksmuseum Kröller-Müller, Otterlo

work emulated through its heavily worked surfaces and vigorously handled pigments. Among the labourers and artisans van Gogh exalted, weavers held a special place, because of the parallel between painting and weaving as crafted planar products with coloured patterns. Van Gogh often tried to make his painted surfaces emulate 'rough cloth' and juxtaposed threads, as he wrote in a famous description of the *Potato Eaters*.[141] In *La Berceuse* the wallpaper is another patterned article, this one with floral motifs that testify that the social utility of visual artisanry is the creation of harmonious surroundings. Wallpaper thus has a bouquet-like function, yet its flatness and abstractness express more explicitly than bouquets their origins in the aesthetic impulse and their status as crafted form.

For Gauguin, by contrast, and sometimes closer to Manet, the hand was often the device for insertion of the artist's selfconscious visual wit. In his portrait of Meyer de Haan (illus. 90), the poet's hand holds a snake which forms the 'G' of the artist's signature, and in his *Self-portrait with Halo* the artist's own hand holds the snake. Though his self-conception is different from van Gogh's – more that of aesthetic conjurer than artisan – Gauguin clearly accepted the motif of the hand as an emblem for artistic input and a vehicle for expressing its character. He also used flowers to allude to artistic creativity, but, taking the craftedness of art for granted, he stressed its origins in the creative mind. Flowers are part of the wallpaper pattern that serves as background for the *Self-portrait (Les Misérables)* sent to van Gogh in 1888, where the less heavily worked surface makes them appear to float as figments of the artist's imaginative power. Gauguin often juxtaposed flower arrangements to other objects or to pictures as suggestions of the relationship between art and nature. The *Still-life with Mug* of 1889 is especially revealing. A ceramic mug Gauguin had made in the shape of a self-portrait is used as a planter from which flowers sprout. It faces an exuberant and brilliantly coloured bouquet that contrasts sharply to its own virtually monochromatic and mysterious seedlings – their 'nocturnal' quality no doubt alluding to Gauguin's insistence on dreaming before nature. Both bouquet and 'mental' flowers overlap with a Japanese print on the wall. Hence the bold and arbitrary manipulations found in Japanese printmaking provide the conceptual common denominator for both terms of a comparison between flower arrangement and imaginative flowering. (Gauguin may have had *ikebana*, the Japanese art of flower arranging, in mind.) In his portrait of *Van Gogh Painting Sunflowers* (illus. 91), Gauguin brings flowers and the hand together. At first glance the painting seems to concentrate on van Gogh's mental processes, for Gauguin shows the artist with an almost somnolent expression, leaning back with his arm outstretched. Yet Gauguin also alludes to van Gogh's respect for handwork, for there is a deliberate confusion between the observed flowers and those on van Gogh's canvas. Does van Gogh's brush trace a painting, or the real flowers? Which is the greater reality, nature or the creation, the perception or the sign?

Cézanne's first reaction to Manet was petulant. The portrait

90 Paul Gauguin, *Meyer de Haan (Nirvana)*, c. 1890, oil and turpentine on silk. The Wadsworth Atheneum, Hartford, CT

91 Paul Gauguin, *Vincent van Gogh Painting Sunflowers*, 1888, oil on canvas. Vincent van Gogh Foundation/Van Gogh Museum, Amsterdam

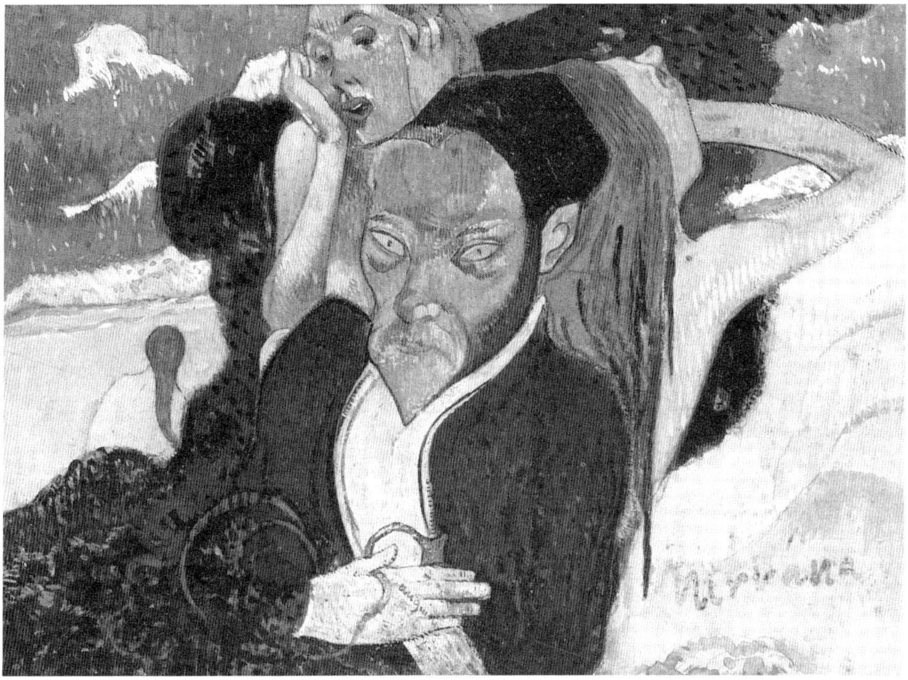

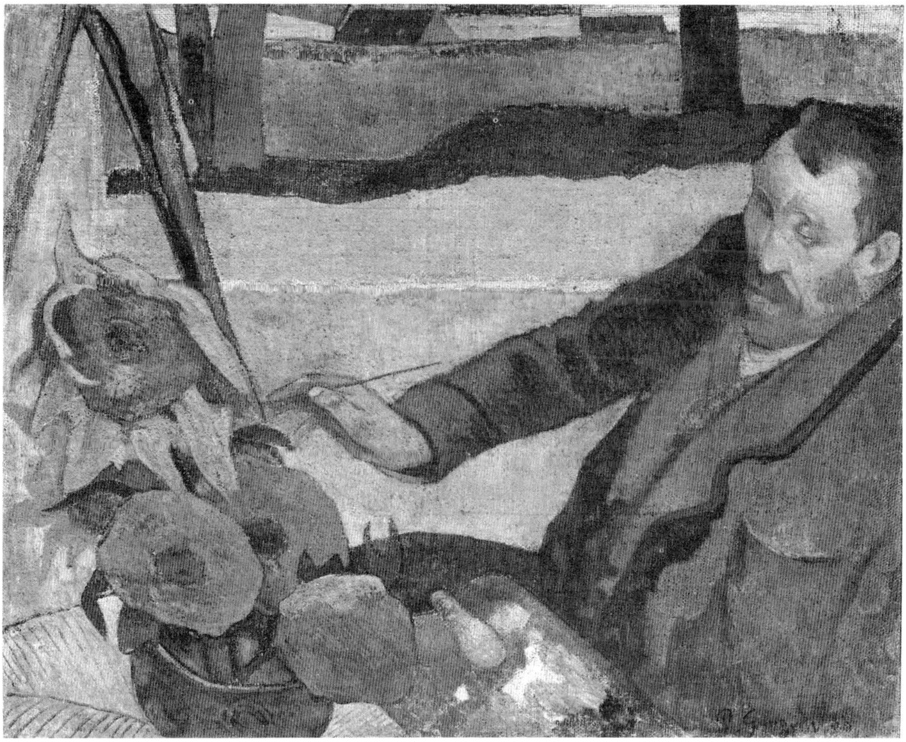

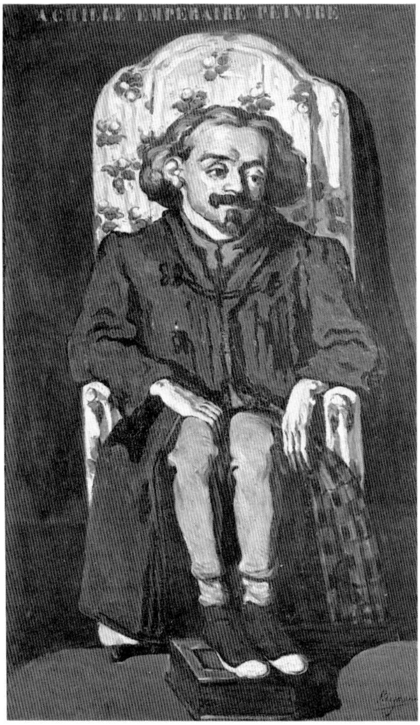

92 Paul Cézanne, *Achille Emperaire*, c. 1868, oil on canvas. Musée d'Orsay, Paris

of *Achille Emperaire* (illus. 92), while profoundly derivative, none the less destructively resisted Manet by its workmanlike handling and the inelegance of its frontally presented and disproportionate figure. The stencil-like lettering of Emperaire's name at the top of the canvas seems an ostentatious expression of Cézanne's anti-fashionable hand. At this time, distance from, yet knowledge of, Manet must have been important to Cézanne's conception of his own position, which he articulated by differentiating the character of his handwork from that of his predecessor. In subsequent years Cézanne's commentaries on Manet would be more direct. In the earlier of his two versions of the theme of the *Déjeuner sur l'herbe*, he placed a spectator (a self-portrait) in the centre of the composition, giving a literal rendering to the exchanges of gaze Manet had created between figures and viewers. The picnickers seemed to contemplate two fruits placed on their blanket, which, by their relationship to Cézanne's hand and body, alludes as much to a still-life that he, as artist, might have arranged on a table as to a naturalistic spread that he, as a member of the party, might have prepared. Although

Cézanne's ostensible stylistic awkwardness again renders his tone ironic, he has clearly understood Manet's theme of painting as bouquet/still-life/picnic for aesthetic delectation.

Cézanne's position as viewer/creator of Manet's painting is similar in his *A Modern Olympia* (illus. 93), where he took up Manet's implications even more programmatically. Seated opposite a dramatically revealed and brightly lit nude, as both artist and client (or keeper) of the courtesan, the self-portrait may allude to appropriation of nature for subjective needs. Cézanne seems like the stage-director of a theatrical tableau. To one side is a table arranged with objects as in a still-life; to the other is a large flower arrangement on a high pedestal. Both still-life and flowers are part of the darkened foreground, which the figure also inhabits. Looking out at them from the centre is a cat. No doubt Cézanne's diagonal composition contradicts and parodies the *Olympia*'s frontal and planar aesthetic of display. But his use of juxtapositions, however shifted from the original, is of the same order as his predecessor's. The comparison between still-life and flower arrangement, and their location in the same realm (or space) as the artist and his perceptions (and the cat), is a literal assemblage and parody of the various motifs we found central to Manet's concerns. While the flowering of plants on one

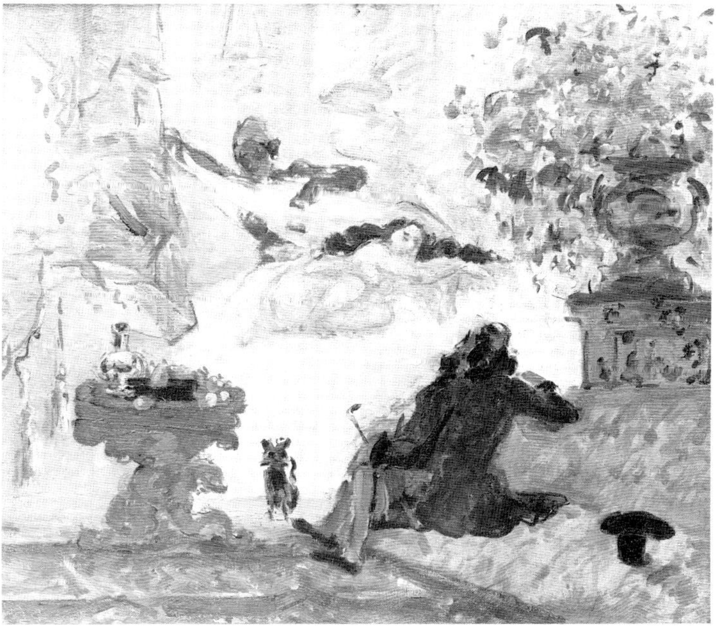

93 Paul Cézanne, *A Modern Olympia*, 1872–3, oil on canvas. Musée d'Orsay, Paris

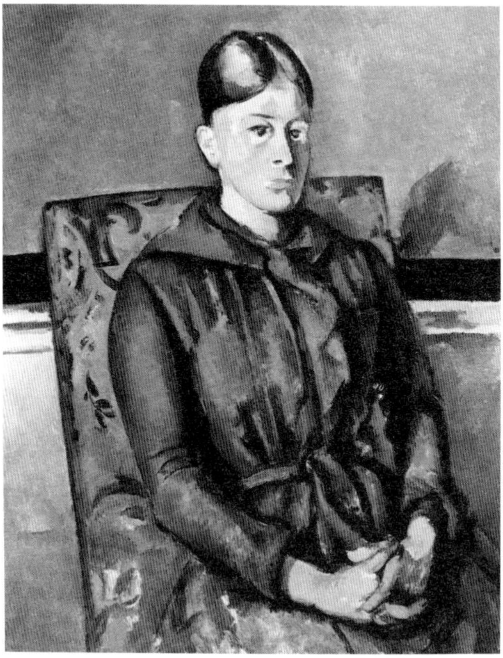

94 Paul Cézanne, *Mme Cézanne in a Yellow Armchair*, c. 1890, oil on canvas. Private collection

level only suggests the client's erotic response to the vision of the nude, it is a suggestion seconded by the phallic form of the walking-stick/paintbrush he (as artist) is gripping in his hand. Cézanne's critique of artistic figuration in what might be called creative self-arousal is unmistakable.

Perhaps Cézanne was seeking a less self-indulgent version of Manet's seminal insights. For him, the natural extension of the eye that senses form, and of the consciousness that arranges it, is the hand that builds form sculpturally. There are numerous paintings in which Cézanne has given particular presence to the hands of figures, from an early version of his Uncle Dominique (called *The Lawyer*) to his portrait of *Madame Cézanne* of about 1890 (illus. 94). In the latter, his wife's hands are both flattened like a map projection and yet seem roughly modelled, as in clay – the analytic and the manual combined. Here, Cézanne's commitment to the tectonic reflects both a more intellectual and a more traditional version of van Gogh's conflation of the effort of labour with artistic thought and creative will. Cézanne is often cited as having said 'I want to make of Impressionism something solid, like the art of the museum'. That is, while respecting Impressionist principles of direct surface observation and of painting from colour, he insisted that his art go beyond the flatness (and decorativeness) he saw as so often the Impressionist result. After all, our experience of being physically in the world teaches us to interpret information from our vision in three-dimensional terms. Here Cézanne was rendering a concept of vision that had been dominant since Descartes and Berkeley. A reconstitution on modern grounds of traditional values would both preserve them and produce a more lasting art. Substituting protracted viewing for the spontaneity of the moment, and using closely related, usually earth-tones rather than contrasting colours, were two means of coercing Impressionist technique to those aims. It is as if Cézanne wanted to reconsolidate the fragmentation through which Impressionism hedonistically celebrated atomistic matter into a more dignified reflection of human aspiration, and it was as if doing so would require leaving traces of the diligent efforts of the hand. Nowhere is Cézanne's gaze more intense than in portraits, such as the *Man with Straw Hat* of *c.* 1870 or a *Self-portrait* of *c.* 1877. In such works, a touch that is reminiscent of Manet for its thickness and viscosity enlivens form with the sense that the eye itself, as an instrument of reason, has had a hand in its building – a 'manual' eye. That is, Cézanne's brushstroke now contains more than merely the sensuous experience of immersion. Without falling prey to classical conventions, it has acquired the ability to express the distancing, rational gaze as well. It accepts the site of representation as the flat canvas, yet it explores the reality effects of everyday perception.

The analytical consciousness we sense in Cézanne's portraits becomes the constructive faculty underlying his still-lifes. Although in *A Modern Olympia* Cézanne had used a floral arrangement for its association with creativity, flowers were tangential to his more austere ethos. His still-lifes tend to concentrate on simply shaped and relatively ordinary objects, though often set in complex, sometimes positively Baroque arrangements; and he deliberately, almost didactically, mixes the natural and the man-made. He took fruits, kitchen articles, furniture, wallpaper and other forms for a fascinating counterpoint of relationships that use sensations of three-dimensionality as their springboard. Compared to such works, flower pieces offered a limited range. His treatment of landscape, which assumed the dominant role in his work as he entered the 1880s, is informed by similar experience. The rough earth, its rock formations, dense stands of trees as well as houses, roads and open fields are the elements in arrangements that metaphorize creativity. It was as if, for him, the expression through painterly touch of the self in seeing became the enactment of nature's own physical formation – one in which human perception is immanent. His handling of pigment acts directly on the viewer to perform rather than describe (following the literary paradigm) the relationship between human consciousness and natural existence. Thought is nature's thought, expressed in art through traces of the hand as an instrument of the eye. In revealing the constructedness of his pictorial composition, Cézanne manually articulates the mental construct of nature's vision within his mind's eye. As in Monet, but through force of intellect rather than gardening tools, nature is the primal still-life. All pictorial representations of nature reveal the fabricating role of human consciousness through manipulation by the visual hand: landscape becomes bouquet.

THE PARADOX OF REALISM

Did realism ever truly exist in art? It was a central concept in the nineteenth century, yet its selfconsciousness always rendered impossible the enterprise it advocated. The theoretical possibility of realist art as objective description of the external world always underlay Western painting. The humanistic theory of art, which claimed the greater moral worth of idealization – of representation of what the world ought to be rather than what it is – none the less took for granted the possibility of representing the world as it is. The prescriptive took the descriptive as its condition, for it presupposed omniscient vision as a certainty. It seems that almost everyone but the Realists themselves, who defended Realism on the basis of human subjectivity, believed there could be realism in art. Such believers conflated two realisms – the nineteenth-century artistic movement designated by the capital 'R'; and the effect of objectivity produced by certain styles, designated by the small 'r' and disparaged by Baudelaire as positivism. The suppression of the signs of seeing that the nineteenth century generally admired in Dutch and Spanish art (though so often exposed and problematized, hence undermined, by the greatest hands – Rembrandt, Hals, Vermeer or Velázquez), was the most important model for the contemporary understanding (or wilful misunderstanding) of Realism. Western art, as sweepingly theorized by Marin and Foucault, seemed to create a universal vantage point, endowing the gaze with sovereignty over matter. The world could seem to represent itself without physical intervention; for the artist/viewer, the mere act of perception appeared to call forth the world.

However, at the same time in the nineteenth century, the subject's relationship to the external world became less certain. Theories of vision, such as in Schopenhauer and Helmholtz, referred to perception as hallucination and to reality as sign – thus questioning 'objective' physiological vision in favour of a more 'subjective' and organic psychological formulation. This new condition provided the context for a paradigm shift. As a selfconscious concept, realism lost its universal status as the condition of representation to become its mere aim or effect. Realism became a prescriptive theory, and as such no more than one of several possibilities. The active dialogue between self and world suppressed by the kind of naturalist description the nineteenth century seems to have believed could be reached, emerged precisely at this point in the art the nineteenth century actually produced. Indeed, in the painting of the most acclaimed Realist, Courbet – the man absent from Fantin-Latour's group of Realists – the perceiving subject reappeared as explicitly expressed presence, as the central figure in his *Studio of the Painter*. For the sake of authenticity, Courbet had to place himself within the world he represented. It might be argued that in taking possession of the world as external to the self through naturalist description, Western vision had to give up its sense of being in the world. This alienation lay behind the growing need to reaffirm that presence constantly. By creating the sensation of human absence – of the objectivity (unsubjectivity) of perception – Western naturalism laid the ground for its own denial *The Studio of the Painter* reaffirmed the artist's presence among peers and his physical dialogue with the stuff of nature.

That move has its equivalent in the creation of the self (as consciousness) as artistic object to which we found Mallarmé alluding. For he advocated Impressionist immersion as an antidote to Realism, hence as a reassertion of being in the world. In accepting its materiality, the self, once in the world, could be the object of reconstruction and manipulation. Realism, not so much as in the art of Courbet but as conceptualized in the practice of Western art, particularly in the nineteenth century, was a distancing strategy, which suppressed the essential concreteness of both artistic perception and practice. Manet and Impressionism, to the contrary, relocated the artist's creativity within the physical and expressed a process rooted in human activities, which are characterized in modern society by both labour and its converse, leisure – and which in the case of the modern artist became the same. Impressionism consisted, Mallarmé might have argued, not in possessing the world by deploying quasi-scientific techniques that subordinate nature through representation, but in a more intuitive process, through which the artist draws manual gestures from himself that testify to empathy with and immersion in the world. Representation is more like a conscious daydream than a certainty. Manet's explicit expression of the world as sign and the Impressionist fragmentation of its conventional coherence constituted the necessary destruction of traditional Western distance; they offer a celebration of worldly matter by transforming seeing into a quasi-physical/tactile spectacle. The *touche* or *tache* performs just such a celebration in offering itself for the viewer's delectation. Manet's counterpart to Courbet's *Studio of the Painter*, then, is his *Claude Monet in the Boat Studio* of 1874 (illus. 50). Almost literally immersed in the middle of his world (Monet is floating), and accompanied not by representatives of political society but by his wife, Camille, Monet exemplifies the painter, like Manet, for whom art is a natural function, centered in leisure and at home in the context of personal relations.

Serious painting generally embodies our relation to the world. It is sometimes said, and Manet's activity might provide the evidence, that the modern artist enacts our society's aspirations to human freedom. We grant the artist more leeway to express himself than we grant to ordinary citizens, because we need to believe in the possibility that human potential can be completely fulfilled within our social system. Where the illusionistic devices of pre-modern Western naturalism seem passively to embody the faith that human dominance over the world of matter can be taken for granted, modernist painting, which is constantly expressing originality and innovation as an active battle with tradition, glorifies the concrete activity of human existence as if its meaning lay in that valiant encounter. Recognizing our human materiality and mere organicity is a discovery that might result in loss of self esteem and confidence. However, the artist is able to recover from that loss by making the manual traces of his performance in the world the sign of an ability (however vicarious) to fragment and reconstitute reality through imagination – an effort paralleling what Baudelaire called the heroism of modern life and, as we know, originally formulated as the so-called Romantic quest. As self and world, spiritual and material, and poetry and commodity become merged, we attach increasing importance to the signs of artistic exertion, as if they are redemptive. The sense of exclusion from power, so commonly associated with ennui, is compensated by the illusion of artistic freedom and the encouragement to defy tradition.

Manet's brushstrokes run against the grain of the professional, academic work ethic signified by smooth and careful finish. They connote a practice, though physical, that appears free from the bonds of such traditional labour and linked, rather, to the casual and the experimental. Indeed, Manet's blatant display of manual physicality implies a renewal of contact with the material continuum (necessitated by accepting the human condition as materially grounded), and yet assures us of our power to mould, change and even to destroy it from a position at its centre. You can have your cake, and eat it too. The primacy in modern painting of our focus on the artist as agent/performer, rather than on reality as dominant and fixed, is therefore ideological. It confirms our sense of purpose in the world. When art could call forth a beholder empowered by the simple act of gazing on an unproblematic reality, the question of sovereignty was moot.

But in the modern world of uncertain identities, contested power and spiritual isolation, we are consoled by the activities of those whose boldness and originality give them the appearance of control, or at least imply its possibility. Art that selfconsciously departs from realism, particularly with styles or strategies that flaunt the creative/destructive or recreative effort – such as Cubism, Dada, Abstract Expressionism and, most recently, Performance Art (of Joseph Beuys, say) – effects an exhilarating substitution of the signs of art for the empirical data of existence. The immersion in the physical implied by Manet's particular style gives his artistic performance the dimensions of real life. Manet's gestures, both the bold and the slight, conflate the moves of art with the operations of social intercourse. Their simultaneous embrace of the world and acting out of artistic freedom from it provide a dialectical model for the conditions by which our own existence appears determined within the social formation. The shift from the descriptive/narrative to the performative/transformative embodies the ideological change from pre-modern representations of self and world as separate and static into a living paradigm, in which their merger, though grounding us in matter, is acclaimed as the condition for fulfilment of human possibility. No longer the omniscient framer of a static and available world, the artist responded to his subjugation by nature in becoming a shaper and producer, interacting organically and physically with nature, and proudly leaving the artistic marks of his handwork behind.

The performative will always precede, underlie and inhere in the normative, hence in constative language (following Austin's terminology), which expresses the status quo. Yet all paradigm shifts in culture are embodied in performative uses of language in which performativity becomes overt and transformative. If perception was a major issue in the second half of the nineteenth century, it is because representation was being redefined, as we saw, in terms of signs and sign manipulation. Such a semiotic conception, despite defences of Impressionism based on claims of its truth to perception, liberated artists from their obligation to description, enabling them to practice *poesis* more as what might be called *semiosis* rather than *mimesis*. Even though they still viewed perception as the root of art, artists endowed it with 'meaning' (now understood as the expression of their individuality) by playing on the opacity of the material sign. Thus, the theory that artistic practice consists of deploying and manipulating a culturally determined vocabulary of signs would be incomplete if it overshadowed the power of certain individuals to invent, to shock and to renew. Artists such as Manet, though circumscribed by the 'prison-house of language', which they cannot found anew, may none the less be capable of intervening within the field of signs to produce new associations, to bring new combinations into prominence, or to found new positions or sites. Of course, any such discoveries will have been latent in contemporary society and ideology, but the artist may bring them forward and make them visible by challenging convention. An artist may discover compelling new uses of language that act powerfully enough on the viewer to contribute to changes in public consciousness, and to establish the validity for the culture as a whole, meanings the artist was the first to perceive and then make into culture's new conventions. Even if we were to grant completely the theoretical possibility that our (and his) conceptions are formed from a pre-existing field of signs – so that Manet could not have acted without the assumption that his acts had some kind of meaning – we still need to understand how representations shape us. Located in the realm of culture, the effect of art is always social.[142]

Featuring the self as performer in artworks that are themselves performative leads, then, to two ostensibly opposed interpretations. The first focuses on the artist as agent and implies his personal freedom and power; the second emphasizes primarily the artwork and sees it functioning more independently of the artist, implicitly denying individual agency in favour of cultural determination. But rather than seeing this circularity as an irresolvable dilemma bound to frustrate and divide art history, we may recognize it as an expression of the complexity of human existence. It is well known that accepting the paradoxes and conflicts within our own consciousness can become a key to personal understanding and enrichment. Similarly, our acceptance of aporia as a poetic element of art can lead to the enrichment of art history. For while art history is constantly seeking the meaning of art, it is itself structured by its presuppositions and its verbal medium. Adopting the historical form of discourse, it operates through a grammar and a syntax that predetermine the nature of the meanings it discovers as conforming more or less to their internal logic. So a further lesson of Post structuralism may be that, just as we cannot construct the artwork as an entity from which the artist is innocently external or which has a neutral effect on the viewer, neither is the art historian's representation an impartial one. Posing as an objective science, art history, and its position of omniscience, has served ultimately to empower its own practitioners and their ideology. A more inclusive art history would recognize the singularity and historicity of its point of view, while accepting the contradictions within artworks and the ambivalences of artists as essential to its core.

The satisfaction we derive from Impressionist paintings is often like a reaffirmation bestowed on us by a loved one; yet at other times we may find our doubts reflected in that loved one's eyes. The lover offers us a bouquet; but it may wither, as may first love. Manet's paintings perform with similar complexity. Like magic mirrors, more than just reflecting, they both generate within us the disquiet of self-knowledge and project on us the confidence of heroism. In that paradox of silently exchanged gazes lies the secret of their spell-binding allure. It is often said that the artists of the nineteenth century were forerunners of modern art, from Cubism and collage to the automatist gestures of Surrealism, and finally to post-World War II abstraction and beyond. But in Impressionism and Post-Impressionism the 'visual' hand was discovered through the 'handling' eye (and vice versa) – that is, through acknowledging the materiality of human perception. Expressing both its contingency and its aspirations toward autonomy, Impressionist style was grounded in human representational processes, and, as such, in experiences of a reality whose accessibility through perception still seems to endow the world with objective status. This continuing link to naturalism, which Manet both affirmed and challenged, was at the heart of both the difficulty and the eventual appeal of his painting and that which followed. The fundamental dialectic such art performs, despite its ostensible *naïveté*, gives it an uplifting, even quasi-metaphysical dimension that sustained its rapid emergence as the leading trend in avant-garde culture. The tension between objective and subjective knowledge is so central to human existence, that once the public became accustomed to its novel forms it would discover in them a profoundly humanistic sympathy. This felicitous combination of the philosophical and the everyday continues to make Impressionism the most popular movement in Western art, and Edouard Manet, as its most visible founder, its most acclaimed and studied champion.

Appendix: Two Texts by Stéphane Mallarmé

L'Après-midi d'un faune

Églogue

LE FAUNE

Ces nymphes, je les veux perpétuer.
                                        Si clair,
Leur incarnat léger, qu'il voltige dans l'air
Assoupi de sommeils touffus.

                                        Aimai-je un rêve?
Mon doute, amas de nuit ancienne, s'achève
En maint rameau subtil, qui, demeuré les vrais
Bois mêmes, prouve, hélas! que bien seul je m'offrais
Pour triomphe la faute idéale de roses –
Réfléchissons . . .

                        ou si les femmes dont tu gloses
Figurent un souhait de tes sens fabuleux!
Faune, l'illusion s'échappe des yeux bleus
Et froids, comme une source en pleurs, de la plus chaste:
Mais, l'autre tout soupirs, dis-tu qu'elle contraste
Comme brise du jour chaude dans ta toison?
Que non! par l'immobile et lasse pâmoison
Suffoquant de chaleurs le matin frais s'il lutte,
Ne murmure point d'eau que ne verse ma flûte
Au bosquet arrosé d'accords; et le seul vent
Hors des deux tuyaux prompt à s'exhaler avant
Qu'il disperse le son dans une pluie aride,
C'est, à l'horizon pas remué d'une ride,
Le visible et serein souffle artificiel
De l'inspiration, qui regagne le ciel.

Ô bords siciliens d'un calme marécage
Qu'à l'envi de soleils ma vanité saccage,
Tacite sous les fleurs d'étincelles, CONTEZ
'Que je coupais ici les creux roseaux domptés
Par le talent; quand, sur l'or glauque de lointaines
Verdures dédiant leur vigne à des fontaines,
Ondoie une blancheur animale au repos:
Et qu'au prélude lent où naissent les pipeaux
Ce vol de cygnes, non! de naïades se sauve
Ou plonge . . .'

Inerte, tout brûle dans l'heure fauve
Sans marquer par quel art ensemble détala
Trop d'hymen souhaité de qui cherche le *la*:
Alors m'éveillerai-je à la ferveur première,
Droit et seul, sous un flot antique de lumière,
Lys! et l'un de vous tous pour l'ingénuité.

Autre que ce doux rien par leur lèvre ébruité,
Le baiser, qui tout bas des perfides assure,
Mon sein, vierge de preuve, atteste une morsure
Mystérieuse, due à quelque auguste dent;
Mais, bast! arcane tel élut pour confident
Le jonc vaste et jumeau dont sous l'azur on joue:
Qui, détournant à soi le trouble de la joue,
Rêve, dans un solo long, que nous amusions
La beauté d'alentour par des confusions
Fausses entre elle-même et notre chant crédule;
Et de faire aussi haut que l'amour se module
Évanouir du songe ordinaire de dos
Ou de flanc pur suivis avec mes regards clos,
Une sonore, vaine et monotone ligne.

Tâche donc, instrument des fuites, ô maligne
Syrinx, de refleurir aux lacs où tu m'attends!
Moi, de ma rumeur fier, je vais parler longtemps
Des déesses; et par d'idolâtres peintures,
A leur ombre enlever encore des ceintures:
Ainsi, quand des raisins j'ai sucé la clarté,
Pour bannir un regret par ma feinte écarté,
Rieur, j'élève au ciel d'été la grappe vide
Et, soufflant dans ses peaux lumineuses, avide
D'ivresse, jusqu'au soir je regarde au travers.

Ô nymphes, regonflons des SOUVENIRS divers.
'Mon œil, trouant les joncs, dardait chaque encolure
Immortelle, qui noie en l'onde sa brûlure
Avec un cri de rage au ciel de la forêt;
Et le splendide bain de cheveux disparaît
Dans les clartés et les frissons, ô pierreries!
J'accours; quand, à mes pieds, s'entrejoignent (meurtries
De la langueur goûtée à ce mal d'être deux)
Des dormeuses parmi leurs seuls bras hasardeux;
Je les ravis, sans les désenlacer, et vole
À ce massif, haï par l'ombrage frivole,
De roses tarissant tout parfum au soleil,
Où notre ébat au jour consumé soit pareil.'
Je t'adore, courroux des vierges, ô délice
Farouche du sacré fardeau nu qui se glisse
Pour fuir ma lèvre en feu buvant, comme un éclair

Tressaille! la frayeur secrète de la chair:
Des pieds de l'inhumaine au cœur de la timide
Que délaisse à la fois une innocence, humide
De larmes folles ou de moins tristes vapeurs.
'Mon crime, c'est d'avoir, gai de vaincre ces peurs
Traîtresses, divisé la touffle échevelée
De baisers que les dieux gardaient si bien mêlée:
Car, à peine j'allais cacher un rire ardent
Sous les replis heureux d'une seule (gardant
Par un doigt simple, afin que sa candeur de plume
Se teignît à l'émoi de sa sœur qui s'allume,
La petite, naïve et ne rougissant pas:)
Que de mes bras, défaits par de vagues trépas,
Cette proie, à jamais ingrate se délivre
Sans pitié du sanglot dont j'étais encore ivre.'

Tant pis! vers le bonheur d'autres m'entraîneront
Par leur tresse nouée aux cornes de mon front:
Tu sais, ma passion, que, pourpre et déjà mûre,
Chaque grenade éclate et d'abeilles murmure;
Et notre sang, épris de qui le va saisir,
Coule pour tout l'essaim éternel du désir.
À l'heure où ce bois d'or et de cendres se teinte
Une fête s'exalte en la feuillée éteinte:
Etna! c'est parmi toi visité de Vénus
Sur ta lave posant ses talons ingénus,
Quand tonne un somme triste ou s'épuise la flamme.
Je tiens la reine!

Ô sûr châtiment . . .

Non, mais l'âme
De paroles vacante et ce corps alourdi
Tard succombent au fier silence de midi:
Sans plus il faut dormir en l'oubli du blasphème,
Sur le sable altéré gisant et comme j'aime
Ouvrir ma bouche à l'astre efficace des vins!

Couple, adieu; je vais voir l'ombre que tu devins.

(1876)

The Afternoon of a Faun

Eclogue

THE FAUN

These nymphs, I want to perpetuate them,
So clear,
Their lightness incarnadine, that it lilts in the air
Drowsy with tufted slumbers.

Did I love a dream?
My doubt, heap of ancient night, culminates
In many a subtle branch, which, remained the true
Woods themselves proves, alas! that quite alone I offered myself
The ideal fault of roses as triumph.
Let us reflect . . .

or if the women you are glossing
Figure a desire of your fabulous senses!
Faun, the illusion breaks free of the eyes blue
And cold, like a spring in tears, of the most chaste:
But, the other, all sighs, do you say she contrasts
Like a hot day's breeze upon your fleece?
But no! by the still and torpid rapture
Suffocating in warmth the cool morning if it struggles,
Murmurs no stream but that poured by my flute
Into the grove sprinkled by chords; and the sole wind
Out of two stems ready to exhale before
Dispersing the sound in an arid rain,
Is, at the horizon unstirred by a wrinkle,
The visible and serene artificial breath
Of inspiration, which returns to heaven.

O Sicilian banks of the calm pool
Which at the yearning of suns my vanity plunders,
Tacit under flowers sparkle, TELL
'That I cut here these tamed and hollow reeds
By talent; when, on the glaucous gold of far-away
Verdure dedicating their vines to fountains,
Ripples an animal whiteness at rest:
And that at the slow prelude where the reeds are born
This flight of swans, no! of naïads flees
Or plunges . . .'

Inert, everything burns in the tawny hour
Without marking by what art together ran off
Too much hymen desired by the one who seeks the *la*:
So I will be awakened by the initial ardour,
Upright and alone, under an ancient flood of light,
Lily! and one of you all for ingenuousness.

Other than the sweet nothing sounded by their lip
The kiss, which quietly the perfidious ones assure,
My breast, virgin of proof, attests to being
Mysteriously bitten, by some august tooth;
But, enough! arcanum so chosen as confident
The reed, vast and twin which under the azure we play:
Which, diverting toward itself the cheek's exertion,
Dreams, in a long solo, that we amused
The beauty of surroundings by false confusions
Between herself and our credulous song;
And to form as high as love can modulate
Vanish the common dream of back
Or of pure flank followed by my closed gaze,
A sonorous, fruitless and monotonous line.

Try then, instrument of flights, o sly
Syrinx, to reflower at the lakes where you await me!
I, emboldened by my murmur, will speak at length
Of goddesses; and with idolatrous paintings,
I will lift bodices from their shadow:
Thus, when from the grapes I have sucked the brightness,
To banish a regret by my ruse discarded,
Laughing, I raise the empty cluster to the sky
And, blowing into its luminous skins, avid
For drunkenness, till evening I gaze through them.

O nymphs, let us reflate these varied MEMORIES.
'My eye, piercing the rushes, darted toward each immortal
Neck, which drowned its burning in the wave
With an enraged cry to the woodland sky;
And the splendid shower of hair disappears
In flashes and shivers, oh jewels!
I rush ahead; when, at my feet, interlocked (bruised
With languor tasted in the evil of being two)
Slumberers only among mere random arms;
I steal them away, without untangling them, and fly
To that mound, hated by frivolous umbrage,
Of roses expending all perfume to the sun,
Where our frolic by day consumed may be as well.'
I adore you, fury of virgins, oh fierce delight
Of the holy naked burden that slips away
Fleeing my fire-drinking lip, like lightning

Quivers! the secret fright of the flesh;
The feet of the inhuman to the heart of the timid
Who abandons at the same time an innocence, damp
With crazed tears or less sorrowful vapours.
'My crime, happy to vanquish these treacherous fears,
Is to have divided the dishevelled tuft
Of kisses that the gods kept so well together:
For, just as I was about to hide a fiery laugh
Under the happy folds of one (keeping
With a single finger, so that with the candour of a feather
She is coloured with the emotion of her sister igniting,
The little one, naïve and not even blushing:)
That my arms, undone by vague expirings,
This prey, forever ungrateful rescues herself
Without pity for the sobs with which I was still drunk.'

A shame! Others will pull me along toward happiness
By their tresses knotted over the horns of my brow:
You know, my passion, which, purple and already ripe,
Each pomegranate bursts and honey-bees murmur;
And our blood, infatuated by whom will seize it,
Flows for every eternal swarm of desire.
At the hour where gold and ashes tint this wood
A feast exults in the extinguished leaves:
Etna! it is with you visited by Venus
On your lava resting her ingenuous heels,
When sounds a sad sleep or burns out the flame.
I hold the queen!

Oh sure punishment . . .

No, but the soul

Vacant of speech and body weighted down
Succumbed late to the proud silence of noon:
With no more ado we must sleep in the forgetting of blasphemy,
Stretched out on the debased sand – and how I love
To open my mouth to that efficacious star which is wine!

Couple, farewell; I am going to see the shade you became.

(Translation by James H. Rubin, with Robert Harvey and Harry Gilonis)

The Impressionists and Edouard Manet

Without any preamble whatsoever, without even a word of explanation to the reader who may be ignorant of the meaning of the title which heads this article, I shall enter at once into its subject, reserving to myself either to draw my deductions, new from an art point of view, as the facts I relate present themselves, or leave them to ooze out when and as they may.

Briefly, then, let us take a short glimpse backward on art history. Rarely do our annual exhibitions abound with novelty, and some few years back such years of abundance were still more rare; but about 1860 a sudden and a lasting light shone forth when Courbet began to exhibit his works. These then in some degree coincided with that movement which had appeared in literature, and which obtained the name of Realism; that is to say, it sought to impress itself upon the mind by the lively depiction of things as they appeared to be, and vigorously excluded all meddlesome imagination. It was a great movement, equal in intensity to that of the Romantic school, just then expiring under the hands of the landscape painters, or to that later one whence issued the bold decorative effects of Henri Regnault; and it then moved many on a new and contemporaneous path. But in the midst of this, there began to appear, sometimes perchance on the walls of the Salon, but far more frequently and certainly on those of the galleries of the rejected, curious and singular paintings – laughable to the many, it is true, from their very faults, but nevertheless very disquieting to the true and reflective critic, who could not refrain from asking himself what manner of man is this? and what the strange doctrine he preaches? For it was evident that the preacher had a meaning; he was persistent in his reiteration, unique in his persistency, and his works were signed by the then new and unknown name of EDOUARD MANET. There was also at that time, alas! that it should have to be written in the past tense, an enlightened amateur, one who loved all arts and lived for one of them. These strange pictures at once won his sympathy; an instinctive and poetic foresight made him love them; and this before their prompt succession and the sufficient exposition of the principles they inculcated had revealed their meaning to the thoughtful few of the public many. But this enlightened amateur died too soon to see these, and before his favourite painter had won a public name.

That amateur was our last poet, Charles Baudelaire.

Following in appreciative turn came the then coming novelist Emile Zola. With that insight into the future which distinguishes his own works, he recognized the light that had arisen, albeit that he was yet too young to then define that which we today call Naturalism, to follow the quest, not merely of that reality which impresses itself in its abstract form on all, but of that absolute and important sentiment which Nature herself impresses on those who have voluntarily abandoned conventionalism.

In 1867 a special exhibition of the works of Manet and some few of his followers, gave to the then nameless school of recent painting which thus grew up, the semblance of a party, and party strife grew high. The struggle with this resolute intruder was preached as a crusade from the rostrum of each school. For several years a firm and implacable front was formed against its advance; until at length vanquished by its good faith and persistency, the jury recognized the name of Manet, welcomed it, and so far recovered from its ridiculous fears, that it reasoned and found it must either declare him a self-created sovereign pontiff, charged by his own faith with the cure of souls, or condemn him as a heretic and a public danger.

The latter of these alternatives being now-a-days definitively adopted, the public exhibition of Manet's works has of late taken place in his own studio. Yet, and notwithstanding all this, and in spite of concurrent Salons, the public rushed with lively curiosity and eagerness to the Boulevard des Italiens and the galleries of Durand Ruel in 1874 and 1876, to see the works of those then styled the Intransigeants, now the Impressionists. And what found they there? A collection of pictures of strange aspect, at first view giving the ordinary impression of the motive which made them, but over beyond this, a peculiar quality outside mere Realism. And here occurs one of those unexpected crises which appear in art. Let us study it in its present condition and its future prospects, and with some attempt to develop its idea.

Manet, when he casts away the cares of art and chats with a friend between the lights in his studio, expresses himself with brilliancy. Then it is that he tells him what he means by Painting; what new destinies are yet in store for it; what it is, and how that it is from an irrepressible instinct that he paints, and that he paints as he does. Each time he begins a picture, says he, he plunges headlong into it, and feels like a man who knows that his surest plan to learn to swim safely, is, dangerous as it may seem, to throw himself into the water. One of his habitual aphorisms then is that no one should paint a landscape and a figure by the same process, with the same knowledge, or in the same fashion; nor what is more, even two landscapes or two figures. Each work should be a new creation of the mind. The hand, it is true, will conserve some of its acquired secrets of manipulation, but the eye should forget all else it has seen, and learn anew from the lesson before it. It should abstract itself from memory, seeing only that which it looks upon, and that as for the first time; and the hand should become an impersonal abstraction guided only by the will, oblivious of all previous cunning. As for the artist himself, his personal feeling, his peculiar tastes, are for the time absorbed, ignored, or set aside for the enjoyment of his personal life. Such a result as this cannot be attained all at once. To reach it the master must pass through many phases ere this self-isolation can be acquired, and this new evolution of art be learnt; and I, who have occupied myself a good deal in its study, can count but two who have gained it.

Wearied by the technicalities of the school in which, under Couture, he studied, Manet, when he recognized the inanity of all he was taught, determined either not to paint at all or to paint entirely from without himself. Yet, in his self-sought insulation, two masters – masters of the past – appeared to him, and befriended him in his revolt. Velasquez, and the painters of the Flemish school, particularly impressed themselves upon him, and the wonderful atmosphere which enshrouds the compositions of the grand old Spaniard, and the brilliant tones which glow from the canvasses of his northern compeers, won the student's admiration, thus presenting to him two art aspects which he has since made himself the master of, and can mingle as he pleases. It is precisely these two aspects which reveal the truth, and give paintings based upon them living reality instead of rendering them the baseless fabric of abstracted and obscure dreams. These have been the tentatives of Manet, and curiously, it was to the foreigners and the past that he turned for friendly council in remedying the evils of his country and his time. And yet truth bids me say that Manet had no pressing need for this; an incomparable copyist, he could have found his game close to hand had he chosen his quarry there; but he sought something more than this, and fresh things are not found all at once; freshness, indeed, frequently consists – and this is especially the case in these critical days – in a co-ordination of widely-scattered elements.

The pictures in which this reversion to the traditions of the old masters of the north and south are found constitute Manet's first manner. Now the old writers on art expressed by the word 'manner', rather the lavish blossoming of genius during one of its intellectual seasons than the fact fathered, found, or sought out by the painter himself. But that in which the painter declares most his views is the choice of his subjects. Literature often departs from its current path to seek for the aspirations of an epoch of the past, and to modernize them for its own purpose, and in painting Manet followed a similarly divergent course, seeking the truth, and loving it when found, because being true it was so strange, especially when compared with old and worn-out ideals of it. Welcomed on his outset, as we have said, by Baudelaire, Manet fell under the influence of the moment, and, to illustrate him at this period, let us take one of his first works, 'Olympia'; that wan, wasted courtesan, showing to the public, for the first time, the non-traditional, unconventional nude. The bouquet, yet enclosed in its paper envelope, the gloomy cat (apparently suggested by one of the prose poems of the author of the 'Fleurs du Mal'), and all the surrounding accessories, were truthful, but not immoral – that is, in the ordinary and foolish sense of the word – but they were undoubtedly intellectually perverse in their tendency. Rarely has any modern work been more applauded by some few, or more deeply damned by the many, than was that of this innovator.

If our humble opinion can have any influence in this impartial history of the work of the chief of the new school of painting, I would say that the transition period in it is by no means to be regretted. Its parallel is found in literature, when our sympathies are suddenly awakened by some new imagery presented to us; and this is what I like in Manet's work. It surprised us all as something long hidden, but suddenly revealed. Captivating and repulsive at the same time, eccentric, and new; such types as he gave us were needed in our ambient life. In them, strange though they were, there was nothing vague, general, conventional, or hackneyed. Often they attracted attention by something peculiar in the physiognomy of his subject, half hiding or sacrificing to those new laws of space and light he set himself to inculcate, some minor details which others would have seized upon.

Bye and bye, if he continues to paint long enough, and to educate the public eye – as yet veiled by conventionality – if that public will then consent to see the true beauties of the people, healthy and solid as they are, the graces which exist in the bourgeoisie will then be recognized and taken as worthy models in art, and then will come the time of peace. As yet it is but one of struggle – a struggle to render those truths in nature which for her are eternal, but which are as yet for the multitude but new.

The reproach which superficial people formulate against Manet, that whereas once he painted ugliness now he paints vulgarity, falls harmlessly to the ground, when we recognize the fact that he paints the truth, and recollect those difficulties he encountered on his way to seek it, and how he conquered them. *Un Déjeuner sur l'Herbe, L'Exécution de Maximilien, Un Coin de Table, Des Gens du monde a la Fenêtre, Le Bon Bock, Un Coin de Bal de l'Opera, Le Chemin de Fer*, and the two *Canotiers* – these are the pictures which step by step have marked each round in the ladder scaled by this bold innovator, and which have led him to the point achieved in his truly marvellous work, this year refused by the Salon, but exhibited to the public by itself, entitled *Le Linge* – a work which marks a date in a life-time perhaps, but certainly one in the history of art.

The whole of the series we have just above enumerated with here and there an exception, demonstrate the painter's aim very exactly; and this aim was not to make a momentary escapade or sensation, but by steadily endeavouring to impress upon his work a natural and a general law, to seek out a type rather than a personality, and to flood it with light and air: and such air! air which despotically dominates over all else. And before attempting to analyse this celebrated picture I should like to comment somewhat on that truism of tomorrow, that paradox of today, which in studio slang is called 'the theory of open air' or at least on that which it becomes with the authoritative evidence of the later efforts of Manet. But here is first of all an objection to overcome. Why is it needful to represent the open air of gardens, shore or street, when it must be owned that the chief part of modern existence is passed within doors? There are many answers; among these I hold the first, that in the atmosphere of any interior, bare or furnished, the reflected lights are mixed and broken and too often discolour the flesh tints. For instance I would remind you of a painting in the salon of 1873 which our painter justly called a *Rêverie*. There a young woman reclines on a divan exhaling all the lassitude of summer time; the jalousies of her room are almost closed, the dreamer's face is dim with shadow, but a vague, deadened daylight suffuses her figure and her muslin dress. This work is altogether exceptional and sympathetic.

Woman is by our civilization consecrated to night, unless she escape from it sometimes to those open air afternoons by the seaside or in an arbour, affectionated by moderns. Yet I think the artist would be in the wrong to represent her among the artificial glories of candle-light or gas, as at that time the only object of art would be the woman herself, set off by the immediate atmosphere, theatrical and active, even beautiful, but utterly inartistic. Those persons much accustomed, whether from the habit of their calling or purely from taste, to fix on a mental canvas the beautiful remembrance of woman, even when thus seen amid the glare of night in the world or at the theatre, must have remarked that some mysterious process despoils the noble phantom of the artificial prestige cast by candelabra or footlights, before she is admitted fresh and simple to the number of every day haunters of the imagination. (Yet I must own that but few of those whom I have consulted on this obscure and delicate point are of my opinion.) The complexion, the special beauty which springs from the very source of life, changes with artificial lights, and it is probably from the desire to preserve this grace in all its integrity, that painting – which concerns itself more about this flesh-pollen than any other human attraction – insists on the mental operation to which I have lately alluded, and demands daylight – that is space with the transparence of air alone. The natural light of day penetrating into and influencing all things, although itself invisible, reigns also on this typical picture called *The Linen*, which we will study next, it being a complete and final repertory of all current ideas and the means of their execution.

Some fresh but even-coloured foliage – that of a town garden – holds imprisoned a flood of summer morning air. Here a young woman, dressed in blue, washes some linen, several pieces of which are already drying; a child coming out from the flowers looks at its mother – that is all the subject. This picture is life-size, though this scale is somewhat lower in the middle distance, the painter wisely recognizing the artificial requirements forced upon him by the arbitrarily fixed point of view imposed on the spectator. It is deluged with air. Everywhere the luminous and transparent atmosphere struggles with the figures, the dresses, and the foliage, and seems to take to itself some of their substance and solidity; whilst their contours, consumed by the hidden sun and wasted by space, tremble, melt, and evaporate into the surrounding atmosphere, which plunders reality from the figures, yet seems to do so in order to preserve their truthful aspect. Air reigns supreme and real, as if it held an enchanted life conferred by the witchery of art; a life neither personal nor sentient, but itself subjected to the phenomena thus called up by science and shown to our astonished eyes, with its perpetual metamorphosis and its invisible action rendered visible. And how? By this fusion or by this struggle ever continued between surface and space, between colour and air. Open air: – that is the beginning and end of the question we are now studying. Aesthetically it is answered by the simple fact that there in open air alone can the flesh tints of a model keep their true qualities, being nearly equally lighted on all sides. On the other hand if one paints in the real or artificial half-light in use in the schools, it is this feature or that feature on which the light strikes and forces into undue relief, affording an easy means for a painter to dispose a face to suit his own fancy and return to by-gone styles.

The search after truth, peculiar to modern artists, which enables them to see nature and reproduce her, such as she appears to just and pure eyes, must lead them to adopt air almost exclusively as their medium, or at all events to habituate themselves to work in it freely and without restraint: there should at least be in the revival of such a medium, if nothing more, an incentive to a new manner of painting. This is the result of our reasoning, and the end I wish to establish. As no artist has on his palette a transparent and neutral colour answering to open air, the desired effect can only be obtained by lightness or heaviness of touch, or by the regulation of tone. Now Manet and his school use simple colour, fresh, or lightly laid on, and their results appear to have been attained at the first stroke, that the ever-present light blends with and vivifies all things. As to the details of the picture, nothing should be absolutely fixed in order that we may feel that the bright gleam which lights the picture, or the diaphanous shadow which veils it, are only seen in passing, and just when the spectator beholds the represented subject, which being composed of a harmony of reflected and ever-changing lights, cannot be supposed always to look the same, but palpitates with movement, light, and life.

But will not this atmosphere – which an artifice of the painter extends over the whole of the object painted – vanish, when the completely finished work is as a repainted picture? If we could find no other way to indicate the presence of air than the partial or repeated application of colour as usually employed, doubtless the representation would be as fleeting as the effect represented, but from the first conception of the work, the space intended to contain the atmosphere has been indicated, so that when this is filled by the represented air, it is as unchangeable as the other parts of the picture. Then composition (to borrow once more the slang of the studio) must play a considerable part in the aesthetics of a master of the

Impressionists? No; certainly not; as a rule the grouping of modern persons does not suggest it, and for this reason our painter is pleased to dispense with it, and at the same time to avoid both affectation and style. Nevertheless he must find something on which to establish his picture, though it be but for a minute – for the one thing needful is the time required by the spectator to see and admire the representation with that promptitude which just suffices for the connection of its truth. If we turn to natural perspective (not that utterly and artificially classic science which makes our eyes the dupes of a civilized education, but rather that artistic perspective which we learn from the extreme East – Japan for example) – and look at these sea-pieces of Manet, where the water at the horizon rises to the height of the frame, which alone interrupts it, we feel a new delight at the recovery of a long obliterated truth.

The secret of this is found in an absolutely new science, and in the manner of cutting down the pictures, and which gives to the frame all the charm of a merely fanciful boundary, such as that which is embraced at one glance of a scene framed in by the hands, or at least all of it found worthy to preserve. This is the picture, and the function of the frame is to isolate it; though I am aware that this is running counter to prejudice. For instance, what need is there to represent this arm, this hat, or that river bank, if they belong to someone or something exterior to the picture; the one thing to be attained is that the spectator accustomed among a crowd or in nature to isolate one bit which pleases him, though at the same time incapable of entirely forgetting the adjured details which unite the part to the whole, shall not miss in the work of art one of his habitual enjoyments, and whilst recognizing that he is before a painting half believes he sees the mirage of some natural scene. Some will probably object that all of these means have been more or less employed in the past, that dexterity – though not pushed so far – of cutting the canvass off so as to produce an illusion – perspective almost conforming to the exotic usage of barbarians – the light touch and fresh tones uniform and equal, or variously trembling with shifting lights – all these ruses and expedients in art have been found more than once in the English school, and elsewhere. But the assemblage for the first time of all these relative processes for an end, visible and suitable to the artistic expression of the needs of our times, this is no inconsiderable achievement in the cause of art, especially since a mighty will has pushed these means to their uttermost limits.

But the chief charm and true characteristic of one of the most singular men of the age is, that Manet (who is a visitor to the principal galleries both French and foreign, and an erudite student of painting) seems to ignore all that has been done in art by others, and draws from his own inner consciousness all his effects of simplification, the whole revealed by effects of light incontestably novel. This is the supreme originality of a painter by whom originality is doubly forsworn, who seeks to lose his personality in nature herself, or in the gaze of a multitude until then ignorant of her charms.

Without making a catalogue of the already very considerable number of Manet's works, it has been necessary to mark the successive order of his pictures, each one of them an exponent of some different effort, yet all connected by the self-same theory; valuable also as illustrating the career of the head of the school of Impressionists, or rather the initiator of the only effective movement in this direction; and as showing how he has patiently mastered the idea of which he is at present in full possession. The absence of all personal obtrusion in the manner of this painter's interpretation of nature, permits the critic to dwell so long as he pleases on his pictures without appearing to be too exclusively occupied by one man; yet we must be careful to remember that each work of a genius, singular because he abjures singularity, is an artistic production, unique of its kind, recognizable at first sight among all the schools of all ages. And can such a painter have pupils? Yes, and worthy ones; notably Mademoiselle Eva Gonzales, who to a just understanding of the master's stand-point unites qualities of youthfulness and grace all her own.

But his influence as from friend to friend is wider spread than that which the master exercises over the pupil, and sways all the painters of the day; for even the manner of those artists most strongly opposed in idea to his theory is in some degree determined by his practice. There is indeed no painter of consequence who during the last few years has not adopted or pondered over some one of the theories advanced by the Impressionists, and notably that of the open air, which influences all modern artistic thought. Some come near us and remain our neighbours; others, like M. Fantin-Latour and the late M. Chintreuil, painters without any common point of resemblance, while working out their own ideas have little by little attained to results often analogous to those of the Impressionists, thus creating between this school and that of academic painting a healthy, evident, true, and conjunctive branch of art, at present upheld even by the generality of art lovers. But the Impressionists themselves, those whom cosy studio chats and an amicable interchange of idea have enabled to push together towards new and unexpected horizons, and fresh-formed truths, such as MM. Claude Monet, Sisley and Pissarro, paint wondrously alike; indeed a rather superficial observer at a pure and simple exhibition of Impressionism would take all their works to be those of one man – and that man, Manet. Rarely have three workers wrought so much alike, and the reason of the similitude is simple enough, for they each endeavour to suppress individuality for the benefit of nature. Nevertheless the visitor would proceed from this first impression, which is quite right as a synthesis, to perceiving that each artist has some favourite piece of execution analogous to the subject accepted rather than chosen by him, and this acceptation fostered by reason of the country of his birth or residence, for these artists as a rule find their subjects close to home, within an easy walk, or in their own gardens.

Claude Monet loves water, and it is his especial gift to portray its mobility and transparency, be it sea or river, grey and monotonous, or coloured by the sky. I have never seen a boat poised more lightly on the water than in his pictures, or a veil more mobile and light than his moving atmosphere. It is in truth a marvel. Sisley seizes the passing moments of the day; watches a fugitive cloud and seems to paint it in its flight; on his canvas the live air moves and the leaves yet thrill and tremble. He loves best to paint them in spring, 'when the yonge leves on the lyte wode, waxen al with wille', or when red and gold and russet-green the last few fall in autumn; for them space and light are one, and the breeze stirring the foliage prevents it from becoming an opaque mass, too heavy for such an impression of mobility and life. On the other hand, Pissarro, the eldest of the three, loves the thick shade of summer woods and the green earth, and does not fear the solidity which sometimes serves to render the atmosphere visible as a luminous haze saturated with sunlight. It is not rare for one of these three to steal a march on Manet, who suddenly perceiving their anticipated or explained tendency, sums up all their ideas in one powerful and masterly work. For them, rather are the subtle and delicate changes of nature, the many variations undergone in some long morning or afternoon by a thicket of trees on the water's side.

The most successful work of these three painters is distinguished by a sure yet wonderfully rapid execution. Unfortunately the picture buyer, though intelligent enough to perceive in these transcripts from nature much more than a mere revel of execution, since in these instantaneous and voluntary pictures all is harmonious, and were spoiled by a touch more or less, is the dupe of this real or apparent promptitude of labour, and though he pays for these paintings a price a thousand times inferior to their real value, yet is disturbed by the after-thought that such light productions might be multiplied *ad infinitum;* a merely commercial misunderstanding from which, doubtless, these artists will have still to suffer. Manet has been more fortunate, and receives an adequate price for his work. As thorough Impressionists, these painters (excepting M. Claude Monet, who treats it superbly) do not usually attempt the natural size of their subjects, neither do they take them from scenes of private life, but are before everything landscape painters, and restrict their pictures to that size easiest to look at, and with shut eyes preserve the remembrance of.

With these, some other artists, whose originality has distanced them from other contemporary painters, frequently, and as a rule, exhibit their paintings, and share in most of the art theories I have reviewed here. These are Degas, Mademoiselle Berthe Morizot, (now Madame Eugène Manet), and Renoir, to whom I should like to join Whistler, who is so well appreciated in France, both by critics and the world of amateurs, had he not chosen England as a field of his success.

The muslin drapery that forms a luminous, ever-moving atmosphere round the semi-nakedness of the young ballet-dancers; the bold, yet profoundly complicated attitudes of these creatures, thus accomplishing one of the at once natural and yet modern functions of women, have enchanted M. Degas, who can, nevertheless, be as delighted with the charms of those little washerwomen, who fresh and fair, though poverty-stricken, and clad but in camisole and petticoat, bend their slender bodies at the hour of work. No voluptuousness there, no sentimentality here; the wise and intuitive artist does not care to explore the trite and hackneyed view of his subject. A master of drawing, he has sought delicate lines and movements exquisite or grotesque, and of a strange new beauty, if I dare employ towards his works an abstract term, which he himself will never employ in his daily conversation.

More given to render, and very succintly, the aspect of things, but with a new charm infused into it by feminine vision, Mademoiselle Berthe Morizot seizes wonderfully the familiar presence of a woman of the world, or a child in the pure atmosphere of the sea-shore, or green lawn. Here a charming couple enjoy all the limpidity of hours where elegance has become artless; and there how pure an atmosphere veils this woman standing out of doors, or that one who reclines under the shade of an umbrella thrown among the grasses and frail flowers which a little girl in a clean dress is busy gathering. The airy foreground, even the furthermost outlines of sea and sky, have the perfection of an actual vision, and that couple yonder, the least details of whose pose is so well painted that one could recognize them by that alone, even if their faces, seen under the shady straw hats, did not prove them to be portrait sketches, give their own characteristics to the place they enliven by their visit. The air of preoccupation, of mundane care or secret sorrows, so generally characteristic of the modern artist's sketches from contemporary life, were never more notably absent than here; one feels that the graceful lady and child are in perfect ignorance that the pose unconsciously adopted to gratify an innate sense of beauty is perpetuated in this charming water-colour.

The shifting shimmer of gleam and shadow which the changing reflected lights, themselves influenced by every neighbouring thing, cast upon each advancing or departing figure, and the fleeting combinations in which these dissimilar reflections form one harmony or many, such are the favourite effects of Renoir – nor can we wonder that this infinite complexity of execution induces him to seek more hazardous success in things widely opposed to nature. A box at a theatre, its gaily-dressed inmates, the women with their flesh tints heightened and displaced by rouge and rice powder, a complication of effects of light – the more so when this scene is fantastically illuminated by an incongruous day-light. Such are the subjects he delights in.

All these various attempts and efforts (sometimes pushed yet farther by the intrepid M. de Césane) are united in the common bond of Impressionism. Incontestably honour is due to these who have brought to the service of art an extraordinary and quasi-original newness of vision, undeterred by a confused and hesitating age. If sometimes they have gone too far in the search of novel and audacious subjects, or have misapplied a freshly discovered principle, it is but another canvas turned to the wall; and as a set off to such an accident they have attained a praiseworthy result, to make us understand when looking on the most accustomed objects the delight that we should experience could we but see them for the first time.

If we try to recall some of the heads of our argument and to draw from them possible conclusions, we must first affirm that Impressionism is the principal and real movement of contemporary painting. The only one? No; since other great talents have been devoted to illustrate some particular phrase or period of bygone art; among these we must class such artists as Moreau, Puvis de Chavannes, etc.

At a time when the romantic tradition of the first half of the century only lingers among a few surviving masters of that time, the transition from the old imaginative artist and dreamer to the energetic modern worker is found in Impressionism.

The participation of a hitherto ignored people in the political life of France is a social fact that will honour the whole of the close of the nineteenth century. A parallel is found in artistic matters, the way being prepared by an evolution which the public with rare prescience dubbed, from its first appearance, Intransigeant, which in political language means radical and democratic.

The noble visionaries of other times, whose works are the semblance of worldly things seen by unworldly eyes, (not the actual representations of real objects) appear as kings and gods in the far dream-ages of mankind; recluses to whom were given the genius of a dominion over an ignorant multitude. But today the multitude demands to see with its own eyes; and if our latter-day art is less glorious, intense, and rich, it is not without the compensation of truth, simplicity and child-like charm.

At that critical hour for the human race when nature desires to work for herself, she requires certain lovers of hers – new and impersonal men placed directly in communion with the sentiment of their time – to loose the restraint of education, to let hand and eye do what they will, and thus through them, reveal herself.

For the mere pleasure of doing so? Certainly not, but to express herself, calm, naked, habitual, to those newcomers of tomorrow, of which each one will consent to be an unknown unit in the mighty numbers of a universal suffrage, and to place in their power a newer and more succinct means of observing her.

Such, to those who can see in this the representative art of a period which cannot isolate itself from the equally characteristic politics and industry, must seem the meaning of the manner of painting which we have discussed here, and which although marking a general phase of art has manifested itself particularly in France.

Now in conclusion I must hastily re-enter the domain of aesthetics, and I trust we shall thoroughly have considered our subject when I have shown the relation of the present crisis – the appearance of the Impressionists – to the actual principles of painting – a point of great importance.

In extremely civilized epochs the following necessity becomes a matter of course, the development of art and thought having nearly reached their far limits – art and thought are obliged to retrace their own footsteps, and to return to their ideal source, which never coincides with their real beginnings. English Preraphaelitism, if I do not mistake, returned to the primitive simplicity of mediaeval ages. The scope and aim (not proclaimed by authority of dogmas, yet not the less clear), of Manet and his followers is that painting shall be steeped again in its cause, and its relation to nature. But what, except to decorate the ceilings of saloons and palaces with a crowd of idealized types in magnificent foreshortening, what can be the aim of a painter before everyday nature? To imitate her? when his best effort can never equal the original with the inestimable advantages of life and space. – Ah no! this fair face, that green landscape, will grow old and wither, but I shall have them always, true as nature, fair as remembrance, and imperishably my own; or the better to satisfy my creative artistic instinct, that which I preserve through the power of Impressionism is not the material portion which already exists, superior to any mere representation of it, but the delight of having recreated nature touch by touch. I leave the massive and tangible solidity to its fitter exponent, sculpture. I content myself with reflecting on the clear and durable mirror of painting, that which perpetually lives yet dies every moment, which only exists by the will of Idea, yet constitutes in my domain the only authentic and certain merit of nature – the Aspect. It is through her that when rudely thrown at the close of an epoch of dreams in the front of reality, I have taken from it only that which properly belongs to my art, an original and exact perception which distinguishes for itself the things it perceives with the steadfast gaze of a vision restored to its simplest perfection.

(from *The Art Monthly Review*, London, 30 September 1876)

References

1 According to, for example, Antonin Proust in his *Edouard Manet, Souvenirs* (Paris, 1913), p. 129.

2 Emile Benveniste, *Problèmes de linguistique générale* (Paris, 1966).

3 Louis Marin, 'Toward a Theory of Reading in the Visual Arts: Poussin's "The Arcadian Shepherds" ', in *Calligram: Essays in New Art History from France*, ed. Norman Bryson (Cambridge, 1988), pp. 63–90, and Marin, *Portrait of the King*, trans. M. M. Houle (Minneapolis, 1988). See also Marin's 'Le Corps glorieux du Roi et son portrait', in *La Parole mangée et autres essais théologico-politiques* (Paris, 1986), pp. 195–225.

4 Michel Foucault, 'Las Meninas', in *The Order of Things: An Archaeology of the Human Sciences* (New York, 1970), pp. 3–16.

5 Jacques Derrida, *The Truth in Painting* (Chicago, 1987).

6 Michel Foucault, *Discipline and Punish: The Birth of the Prison* (New York, 1977).

7 Svetlana Alpers, *The Art of Describing: Dutch Art in the Seventeenth Century* (Chicago, 1983); Michael Fried, *Absorption and Theatricality: Painting and Beholder in the Age of Diderot* (Berkeley, 1980).

8 This parallel was first suggested by Don Ihde of the Department of Philosophy, Stony Brook, the State of University of New York, in a lecture given there in 1987.

9 Georges Didi-Huberman, *Devant l'image: question posée aux fins d'une histoire de l'art* (Paris, 1990).

10 Ibid, pp. 26–9.

11 J. L. Austin, *How to do Things with Words* (Cambridge, 1962), the William James lectures delivered at Harvard University in 1955.

12 Jacques Derrida, 'Signature Event Context', *Glyph: John Hopkins Textual Studies*, I (1977), pp. 172–97.

13 I have made a related argument in my 'David et la main du peuple: saisir le site de la représentation', in *Actes du Colloque: David Contre David*, Actes du Colloque du Musée du Louvre, December 1989; La Documentation Française, Paris, 1993, II, pp. 783–803.

14 See Julia Kristeva, *La Révolution du langage poétique: L'Avant-Garde à la fin du XIXe siècle: Lautréamont et Mallarmé* (Paris, 1974).

15 I would distinguish my point of view from that of Richard Wollheim (*Painting as an Art*, Princeton, 1987, pp. 141–64), who takes the idea of the viewer in the picture so literally that I cannot verify it by his evidence, nor by my own experience, except insofar as he supports the idea of Manet's pictures harbouring a 'physical presence'. On similar grounds, I would differentiate Michael Fried's hypotheses on Courbet from mine on Manet (Fried, *Courbet's Realism*, London, 1990), though we agree, of course, on the idea of overcoming distance. Unlike Fried's concept of 'absorption', Mallarmé's 'immersion' refers to a depersonalization and transcendence of the personal – an effacement of the boundaries of the subject – and acquires a historical valency, as we shall see, through its connection to Hegel.

16 Jules Laforgue, 'L'Impressionisme' (1883), in *Oeuvres complètes*, III: *Mélanges posthumes* (Paris, 1902–3), pp. 133–45.

17 René Descartes, 'La Dioptrique', in *Discours sur la méthode et essais* (Leiden, 1637), I, 'De la lumière', *passim*.

18 Michael Baxandall, *Patterns of Intention: On the Historical Explanation of Pictures* (London, 1985), pp. 74–104.
19 Jonathan Crary, 'Modernizing Vision', in *Vision and Visuality*, ed. Hal Foster (Seattle, 1988), pp. 29–44, expanded in *Techniques of the Observer: On Vision and Modernity in the Nineteenth Century* (London, 1990).
20 See *Mémoires d'un aveugle: L'autoportrait et autres ruines*, exhibition catalogue by Jacques Derrida: Paris, Musée du Louvre, 1990, p. 11.
21 Cited by Emile Zola in *Mon Salon, Edouard Manet* (1868); see *Mon Salon, Manet: Ecrits sur l'art* (Paris, 1970), p. 139.
22 Pierre Bourdieu, 'L'Institutionalisation de l'anomie', *Cahiers du Musée National d'Art Moderne*, v (19–20 June 1987), pp. 6–19.
23 See Rosalind E. Krauss, 'Manet's "Nymph Surprised" ', *The Burlington Magazine*, CIX (1967), pp. 622–7.
24 According to Proust, *Souvenirs*, p. 126.
25 J.B.C. de Chantal, *La Civilité des jeunes personnes* (Paris, 1843), p. 39.
26 Maury, 'Le Somnambulisme naturel et l'hypnotisme', *Revue des Deux-Mondes*, I (1860), p. 705.
27 Benjamin, 'On Some Motifs in Baudelaire', in *Illuminations*, ed. Hannah Arendt (New York, 1969), pp. 190–1.
28 A. Clairet, 'Le Bracelet de l'Olympia – Genèse et destinée d'un chef d'oeuvre', *L'Oeil*, 333 (April 1983), p. 37, cited in Juliet Wilson-Bareau *et al.*, *The Hidden Face of Manet: An Investigation of the Artist's Working Processes* (London, 1986), p. 45.
29 Carol Armstrong, 'Manet/Manette: Encoloring the I/Eye', *Stanford Humanities Review* (1992), pp. 1–46, suggests the possibility of the *Olympia* as self-portrait while eloquently demonstrating the ambiguity of identity in Manet's figure representations. I adopt her use of 'I/Eye' later in this chapter.
30 Sharon Flescher, *Zacharie Astruc: Critic, Artist and Japonist* (London, 1978), p. 173.
31 For helping to define my characterizations of Manet's politics, I am indebted to John House, 'Manet's Maximilian: History Painting, Censorship and Ambiguity', in Juliet Wilson-Bareau *et al.*, *Manet: 'The Execution of Maximilian'; Painting, Politics and Censorship* (London, 1992), pp. 87–111.
32 As in *Le Journal d'Eugène Delacroix*, ed. André Joubin (Paris, 1932), 8 October 1822 and 19 May 1853; Baudelaire, 'Salon of 1846', in *Art in Paris, 1845–1862*, trans. and ed. by J. Mayne (London, 1965), pp. 48–52, 'On Colour'.
33 Desnoyers, in *L'Artiste* (1855), quoted by Bernard Weinberg, *French Realism: The Critical Reaction, 1830–1870* (New York, 1937), p. 121.
34 Duranty, *Le Réalisme*, I (15 November 1856).
35 Castagnary, 'Philosophie du Salon de 1857', in *Salons* (Paris, 1892), I, pp. 4–5.
36 Duranty, *La Nouvelle Peinture, à propos d'un groupe d'artistes qui exposé dans les galeries Durand-Ruel* (Paris, 1876), p. 30.
37 Duret, *Les Peintres impressionistes: Monet, Sisley, Renoir, Morisot* [1878], in his *Critique d'avant-garde* (Paris, 1885), p. 69.
38 Duret, *Les Peintres français en 1867* (Paris, 1867), pp. 89–111.
39 Duret, 'Salon de 1870', in *Critique d'avant-garde*, pp. 36–37.
40 Duranty, *Le Réalisme*, I, (15 November 1856).
41 Duranty, *La Nouvelle Peinture*, p. 17.
42 Chesnau, *Le Constitutionnel* (16 May 1865).
43 Desnoyers, *Salon des Refusés, la peinture en 1863* (1863), pp. 40–1.
44 Proust, *Souvenirs*, p. 128.
45 Baudelaire, 'Peintres et Aquafortistes' (September 1862), in *Curiosités esthétiques, L'Art romantique*, ed. H. Lemaître (Paris, 1962), pp. 410–11.

46 Baudelaire, letter to Thoré (*c*. 20 June 1864), *Correspondance de Baudelaire* (Paris, 1973), II, pp. 386–7.
47 Baudelaire, letter to Manet (11 May 1865), *Correspondance*, II, pp. 496–7.
48 Baudelaire, letter to Mme Paul Meurice (24 May 1865), *Correspondance*, II, pp. 500–1.
49 Baudelaire, 'Salon of 1846', in *Art in Paris*, pp. 58–9.
50 Baudelaire, 'Salon of 1859', in ibid., p. 162.
51 Baudelaire, 'The Painter of Modern Life', in *The Painter of Modern Life and Other Essays*, trans. and ed. by J. Mayne (London, 1965), p. 8 and pp. 31–2.
52 Astruc, *Le Salon quotidien* (20 May 1863), p. 5.
53 Claretie, 'Salon de 1875', *L'Art et les artistes français contemporains* (1876), pp. 337–8.
54 Zola, letter to Cézanne (25 March 1860), in *Le Bon Combat, de Courbet aux Impressionistes*, ed. Gaëton Picon and Jean-Paul Bouillon (Paris, 1974), p. 295.
55 Zola, letter to Antonin Valabrégue (18 August 1864), in ibid., p. 298.
56 Ibid., p. 299.
57 Ibid., p. 302.
58 Taine, *La Philosophie de l'art* (Paris, 1867; 1904 edn), II, p. 225.
59 Duret, 'Schopenhauer', (*Le Siècle*, 1878), in *Critique d'avant-garde*, pp. 299–313.
60 Taine, *De L'Intelligence* (Paris, 1870; 1888 edn), II, p. 13.
61 Ibid., p. 71.
62 Helmholtz, *Optique physiologique*, trans. E. Javal and N. Th. Klein (Paris, 1867), pp. 1001–2.
63 Ibid., p. 877.
64 James Sully, *Les Illusions des sens et de l'esprit* (Paris, 1883), p. 53.
65 Ribot, *La Philosophie de Schopenhauer* (Paris, 1874), II, pp. 156–7.
66 Ibid., p. 161.
67 Ibid., p. 189.
68 Castagnary, 'Salon de 1879', *Salons*, II, p. 362.
69 Castagnary, 'Salon de 1868', *Salons*, I, p. 291.
70 Zola, review of Proudhon, in *Le Bon Combat*, p. 38.
71 Castagnary, 'Salon de 1863', *Salons*, I, p. 140.
72 Zola, *Une Nouvelle Manière de peindre: Edouard Manet* (1867), in *Mon Salon, Manet*, p. 101.
73 Ibid., pp. 96–101.
74 Zola, *Mon Salon* (1866), in *Mon Salon, Manet*, pp. 73–4.
75 Zola, *Une Nouvelle Manière de peindre*, p. 103.
76 Ibid., pp. 98–9.
77 Zola, *Mon Salon* (1866), p. 69.
78 Zola, *Une Nouvelle Manière de peindre*, pp. 100–1.
79 Ibid., pp. 101–2.
80 Ibid., p. 97.
81 Ibid., p. 100.
82 Zola, Preface to *Thérèse Raquin* (1867), quoted by George J. Becker, *Documents of Modern Literary Realism* (Princeton, 1963), p. 159.
83 Zola, *Une Nouvelle Manière de peindre*, p. 102.
84 Ibid., p. 109.
85 Zola, *Mon Salon, Edouard Manet* (1868), pp. 141–2.
86 Zola, 'Salon de 1879', in *Le Bon Combat*, p. 205.
87 Mallarmé, 'The Impressionists and Edouard Manet', *Art Monthly Review* (30 Sept 1876), see the Appendix, p. 232.
88 Mallarmé, 'Le Jury de Peinture pour 1874 et M. Manet', in *Oeuvres complètes*, ed. H. Mondor and G. Jean-Aubry (Paris, 1970), p. 698.

89 Mallarmé, 'Artistic Gossip' (25 November 1875), in *Les Gossips de Mallarmé*, ed. H. Mondor and L. J. Austin (Paris, 1962), p. 42.
90 Mallarmé, 'Fine-Art Gossip' (20 March 1876), in ibid., p. 70.
91 Mallarmé, 'The Impressionists and Edouard Manet', Appx, pp. 232–3.
92 Appx, p. 234. On the significance of the two-stage process described by Mallarmé, in which the artist first embraces modernity and then seeks a more universal, a-historical and consequently conservative basis for art, see Thomas Crow, 'Modernism and Mass Culture in the Visual Arts', in Benjamin H. D. Buchloh and Serge Guilbaut, eds, *Modernism and Modernity: The Vancouver Conference Papers* (Nova Scotia, 1983), pp. 215–64.
93 Clay, 'Onguets, fards, pollens', in *Bonjour, Monsieur Manet*, exhibition catalogue: Paris, Centre Georges Pompidou, 1983, p. 17.
94 Mallarmé, 'The Impressionists and Edouard Manet', Appx, pp. 235–6.
95 Richard Shiff gives a somewhat different, but related, account of the relationship between Impressionism and Abstract Expressionism in 'Performing an Appearance: On the Surface of Abstract Expressionism', in *Abstract Expressionism: The Critical Developments*, exhibition catalogue: Albright-Knox Art Gallery, Buffalo, NY, 1967, pp. 94–123.
96 Mallarmé, 'The Impressionists and Edouard Manet', Appx, p. 237.
97 Appx, p. 241. Stephen F. Eisenman, 'The Intransigent Artist *or* How the Impressionists Got Their Name', in *The New Painting: Impressionism 1874–1886*, exhibition catalogue by Charles S. Moffet, *et al.*: Fine Arts Museums of San Francisco, 1986, pp. 51–9, argues the specifically political dimension of the label 'intransigent', which he shows to have been an unsuccessful alternative to the more neutral term, 'impressionism'.
98 Mallarmé, 'The Impressionists and Edouard Manet', Appx, p. 242.
99 Littré, *Dictionnaire de la langue française* (Paris, 1863), under 'aspect'.
100 Mallarmé, letter to Cazalis (14 May 1867), *Correspondance*, quoted by Guy Michaud, *Mallarmé, l'homme et l'oeuvre* (Paris, 1953), p. 58.
101 Mallarmé, 'Les Impressionistes et Edouard Manet', Appx, p. 242.
102 Guillemin, *La Lumière et les couleurs* (Paris, 1874), pp. 10–12.
103 Mallarmé, 'Les Impressionistes et Edouard Manet', Appx, p. 239.
104 Mallarmé, *Correspondance, 1862–1871*, p. 154; Michaud, *Mallarmé*, pp. 35–9.
105 Baudelaire, 'Notes nouvelles sur Edgar Poe', 1857, in *Curiosités esthétiques*, p. 633.
106 All translations are mine, with the aid of Robert Harvey and Harry Gilonis.
107 This point is among many astute observations found in Penny Florence, *Mallarmé, Manet and Redon: Visual and Aural Signs and the Generation of Meaning* (Cambridge, 1986), p. 36.
108 Chesnau, 'Salon de 1852', *Le Constitutionnel* (30 March 1852), and Perrier, *L'Artiste* (14 October 1855), both quoted by Weinberg, *French Realism*, p. 103.
109 Baudelaire, *La Vie et l'œuvre d'Eugène Delacroix*, in *Curiosités esthétiques*, p. 438.
110 Ibid., p. 428.
111 Blanc, *Histoire des peintres de toutes les écoles, Ecole flamande* (Paris, 1864), under 'Rubens'.
112 Blanc, *Histoire . . . Ecole hollandaise*, II (Paris 1861), under 'Van Huysum'.
113 For many excellent examples, from which I have chosen a few, see Michel Faré, *La Nature-Morte en France, son histoire et son évolution du XVIIe au XXe siècle* (Geneva, 1962).
114 Castagnary, 'Salon de 1873', *Salons*, II, p. 57.

115 Louis de Godefroy, 'Le Salon de 1850', *La Revue des Deux-Mondes* (1851), p. 927.
116 Blanc, *Histoire . . . Ecole hollandaise*, II, under 'Kalf'.
117 Thoré, 'Salon de 1861', *Salons de W. Bürger* (Paris, 1870), I, p. 87.
118 Castagnary, 'Salon de 1872', *Salons*, II, p. 14.
119 Rivière, *Renoir et ses amis* (Paris, 1921), p. 81.
120 Henri Fantin-Latour, letter of November 1862, quoted in *Fantin-Latour*, exhibition catalogue: Paris, Grand Palais, 1982–3, p. 111.
121 Thoré, review of exhibition at the Galerie Martinet, in *Gazette des Beaux-Arts* (1860), pp. 333–5.
122 Blanc, *Histoire . . . Ecole française*, II (Paris, 1862), under 'Chardin'. The point is substantiated by Baxandall, *Patterns of Intention*, pp. 74–104.
123 Jules and Edmond de Goncourt, *L'Art du dix-huitième siècle* (1864; Paris, 1967), pp. 81–4.
124 The expression is Baxandall's, in *Patterns of Intention*, p. 102.
125 Zola, *Une Nouvelle Manière de peindre*, p. 110.
126 Thoré, 'Salon de 1868', *Salons de W. Bürger*, II, pp. 531–2.
127 Castagnary, 'Salon de 1868', *Salons*, I, p. 314.
128 Mantz, 'Salon de 1869', *Gazette des Beaux-Arts*, II (1869), p. 13.
129 On the frontispiece etchings, see Theodore Reff, 'The Symbolism of Manet's Frontispiece Etchings', *The Burlington Magazine*, CIV (1962), pp. 182–6.
130 Proust, *Souvenirs*, p. 201.
131 Chesnau, 'Salon de 1865', *Le Constitutionnel* (16 May 1865).
132 Duret, *Histoire d'Edouard Manet et de son œuvre* (Paris, 1902; 1926 edn), pp. 88–9.
133 Castagnary, 'Salon de 1869', *Salons*, I, p. 364.
134 Wollheim, *Painting as an Art*, pp. 141–64.
135 Bryson, *Looking at the Overlooked: Four Essays on Still Life Painting* (London and Cambridge, MA, 1990).
136 Baudelaire, *Paris Spleen* (1869), trans. Louise Varèse (New York, 1970), p. 64.
137 See my *Realism and Social Vision in Courbet and Proudhon*, Princeton Essays on the Arts, 10 (Princeton, 1981).
138 Proust gives these various opinions and details of the encounter in his *Souvenirs*, p. 129.
139 Delacroix, *Journal* (11 January 1857).
140 Van Gogh, letter to Theo, no. 528, *Correspondance complète* (Paris, 1960), quoted in *Manet, 1832–1883*, exhibition catalogue by Françoise Cachin *et al.*: New York, Metropolitan Museum of Art, and Paris, Grand Palais, 1983, p. 208.
141 Van Gogh, letter to Theo, no. 404, *The Complete Letters of Vincent van Gogh*, ed. V. W. van Gogh and J. van Gogh (Greenwich, CT, 1958), quoted by Nochlin, *Impressionism and Post-Impressionism*, pp. 140–3.
142 The term is Fredric Jameson's in *The Prison-House of Language: A Critical Account of Structuralism and Russian Formalism* (Princeton, 1972), esp. pp. 3–39; Norman Bryson, *Vision and Painting: The Logic of the Gaze* (London, 1983); idem, 'Introduction', in Bryson, ed., *Calligram*, pp. xiii–xxix.

Bibliography

MANET

Armstrong, Carol, 'Manet/Manette: Encoloring the I/Eye', in *Stanford Humanities Review*, 1992, pp. 1–46.
Clark, T. J., *The Painting of Modern Life: Paris in the Art of Manet and his Followers*, Princeton, 1984.
Clay, Jean, 'Onguets, fards, pollens', in *Bonjour, Monsieur Manet*, exhibition catalogue: Paris, Centre Georges Pompidou, 1983, pp. 6–24.
Duret, Théodore, *Histoire d'Edouard Manet et de son oeuvre*, Paris, 1926 edn.
Forge, Andrew & Gordon, Robert *The Last Flowers of Manet*, New York, 1986.
Fried, Michael, 'Manet's Sources: Aspects of his Art, 1859–1865', *Artforum*, VII, 1969, pp. 28–82.
Friedrich, Otto, *Olympia: Paris in the Age of Manet*, New York, 1992.
Hamilton, George Heard, *Manet and his Critics*, New Haven, 1954.
Hanson, Anne Coffin, *Manet and the Modern Tradition*, New York, 1977.
Hofmann, Werner, *Edouard Manet: Das Frühstück im Atelier*, Frankfurt, 1984.
Krauss, Rosalind E., 'Manet's "Nymph Surprised" ', *The Burlington Magazine*, CIX, 1967, pp. 622–7.
Manet, 1832–1883, exhibition catalogue by Françoise Cachin *et al.*: New York, Metropolitan Museum of Art, and Paris, Grand Palais, 1983.
Manet and Modern Paris, exhibition catalogue by Theodore Reff: National Gallery of Art, Washington, D.C., 1982.
Nochlin, Linda, 'Manet's "Masked Ball at the Opéra" ', in *The Politics of Vision: Essays on Nineteenth-century Art and Society*, New York, 1989, pp. 75–96.
Proust, Antonin, *Edouard Manet, Souvenirs*, Paris, 1913.
Rand, Harry, *Manet's Contemplation at the Gare Saint-Lazare*, Berkeley and Los Angeles, 1987.
Reff, Theodore, 'The Symbolism of Manet's Frontispiece Etchings', *The Burlington Magazine*, CIV, 1962, pp. 182–6.
——, *Manet: Olympia*, London, 1976.
Sandblad, Nils Gösta, *Manet: Three Studies in Artistic Conception*, Lund, 1954.
Wilson-Bareau, Juliet, *The Hidden Face of Manet: An Investigation of the Artist's Working Processes*, with an introduction by John House, London, 1986.
——, *Manet: 'The Execution of Maximilian'; Painting, Politics and Censorship*, London, 1992.

BAUDELAIRE

Baudelaire, Charles, *Le Peintre de la vie moderne*, in *Oeuvres complètes*, ed. Claude Pichois, Paris, 1975.
——, *Correspondance*, ed. Claude Pichois & Jean Ziegler, Paris, 1973.
——, *Les Fleurs du mal*, Paris, 1857.
Benjamin, Walter, 'On Some Motifs in Baudelaire', in *Illuminations*, ed. Hannah Arendt, New York, 1969, pp. 155–94.
Gilman, Margaret, *The Idea of Poetry in France from Houdar de la Motte to Baudelaire*, Cambridge, MA, 1958.
——, *Baudelaire, the Critic* (New York, 1943).

Hyslop, Robert, 'Baudelaire and Manet: A Re-appraisal', in *Baudelaire as a Love Poet and Other Essays*, University Park, PA, 1969, pp. 87–130.

ZOLA

Brunius, Teddy, *Mutual Aid in the Arts, from the Second Empire to Fin-de-Siècle, Figura*, Uppsala Studies in Art History IX, Stockholm, 1972.
Suwata, Halina, *Naissance d'une doctrine: Formation des idées littéraires et esthétiques de Zola (1859–1865)*, Warsaw, 1976.
Zola, Emile, *Le Bon Combat, de Courbet aux Impressionistes, Anthologie des écrits sur l'art*, ed. Gaëton Picon & Jean-Paul Bouillon, Paris, 1974.
——, *Mon Salon, Manet, Écrits sur l'art*, ed. Antoinette Ehrard, Paris, 1970.

MALLARMÉ

Mallarmé, Stéphane, *Oeuvres complètes*, ed. Henri Mondor & G. Jean-Aubry, Paris, 1945.
——, *Oeuvres*, ed. Yves-Alain Favre, Paris, 1985.
Cohn, Robert Greer, *Toward the Poems of Mallarmé*, Berkeley and Los Angeles, 1965.
Eisenman, Stephen F., 'The Intransigent Artist *or* How the Impressionists Got Their Name', in *The New Painting: Impressionism 1874–1886*, exhibition catalogue by Charles S. Moffet, *et al*.: Fine Arts Museums of San Francisco, 1986, pp. 51–9.
Florence, Penny, *Mallarmé, Manet and Redon: Visual and Aural Signs and the Generation of Meaning*, Cambridge, 1986.
Kristeva, Julia, *La Révolution du langage poétique: L'Avant-Garde à la fin du XIXe siècle: Lautréamont et Mallarmé*, Paris, 1974.
Langan, Janine D., *Hegel and Mallarmé*, Lanham, MD, 1986.
Lewis, Paula Gilbert, *The Aesthetics of Stéphane Mallarmé in Relation to his Public*, Cranbury, NJ, 1976.
Michaud, Guy, *Mallarmé, l'homme et l'œuvre*, Paris, 1953.
Mondor, Henri, *Histoire d'un Faune*, Paris, 1948.

OTHER WORKS

Alpers, Svetlana, *The Art of Describing: Dutch Art in the Seventeenth Century*, Chicago, 1983.
Armstrong, Carol, *Odd Man Out: Readings of the Work and Reputation of Edgar Degas*, Chicago, 1991
Austin, James Lloyd, *How to do Things with Words*, the William James lectures delivered at Harvard University in 1955, Cambridge, 1962.
Baxandall, Michael, *Patterns of Intention: On the Historical Explanation of Pictures*, London, 1985.
Benveniste, Emile, *Problèmes de linguistique générale*, Paris, 1966.
Blanc, Charles, *Grammaire des arts du dessin*, Paris, 1867.
——, *Histoire des peintres de toutes les écoles*, Paris, 1861 76.
Bryson, Norman, 'Introduction', in *Calligram: Essays in New Art History from France*, ed. N. Bryson, Cambridge, 1988, pp. xiii-xxix.
——, *Looking at the Overlooked: Four Essays on Still-Life Painting*, London and Cambridge, MA, 1990).
——, *Vision and Painting: The Logic of the Gaze*, London, 1983.
Castagnary, Jules-Antoine, *Salons*, 2 vols, Paris, 1892.
Chantal, J.B.C. de, *La Civilité des jeunes personnes*, Paris, 1843.
Chardin and the Still-life Tradition in France, exhibition catalogue by Gabriel P. Weisberg: Cleveland Museum of Art, 1979.

Charlton, Donald G., *Positivist Thought in France during the Second Empire*, Oxford, 1959.
Chevreul, Michel-Eugène, *De l'abstraction considérée relativement aux beaux-arts et à la littérature*, Dijon, 1864.
Claretie, Arsène-Jules, *Peintres et sculpteurs contemporains*, Paris, 1873.
Colin, René-Pierre, *Schopenhauer en France*, Lyon, 1979.
Crary, Jonathan, 'Modernizing Vision', in *Vision and Visuality*, ed. Hal Foster, Seattle, 1988, pp. 29–44.
——, *Techniques of the Observer: On Vision and Modernity in the Nineteenth Century*, London, 1990.
Crouzet, Marcel, *Un Méconnu du réalisme: Duranty (1883–1880)*, Paris, 1964.
Debord, Guy, *La Société du spectacle*, Paris, 1967.
Derrida, Jacques, *The Truth in Painting*, trans. by Geoff Bennington & Ian McLeod, Chicago, 1987.
——, 'Signature, Event, Context', in *Glyph: John Hopkins Textual Studies* I, 1977, pp. 172–97.
Descartes, René, 'La Dioptrique', in *Discours sur la méthode et essais*, Leiden, 1637.
Didi-Huberman, Georges, *Devant l'image: question posée aux fins d'une histoire de l'art*, Paris, 1990.
——, *La peinture incarnée*, Paris, 1985.
Duranty, Edmond, *La Nouvelle Peinture*, Paris, 1876.
Duret, Théodore, *Critique d'avant-garde*, Paris, 1885.
——, *Les Peintres impressionistes*, Paris, 1878.
Ellenberger, Henri F., *The Discovery of the Unconscious*, New York, 1970.
Erasmus, *La Civilité puérile*, Paris, 1977.
Fantin-Latour, exhibition catalogue: Paris, Grand Palais, 1982–3.
Faré, Michel, *La Nature-Morte en France, son histoire et son évolution du XVIIe au XXe siècle*, Geneva, 1962.
Flescher, Sharon, *Zacharie Astruc: Critic, Artist and Japonist*, London, 1978.
Foucault, Michel, 'Las Meninas', in *Calligram: Essays in New Art History from France*, ed. Norman Bryson, Cambridge, 1988, pp. 91–105.
Goncourt, Jules & Edmond de, *L'Art du dix-huitième siècle*, Paris, 1859–76.
Guillemin, Amédée, *La Lumière et les couleurs*, Paris, 1874.
Helmholtz, Hermann L. F. von, *Optique physiologique*, Paris, 1867.
——, *L'Optique et la peinture*, Paris, 1878.
Herbert, Robert L., *Impressionism: Art, Leisure and Parisian Society*, New Haven, 1988.
Jameson, Fredric, *The Prison-House of Language: A Critical Account of Structuralism and Russian Formalism*, Princeton, 1972.
Laforgue, Jules, 'Impressionisme', (1883) in *Mélanges posthumes*, Paris, 7th edn, 1919.
Lucie-Smith, Edward, *Fantin-Latour*, Oxford, 1977.
Marcussen, Marianne, *Duranty et les Impressionistes*, Hafnia, Copenhagen Papers in the History of Art, 1978, pp. 24–42; 1979, pp. 27–49.
Marin, Louis, 'Towards a Theory of Reading in the Visual Arts: Poussin's "The Arcadian Shepherds" ', in *Calligram: Essays in New Art History from France*, ed. Norman Bryson, Cambridge, 1988, pp. 63–90.
McCoubrey, John, 'The Revival of Chardin in French Still-life Painting, 1850–1870', *Art Bulletin*, XLVI, 1964, pp. 39–53.
Mémoires d'un aveugle: L'autoportrait et autres ruines, exhibition catalogue by Jacques Derrida: Paris, Musée du Louvre, Départment des arts graphiques, Paris, 1990.
The New Painting: Impressionism 1874–1886, exhibition catalogue by Charles S. Moffet, *et al.*: Fine Arts Museums of San Francisco, 1986.
Pastore, Nicholas, *Selective History of Theories of Visual Perception*, New York, 1971.

Ribot, Théodule, *La Philosophie de Schopenhauer*, Paris, 1874.
Rubin, James H., *Realism and Social Vision in Courbet and Proudhon*, Princeton Essays on the Arts 10, Princeton, 1981.
Scherer, Edmond, 'Hegel and l'Hégelianisme', *Review des Deux-Mondes*, I, 1861.
Shiff, Richard, *Cézanne and the End of Impressionism*, Chicago, 1984.
——, 'Performing an Appearance: On the Surface of Abstract Expressionism', in *Abstract Expressionism: The Critical Developments*, exhibition catalogue: Buffalo, NY, Albright-Knox Art Gallery, 1967, pp. 94–123.
Sully, James, *Les Illusions des sens et de l'esprit*, Paris, 1883.
Taine, Hippolyte, *De L'Intelligence*, Paris, 1870.
——, *Philosophie de l'art*, Paris, 1865.
Thoré, Théophile, *Salons de W. Bürger, 1861–1868*, 2 vols, Paris, 1870.
Weinberg, Bernard, *French Realism: The Critical Reaction, 1830–1870*, New York, 1937.

List of Illustrations

Measurements are given in centimetres

1 *Self-portrait with Palette*, 1878–9, oil on canvas, 83 × 67. Private collection.

2 *The Absinthe Drinker*, 1859, oil on canvas, 180.5 × 105.6, Ny Carlsberg Glyptotek, Copenhagen.

3 *The Guitar Player*, 1861, oil on canvas, 147.3 × 114.3. Metropolitan Museum of Art, New York, gift of William Church Osborn, 1949.

4 *The Old Musician*, 1862, oil on canvas, 187.4 × 248.3. National Gallery of Art, Washington, DC; Chester Dale Collection.

5 *The Little Cavaliers*, 1861–2, etching with drypoint (third state) after Manet's own oil copy of a painting in the Louvre formerly attributed to Velázquez, 24.8 × 39. Bibliothèque Nationale, Paris.

6 *The Concert in the Tuileries*, 1862, oil on canvas, 76.2 × 118.1. National Gallery, London.

7 Constantin Guys, *Meeting in a Park*, c. 1855, watercolour, 21.7 × 30. Metropolitan Museum of Art, New York, Rogers Fund, 1937.

8 *Reclining Woman in Spanish Costume*, 1862, oil on canvas, 94.7 × 113.7. Yale University Art Gallery, New Haven, bequest of Stephen Carlton Clark, BA, 1903.

9 Marcantonio Raimondi, *The Judgement of Paris*, c. 1518, detail from an engraving after a lost cartoon by Raphael, Metropolitan Museum of Art, New York, Rogers Fund, 1919.

10 *The Surprised Nymph*, 1859–61, oil on canvas, 144.5 × 112.5. Museo Nacional de Bellas Artes de la Escuela, Buenos Aires. Photo: Grete Stern.

11 Giorgione, *Concert champêtre*, c. 1510, oil on canvas, 105 × 136.5. Musée du Louvre, Paris. Photo: Cliché des Musées Nationaux.

12 Titian, *The Venus of Urbino*, 1538, oil on canvas, 119 × 165. Galleria degli Uffizi, Florence.

13 *Cats' Rendezvous*, lithograph for a poster for Champfleury, *Les Chats*, 1868, 43.5 × 33.2. The New York Public Library, print collection, Miriam and Ira D. Wallach Division of Art, Prints and Photographs; Astor, Lenox and Tilden Foundations.

14 Alexandre Cabanel, *The Birth of Venus*, 1863, oil on canvas, 106 × 182.6. Metropolitan Museum of Art, New York, gift of John Wolfe, 1893.

15 *Zacharie Astruc*, 1866, oil on canvas, 89 × 116. Kunsthalle Bremen.

16 *M. and Mme Auguste Manet*, 1860, oil on canvas, 110 × 90. Musée d'Orsay, Paris. Photo: Cliché des Musées Nationaux.

17 Diego Velázquez, *Bacchus* (*The Drunkards*), c. 1629, oil on canvas, 165 × 225. Museo del Prado, Madrid.

18 *Théodore Duret*, 1868, oil on canvas, 46.5 × 35.5. Musée du Petit Palais, Paris. Photo: Photothèque des Musées de la Ville de Paris.

19 Francisco de Goya, *The Duchess of Alba*, 1797, oil on canvas, 210 × 148. Collection of The Hispanic Society of America, New York.

20 *Lola de Valence*, 1862, oil on canvas, 123 × 92. Musée d'Orsay, Paris. Photo: Cliché des Musées Nationaux.

21 *Philibert Rouvière as a Tragic Actor*, 1865–6, oil on canvas, 187.2 × 108.1. National Gallery of Art, Washington, DC, gift of Edith Stuyvesant Gerry.

22 *Victorine as an Espada*, 1862, oil on canvas, 165.1 × 127.6. Metropolitan Museum of Art, New York, bequest of Mrs H. O. Havemeyer, 1929; the H. O. Havemeyer Collection.

23 Katsushika Hokusai (1760–1849), *Wild Horses*, *c.* 1833, colour woodblock print, sheet size 52.1 × 23.3. Bigelow Collection, courtesy of the Museum of Fine Arts, Boston.

24 *Still-life with Fish*, 1864, oil on canvas, 73.4 × 92.1. Art Institute of Chicago, Mr and Mrs Lewis Larned Coburn Memorial Collection.

25 *The Execution of Emperor Maximilian*, 1868, oil on canvas, 252 × 302. Städtische Kunsthalle, Mannheim.

26 Compositional sketch for *The Execution of Emperor Maximilian*, 1867, oil on canvas, 196 × 259.8. Museum of Fine Arts, Boston, gift of Mr and Mrs Frank Gair Macomber.

27 Francisco de Goya, *The Executions of 3 May 1808*, 1814, oil on canvas, 268 × 347. Museo del Prado, Madrid.

28 *The Escape of Rochefort*, 1880–81, oil on canvas, 143 × 114. Kunsthaus, Zürich. Photo: Kunsthaus Zürich, Society of Zürich Friends of Art.

29 *Luncheon in the Studio*, 1868, oil on canvas, 118.3 × 153.9. Neue Pinakothek, Bayerische Staatsgemäldesammlungen, Munich.

30 *The Balcony*, 1868–9, oil on canvas, 170 × 124.5. Musée d'Orsay, Paris. Photo: Cliché des Musées Nationaux.

31 Edgar Degas, *The Bellelli Family*, *c.* 1860, oil on canvas, 200 × 250. Musée d'Orsay, Paris. Photo: Cliché des Musées Nationaux.

32 *La Gare Saint-Lazare*, 1872–3, oil on canvas, 93 × 114. National Gallery of Art, Washington, DC, gift of Horace Havemeyer, in memory of his mother, Louisine W. Havemeyer.

33 *In the Conservatory*, 1879, oil on canvas, 115 × 150. Nationalgalerie, Staatliche Museen zu Berlin, Preußischer Kulturbesitz. Photo: Jörg P. Anders.

34 *A Masked Ball at the Opéra*, 1873–4, oil on canvas, 59 × 72.5. National Gallery of Art, Washington, DC, gift of Mrs Horace Havemeyer, in memory of her mother-in-law, Louisine W. Havemeyer.

35 *The Prune*, *c.* 1878, oil on canvas, 73.6 × 50.2. National Gallery of Art, Washington, DC, collection of Mr and Mrs Paul Mellon.

36 *Nana*, 1877, oil on canvas, 154 × 115. Kunsthalle, Hamburg. Photo: Elke Walford.

37 Gustave Courbet, *The Studio of the Painter*, 1855, oil on canvas, 359 × 598. Musée d'Orsay, Paris. Photo: Cliché des Musées Nationaux.

38 Study for *A Bar at the Folies-Bergère*, 1881, oil on canvas, 47 × 56. F.F.R. Koenigs Collection, Bennekom, Netherlands.

39 Henri Fantin-Latour, *Homage to Delacroix*, 1864, oil on canvas, 160 × 250. Musée d'Orsay, Paris. Photo: Cliché des Musées Nationaux.

40 *Le Déjeuner sur l'herbe*, 1863, oil on canvas, 208 × 264.5. Musée d'Orsay, Paris. Photo: Cliché des Musées Nationaux.

41 *Olympia*, 1863, oil on canvas, 130.5 × 190. Musée d'Orsay, Paris. Photo: Cliché des Musées Nationaux.

42 *Emile Zola*, 1868, oil on canvas, 146.5 × 114. Musée d'Orsay, Paris. Photo: Cliché des Musées Nationaux.

43 *The Fifer Boy*, 1866, oil on canvas, 161 × 97. Musée d'Orsay, Paris. Photo: Cliché des Musées Nationaux.

44 *Stéphane Mallarmé*, 1876, oil on canvas, 27.5 × 36. Musée d'Orsay, Paris. Photo: Cliché des Musées Nationaux.

45 *A Bar at the Folies-Bergère*, 1881–2, oil on canvas, 96 × 130. Courtauld Galleries, London (Courtauld gift, 1934).

46 *The Dead Toreador*, 1864–5, oil on canvas, 76 × 153.3. © 1993, National Gallery of Art, Washington, DC; Widener Collection.

47 *A Bunch of Violets with a Fan*, 1872, oil on canvas, 22 × 27. Private collection. Photo: Cliché des Musées Nationaux.

48 *The Bunch of Asparagus*, 1880, oil on canvas, 44 × 54. Wallraf-Richartz-Museum, Cologne. Photo: Rheinisches Bildarchiv, Cologne.

49 *Pinks and Clematis in a Crystal Vase*, 1882, oil on canvas, 56 × 35. Musée d'Orsay, Paris. Photo: Cliché des Musées Nationaux.

50 *Claude Monet in the Boat Studio*, 1874, oil on canvas, 82.5 × 100.5. Bayerische Staatsgemäldesammlungen, Munich. Photo: Artothek.

51 *Boating*, 1874, oil on canvas, 97.2 × 130.2. Metropolitan Museum of Art, New York, bequest of Mrs H. O. Havemeyer, 1929; the H. O. Havemeyer Collection.

52 *The Washing*, 1875, oil on canvas, 143.5 × 113.7. The Barnes Collection, Merion, PA.

53 *'Once upon a midnight dreary . . .'*, illustration for *Le Corbeau*, 1875, brush and ink transfer relief-plate, unique state, 27.5 × 37. The New York Public Library, print collection, Miriam and Ira D. Wallach Division of Art, Prints and Photographs; Astor, Lenox and Tilden Foundations.

54 *'Open here I flung the shutter . . .'*, illustration for *Le Corbeau*, 1875, brush and ink transfer relief-plate, second state, 38.5 × 30. The New York Public Library, print collection, Miriam and Ira D. Wallach Division of Art, Prints and Photographs; Astor, Lenox and Tilden Foundations.

55 *'Perched upon a bust of Pallas . . .'*, illustration for *Le Corbeau*, 1875, brush and ink transfer relief-plate, second state, 47.5 × 31.6. The New York Public Library, print collection, Miriam and Ira D. Wallach Division of Art, Prints and Photographs; Astor, Lenox and Tilden Foundations.

56 *'That Shadow that lies floating on the floor . . .'*, illustration for *Le Corbeau*, 1875, brush and ink transfer relief-plate, unique state, 29 × 27.6. The New York Public Library, print collection, Miriam and Ira D. Wallach Division of Art, Prints and Photographs; Astor, Lenox and Tilden Foundations.

57 *Satyr*, illustration for *L'Après-midi d'un faune*, 1876, woodcut, 4.8 × 7.8.

The New York Public Library, print collection, Miriam and Ira D. Wallach Division of Art, Prints and Photographs; Astor, Lenox and Tilden Foundations.

58 *Nymphs*, illustration for *L'Après-midi d'un faune*, 1876 woodcut, 3.0 × 6.3. The New York Public Library, print collection, Miriam and Ira D. Wallach Division of Art, Prints and Photographs; Astor, Lenox and Tilden Foundations.

59 *Grapes*, illustration for *L'Après-midi d'un faune*, 1876, woodcut, 2.5 × 2.0. The New York Public Library, print collection, Miriam and Ira D. Wallach Division of Art, Prints and Photographs; Astor, Lenox and Tilden Foundations.

60 *Wild Flowers*, illustration for *L' Après-midi d'un faune*, 1876, woodcut, 3.5 × 3.3. The New York Public Library, print collection, Miriam and Ira D. Wallach Division of Art, Prints and Photographs; Astor, Lenox and Tilden Foundations.

61 Pierre-Auguste Renoir, *Still-life with Bouquet*, 1871, oil on canvas, 73.2 × 58.9. Museum of Fine Arts, Houston, Robert Lee Blaffer Memorial Collection, gift of Mrs Sarah Campbell Blaffer.

62 First cover design for *Les Eaux-fortes par Edouard Manet*, 1862, etching, 27 × 19. The New York Public Library, print collection, Miriam and Ira D. Wallach Division of Art, Prints and Photographs; Astor, Lenox and Tilden Foundations.

63 Second cover design for *Les Eaux-fortes par Edouard Manet*, 1862, etching, 32.7 × 24. The New York Public Library, print collection, Miriam and Ira D. Wallach Division of Art, Prints and Photographs; Astor, Lenox and Tilden Foundations.

64 *Boy with a Sword*, 1861, oil on canvas, 131.1 × 92.3. Metropolitan Museum of Art, New York, gift of Erwin Davis, 1889.

65 Proof for the frontispiece of *Les Eaux-fortes par Edouard Manet*, 1862–3, etching with aquatint and drypoint, first state, 44.1 × 29.8. Nationalmuseum, Stockholm. Photo: Statens Konstmuseer.

66 Bertall's caricature of *Olympia*, from *Le Journal amusant*, 27 May 1865, Paris. Photo: Bibliothèque Nationale (Cabinet d'Estampes), Paris.

67 *Dead Christ with Angels*, 1864, oil on canvas, 179.4 × 149.9. Metropolitan Museum of Art, New York, bequest of Mrs H. O. Havemeyer, 1929; the H. O. Havemeyer Collection.

68 *Cat and Flowers*, 1869, etching and aquatint, second state, 20.3 × 15.2. The New York Public Library, print collection, Miriam and Ira D. Wallach Division of Art, Prints and Photographs; Astor, Lenox and Tilden Foundations.

69 *Salmon, Pike and Shrimp*, 1864, oil on canvas, 39 × 62.3. Norton Simon Art Foundation, Pasadena.

70 *Fruit on a Table*, 1864, oil on canvas, 45 × 73.5. Musée d'Orsay, Paris. Photo: Cliché des Musées Nationaux.

71 *Peonies in a Vase*, 1864, oil on canvas, 93 × 70. Musée d'Orsay, Paris. Photo: Cliché des Musées Nationaux.

72 *Peony Stems and Pruning Shears*, 1864, oil on canvas, 56.8 × 46.2. Musée d'Orsay, Paris. Photo: Cliché des Musées Nationaux.

73 *Woman with a Parrot*, 1866, oil on canvas, 185.1 × 128.6. Metropolitan Museum of Art, New York, gift of Erwin Davis, 1889.

74 *The Universal Fairgrounds in 1867*, 1867, oil on canvas, 108 × 196.5. Nasjonalgalleriet, Oslo. Photo: J. Lathion.

75 *Rue Mosnier with Flags*, 1878, oil on canvas, 65 × 81. J. Paul Getty Museum, Malibu.

76 *The Monet Family in the Garden*, 1874, oil on canvas, 61 × 99.7. Metropolitan Museum of Art, New York, bequest of Joan Whitney Payson, 1975.

77 *Reading*, *c.* 1865–73, oil on canvas, 60.5 × 73.5. Musée d'Orsay, Paris. Photo: Cliché des Musées Nationaux.

78 *George Moore*, 1879, pastel on canvas, 55.3 × 35.3. Metropolitan Museum of Art, New York, bequest of Mrs H. O. Havemeyer; the H. O. Havemeyer collection.

79 *Asparagus*, 1880, oil on canvas, 16.5 × 21.5. Musée d'Orsay, Paris. Photo: Cliché des Musées Nationaux.

80 *Mirabelle*, 1880, watercolour, 20 × 12.5. Musée du Louvre (Cabinet des Dessins), Paris. Photo: Cliché des Musées Nationaux.

81 *Philippine*, 1880, watercolour, 20 × 12.5. Musée du Louvre (Cabinet des Dessins), Paris. Photo: Cliché des Musées Nationaux.

82 *White Lilacs*, 1883, oil on canvas, 54 × 42. Nationalgalerie, Staatliche Museen zu Berlin, Preußischer Kulturbesitz. Photo: Jörg P. Anders.

83 Eugène Delacroix, *Still-life with Lobster*, 1827, oil on canvas, 80.5 × 106.5. Musée du Louvre, Paris. Photo: Cliché des Musées Nationaux.

84 Delacroix, detail of foreground still-life in *The Death of Sardanapalus*, 1827, oil on canvas, 392 × 496. Musée du Louvre, Paris. Photo: Cliché des Musées Nationaux.

85 Edgar Degas, *The Duke and Duchess of Morbilli*, *c.* 1865, oil on canvas, 116.5 × 88.3. Museum of Fine Arts, Boston, gift of Robert Treat Paine II.

86 Claude Monet, *Women in the Garden*, 1866–7, oil on canvas, 255 × 205. Musée d'Orsay, Paris. Photo: Cliché des Musées Nationaux.

87 Vincent van Gogh, *Fritillaries in a Copper Vase*, 1887, oil on canvas, 73 × 60.5. Musée d'Orsay, Paris. Photo: Cliché des Musées Nationaux.

88 Vincent van Gogh, *Sunflowers*, 1887, oil on canvas, 43.2 × 61. Metropolitan Museum of Art, New York, Rogers Fund, 1949.

89 Vincent van Gogh, *Le Berceuse* (*Augustine Rollin*), 1889, oil on canvas, 92 × 73. Rijksmuseum Kröller-Müller, Otterlo, Netherlands. Photo: Tom Haartsen.

90 Paul Gauguin, *Meyer de Haan* (*Nirvana*), *c.* 1890, oil and turpentine on silk, 21.6 × 29.2. The Wadsworth Atheneum, Hartford, CT. Photo: Joseph Szaszfai.

91 Paul Gauguin, *Vincent van Gogh Painting Sunflowers*, 1888, oil on canvas, 73 × 91. Vincent van Gogh Foundation/Van Gogh Museum, Amsterdam. Photo: Rene Gerritsen.

92 Paul Cézanne, *Achille Emperaire*, *c.* 1868, oil on canvas, 200 × 120. Musée d'Orsay, Paris. Photo: Cliché des Musées Nationaux.

93 Paul Cézanne, *A Modern Olympia*, 1872–3, oil on canvas, 46 × 55.5. Musée d'Orsay, Paris. Photo: Cliché des Musées Nationaux.

94 Paul Cézanne, *Mme Cézanne in a Yellow Armchair*, *c.* 1890, oil on canvas, 80.3 × 65.4. Private collection.